THE AMERICAN
C·O·U·N·T·R·Y
WOODWORKER

THE AMERICAN C·O·U·N·T·R·Y WOODWORKER

50 Country Accents You Can Build in a Weekend

BY MICHAEL DUNBAR

Rodale Press, Emmaus, Pennsylvania

Our Mission

We publish books that empower people's lives.

RODALE BOOKS

The author and editors who compiled this book have tried to make all the contents as accurate and as correct as possible. Plans, illustrations, photographs, and text have all been carefully checked and cross-checked. However, due to the variability of local conditions, construction materials, personal skill, and so on, neither the author nor Rodale Press assumes any responsibility for any injuries suffered or for damages or other losses incurred that result from the material presented herein. All instructions and plans should be carefully studied and clearly understood before beginning construction.

Library of Congress Cataloging-in-Publication Data

Dunbar, Michael.
    The American country woodworker :
    50 country accents you can build in a weekend / by Michael Dunbar.
        p.   cm.
    ISBN 0-87596-568-7   hardcover
    1. Woodwork.   I. Title.
TT180.D78   1993
684'.08—dc20   92-30997
                                    CIP

Distributed in the book trade by St. Martin's Press

2 4 6 8 10 9 7 5 3 1   hardcover

If you have any questions or comments concerning this book, please write:
    Rodale Press
    Book Readers' Service
    33 East Minor Street
    Emmaus, PA 18098

∎

Executive Editor: **Margaret Lydic Balitas**
Senior Editor: **Jeff Day**
Editor: **Robert A. Yoder**
Copy Manager: **Dolores Plikaitis**
Copy Editor: **Sarah S. Dunn**
Administrative assistance: **Susan L. Nickol**
Office Manager: **Karen Earl-Braymer**
Art Director: **Anita Patterson**
Book Designer: **Frank M. Milloni**
Cover Designer: **Jerry O'Brien**
Photographer: **Mitch Mandel**
Photo Stylist: **Marianne G. Laubach**
Illustrator: **Frank Rohrbach**

∎

Special thanks to Edward G. Hyder

Cover Projects: The projects shown on the front cover include (*clockwise from top left*): Standing Quilt Rack (page 91), Turned Breadboard (page 111), Closed Shelf (page 172), Pasta Roller (page 118), Clothespin (page 128), Bucket Bench (page 38), Toy Horse (page 280), Spinning Top (page 270), and Child's Wing Chair (page 295).

■

To Michael

■

CONTENTS

Treenware

Boxes

Wall-Hung Shelves and Racks

Kids' Stuff

INTRODUCTION
WHAT IS COUNTRY?

Country is the most popular decorating style in America today. I think it's safe to say that more people decorate their homes with country furniture than with any other single style. But the purpose of this book is not to tell you how to make country furniture. Instead, it will tell you how to make the small, everyday pieces that collectors and antique dealers call accents. These are the pieces that create depth in a decor. They are the pieces that give a home a lived-in appearance. They are the pieces that make a home more interesting.

You can create depth in your country decor not only by the accents you choose but also by being attentive to the tools and materials you use to make them. I'll talk more about that in the next two chapters. For now, I'd like to examine the country look.

There is a very good reason that country decorating is so popular. Country is exactly what America is—a rich and flavorful stew resulting from many cultures blended together. Some of the cultural influences that resulted in what we call country today came from the English in New England, the Dutch in New York, the Spanish in Florida and the Southwest, the Scandinavians in the upper Midwest, the Germans in Delaware and Pennsylvania, and the French in Canada, the Mississippi River Valley, and New Orleans. Other influences on the country look include America's religious, Utopian, and philosophical movements that produced their own distinctive woodworking styles—the Shakers, Mennonites, Zoarites, Harmonists, and Mormons.

Like America and Americans, the country style is so diverse it is impossible to define or describe, even though everyone knows what it is and easily recognizes it. In fact, in 1969, Winterthur, one of America's most prestigious museums, held a conference of eminent scholars to discuss what country furniture is. They had the same problem as everyone else—country is hard to define.

Country is hard to define because it is a *look* more than a *style*. As a look, it affects everything that goes into a house—including the house itself. There is even a country look in clothing, makeup, and hairdressing. In fact, country is so popular there are magazines dedicated to showing people how to create and decorate in this unique American way. Entire books are limited to individual aspects of country—for example, making country wooden accents like those in this book.

COUNTRY GOES COMMERCIAL

Because country is so popular, commercialism has crept into it. As the many pine furniture stores that dot the countryside indicate, this is especially true in country woodworking. Commercialism in country woodworking is nothing new, having been around since the 1930s. Commercial country is highly stylized, however, and is constantly changing. It is therefore quickly dated. During the 1960s, commercial country was embodied in the rock maple look in which the wood was always covered with an opaque, brownish yellow "maple" stain. During the 1970s, commercial country was typified by dark pine. This furniture was made of 2-inch-thick, rough-edged pine slabs stained a dark brown so they looked almost burnt.

1

Woodworking books have been showing woodworkers how to make country furniture and furnishings since at least the 1940s. I spend a lot of time rummaging in antique shops, where I regularly find copies of these old books. I am always amused by them. Even though they are only 40 or 50 years old, they look so old-fashioned. Why? Because their authors showed how to make pieces that mimicked the then-current commercial country look, which quickly became dated.

Books that mimic the commercial country look are still being published, although I am unable to understand why. Why would a woodworker be willing to go through all the effort of making a project that looks exactly like what is sold in mid-price furniture stores? My desire to work wood has always, at least in part, been a reaction to what is mass-produced. Unable to buy the quality of furniture and woodworking I wanted, I learned to make it myself. Perhaps the commercial country books succeed because we have grown up surrounded by mass-produced furniture. As a result, we automatically assume that that's how furniture is supposed to look and, consequently, that this is how our own work should look.

COUNTRY COMES HOME

Despite the commercialism, there are places where well-built and well-designed furniture is still made. To see one, visit a small custom shop that makes one-of-a-kind pieces and that sells directly to the customer. These are the types of shops in which country woodworking was originally done, and I am very familiar with them. I have been a professional woodworker for 20 years, and I used to run a small, one-man shop where I made exact copies of period and country furniture.

My reaction to mass-produced woodwork-

ing and my experience as a small shop owner led me to this book's point of view. Instead of turning toward commercial country woodworking as the source for these projects, I returned to the originals. They are far better than their commercial cousins. Because they are classics, their designs are timeless. Twenty years from now the pieces you make using this book will not be humorously out of date, but will be as desirable as the originals from which they were copied.

For a woodworker, the pieces in this book are timeless in an even more interesting way. Each piece was measured from an original that has been in use for generations. If a piece survives 100 to 200 years, it is good woodworking. Its very survival proves that the piece was well constructed — that the joints are sufficiently strong and the use of materials was properly considered.

Where did the country furniture come from? As I mentioned earlier, the folk and ethnic cultures that created America brought unique styles with them. The woodworking of various religious groups such as the Shakers and Zoarites reflected their beliefs. These influences eventually extended beyond individual settlements and colonies into the mainstream. However, country design also developed to meet the needs and tastes of the dominant secular culture.

Before the Industrial Revolution, every city and town supported small woodworking shops. Rural craftsmen were usually as skilled as their urban counterparts. But because rural woodworkers lacked the training given to urban apprentices, they didn't understand formal design. They produced highly individualized, unelaborate furniture that makes up part of what we call country woodworking.

But not all country woodworking comes from the country. In cities, America's cabinetmaking geniuses — men like Duncan Phyfe, the Goddards and Townsends, and the Seymours—produced their expensive mahogany masterpieces. Even the wealthiest homes, however, needed simple, everyday furniture for the kitchen and service rooms. A less affluent urban family would furnish their entire house with this type of plain furniture. Scholars use the word "informal" to describe this unelaborate city-made furniture. Since it is practically indistinguishable from the furniture made in small towns, it, too, contributed to today's country look.

The projects in this book contain another category of woodworking that was made and used in both the city and country. This work, called "treen," is generally associated only with country. Treen—a corruption of "tree ware"—means everyday household utensils. The Pasta Roller (page 118), Potato Masher (page 133), Clothespin (page 128), and Mitten and Sock Stretchers (page 142) are treen.

The woodworking that we call country today had one other important influence. Until this century America was dotted with individual family farms. Many were located on the frontier or were otherwise isolated. Every farmer had to be able to perform some level of woodworking just to keep his family going. These everyday objects that were made by untrained farm woodworkers are what antique dealers today call primitives. They are often anything but primitive. In fact, they are highly individualistic and imaginative, finding very clever solutions to common woodworking problems. You will see examples in the Pyramid Shelf (page 250) and the Primitive Coatrack (page 218).

All these influences—social, religious, geographic, and economic—resulted in the country look that interests us so much today. Taken as a whole, this look has two important attributes: It is very individualistic, and it is quite functional.

RUGGED INDIVIDUALISM

One of the reasons country woodwork is timeless is that it provides few clues as to when it was made. Formal, city-made furniture tells the informed eye exactly when it was produced. Each period lasted for a certain number of years before being replaced by another and had a well-established vocabulary. For example, the claw-and-ball foot is part of the Chippendale period's (1775 to 1790) vocabulary. Reeding, on the other hand, is associated with the Sheraton period (1790 to 1815).

Country woodwork is difficult to date because it either has no recognizable style or borrows styles out of context from various furniture periods. Often, the craftsmen who made these pieces were trying to copy the furniture they had seen on visits to the city. On the frontier, settlers tried to re-create from memory what they had left behind. What they were trying to copy had often been made years before and had long since gone out of fashion.

When their memories failed them, these woodworkers worked out their own solutions. It was not uncommon for them to borrow elements from several different periods and use them all in the same piece. The Watch Hutch (page 96) and the Child's Wing Chair (page 295) in this book were attempts to copy city forms. The ovolo molding and tapered legs on the Splay-Leg Table (page 84) associate it with the neoclassical period's Hepplewhite style.

While city woodworkers relied on design books by Chippendale, Hepplewhite, and Sheraton for their inspiration, country woodworkers were more likely to turn to the source they knew and understood—geometry. With some simple tools, such as a pair of dividers, a miter square, and a try square, country woodworkers could quickly lay out an infinite variety of interwoven geometric shapes. As I look at country furniture, I am always fascinated by how many different ways these woodworkers could use just a few simple shapes. You will see the results in many of the pieces in this book, such as the Open Wall Box (page 168), the Corner Candle Shelf (page 214), and the Keeping Bin (page 176).

Architecture was another source of inspiration for country woodworkers. A favorite trick was to incorporate a popular molding profile into a piece's outline. This way, the object was cleverly related to the room in which it was used. This technique is seen in the Pipe Box (page 159), the Serving Tray (page 189), the Towel Roller (page 259), and the door of the Watch Hutch (page 96).

In still other pieces, country woodworkers seemed to pull a design out of thin air. They relied only on individual expression and their own personal inspiration. You will see an example of this in the Corner Shelf (page 264).

Country families were large. Many hands were needed to work a farm, and rural couples found it cheaper to raise their own help than to hire it. Rural people have always loved their children, and country woodworkers invested a lot of effort in making furniture and toys for their little ones. Many of the projects you will find in this book are intended for children. In making these objects, country woodworkers relied on all the sources of inspiration listed above.

Be inspired by whatever sources speak to you. Just as these objects were the original makers' personal statements, you can make your own statements. Do not feel you have to make slavish copies of the projects presented here, never varying from the drawings. Feel free to express yourself. Change a shape or add details if you want. The next two chapters will explain other ways you can individualize your pieces. Many of the project chapters will also contain other options you can consider.

FORM FOLLOWS FUNCTION

Besides being highly individualistic, the accent projects in this book are also functional. Even though the term "country accents" sounds like a decorator term, the projects in this book are not mere decorations. Even though we live in a technological age, many of these pieces still provide a very practical way to accomplish the object's original purpose.

You will find that the Turned Breadboard (page 111) still makes a very good surface on which to slice and serve bread. Although pasta is available packaged at the supermarket, the Pasta Roller (page 118) still works very nicely. The Hanging Quilt Rack (page 241) still stores quilts and dries towels. The various display shelves still provide an excellent place to store the precious and sentimental objects we all own.

Even when an object's original purpose is no longer part of our daily lives, the project can fill another need. Most of us have running water and no longer have to keep buckets of well water by the back door. However, a Bucket Bench (pages 38 and 42) can be used for holding garden supplies, or kids can sit on it to pull on their boots.

I have one last thought that underscores how comfortable Americans are with country woodworking. We have developed a vocabulary of colloquial terms to describe and define some of these objects or parts of them. Names such as bootjack end, tombstone door, and grandfather clock make scholars and academics squirm. To me, they are the nicknames and other terms of endearment that Americans create for things that are fond and familiar. Throughout the book I will introduce you to many more of these colloquialisms that Americans have devised for their favorite form of woodworking—country woodworking.

COUNTRY FINISHING

As I emphasized in the introduction, country woodwork is both highly individualistic and utilitarian, and these qualities can be seen in the finishes and finishing techniques that were traditionally used on country woodwork. The finishes chosen by country woodworkers are functional and, at the same time, very imaginative.

Country woodworkers viewed finishes far differently than we do, and their choices were far more diverse than ours. For the past half-century Americans have thought that a clear finish was the only proper treatment for wood. We are surrounded by modern metals and plastics, so wood remains one of our last links to the natural world. The ability to see wood's grain, texture, and color is reassuring to us. As a result, we automatically give wood a clear finish and consider any finish that obscures its "natural beauty" a desecration.

Country woodworkers used clear finishes much less often than we do today for a couple of very practical reasons. First, the clear finishes that were available to country woodworkers (varnish and shellac) were not durable. A shellac finish, for example, would not hold up long on a bucket bench that held buckets of well water. Second, these clear finishes were too expensive to use on purely utilitarian objects.

The circumstances of daily life also affected the way country folk viewed finishes. They lived and worked in a pre-technological age. Theirs was an age of wood—a time when nearly everything people used was made of wood. Country folk lived in wooden houses with wooden floors and wooden walls. All of their furniture and most of their implements, tools, and utensils were made of wood.

A large percentage of a community's adult and adolescent males worked wood for a living as cabinetmakers, chairmakers, housewrights, joiners, wagonwrights, wheelwrights, wet and dry coopers, and the list goes on. And all farmers (the most common occupation) also had substantial woodworking experience. To country folk, wood was the most common material in their lives. In a world of wood that came in several shades of brown, it was only natural to yearn for bright painted colors; furthermore, on the practical side, paint gave wood the durable finish that it needed.

OIL PAINT

There are no mysteries to old oil paint but, for some reason, it is surrounded by old wives' tales. For example, it is often repeated that old paints were made from berry juices or animal blood. Actually, the formula was much less "colorful." Boiled linseed oil acted as the vehicle and white lead as the binder. Turpentine was both the thinner and drier. Various earthen pigments gave the paint its color. Because iron oxide is readily available everywhere, red was a common color. During the late 18th century, advances in chemistry resulted in the first man-made pigments.

Paint was used so much that almost every woodworker knew how to mix and tint his own. This contrasts with today's paints, which are mass-produced and mass-distributed. They are sold not only by paint and hardware stores but also by department stores and even large pharmacies. Modern paints tend to follow current fashion trends, but some companies produce "reproduction" paints that are copies of traditional colors. Some museums also license their name to paints that reproduce colors found on furniture in their collections. These high-quality paints are more expensive, but after all the effort and care you put into your woodworking, they are worth the cost. You can order reproduction paints from Olde Mill Cabinet Shoppe, R.D. 2, Box 577A, York, PA 17402.

To prepare a project for oil paint, sand it with 220-grit sandpaper. Wipe off any dust with a tack rag, which is a sticky cloth that can be purchased at any paint store. Apply the paint with a high-quality, natural-bristle brush. If you need to paint a fine line (a process known as cutting in), use a sash brush.

To avoid lifting too much paint, submerge only about ½ inch of the bristles. Begin in the middle of a surface rather than on an edge. Draw the paint in both directions, following the wood's grain. To avoid runs, do not try to cover the wood in one coat. Instead, apply two thin coats. Allow the first layer to dry at least 24 hours. If this layer requires any smoothing, rub it down with #000 steel wool.

MILK PAINT

While berry juice and animal blood are myths, milk paint is not. Country woodworkers often made and used this paint mixture, which is also called casein paint. I still use milk paint because it has many of the properties of old lead and oil paints. I buy milk paint from The Old Fashioned Milk Paint Company, 436 Main Street, Box 222, Groton, MA 01540. This milk paint comes in a powdered form and has to be mixed with water, following the manufacturer's directions. Unlike oil paint,

milk paint cannot be stored in liquid form because it goes sour in about a day. In a pinch you can store it overnight in the refrigerator.

Prepare the wood's surface for milk paint by sanding it with 220-grit sandpaper and wiping it clean with a tack rag. I usually apply the paint over dry wood rather than wetting the wood as the manufacturer recommends. Wetting the wood in advance does make the milk paint's first coat go on faster, but the extra water makes this coat so thin that three layers of paint (rather than two) are required for complete coverage. As a result, this step ends up requiring more time rather than less.

Because milk paint is water-based, using it is very different from any finishing experience you are likely to have had. Before starting, please read this section to avoid becoming so frustrated by unexpected differences that you give up too soon on a very good product.

Apply milk paint with a natural-bristle brush. Milk paint is immediately absorbed by raw wood and cannot be drawn out with the brush like an oil paint. The brush's action is more a daub than a stroke (*Photo 1*). As a result, it is difficult to paint thin lines or details with milk paint. Milk paint also has much less body than an oil paint and will not fill small blemishes or gaps around joints. Milk paint should only be used on fresh, raw wood. It will not bind well to any other finishes, to glue, or to a surface that has been stripped. When applying the first coat of milk paint, I keep a cabinet scraper handy to scrape away excess glue, then I brush paint over the freshly exposed wood.

Milk paint dries in as little as 20 minutes, so on a warm day or in a heated shop you can complete the finish in a couple of hours. When the first coat of milk paint dries, it looks terrible. It is thin and blotchy (*Photo 2*). Brave heart! Rub the first coat with #000 steel wool to smooth any grain that was raised by the

Photo 1: The first coat of milk paint should be daubed on with an up-and-down motion of the brush rather than a back-and-forth motion.

Photo 2: When the first coat of milk paint dries, it will look horribly thin and blotchy. Don't worry! The second coat will produce a much more even paint texture.

water in the milk paint. Blow away most of the steel wool filings and pick up the rest with a tack rag. Because it lacks body, milk paint will always be somewhat transparent. Oil paints sit on the wood like a thin shell and, except on coarse woods like oak, hide the material's texture. The texture of the most even-grained woods, like birch and maple, will still show through milk paint.

Apply a second coat. The first coat sealed the wood, so this coat can be drawn out with the brush in a manner similar to (but not exactly like) oil paint (*Photo 3*). Once this second coat has dried, it will be much more uniform than the first, as testified to by the milk-paint-finished Splay-Leg Table (page 84). Usually, there is no need to rub down the second coat with steel wool.

Milk paint dries quite flat. To give it a sheen, brush on a coat of boiled linseed oil thinned 4 parts oil to 1 part turpentine or paint thinner. Wipe the oil dry immediately

Photo 3: The second coat of milk paint can be drawn over the first coat with the more normal or familiar back-and-forth brush stroke.

with a soft, absorbent rag. The oil on the paint will harden in a couple of days, creating a pleasing, soft gloss. Over time, friction from handling or body contact will polish the hardened oil, creating shiny highlights, an effect that I find appealing.

SAFETY TIP

Spontaneous combustion can occur in oil-soaked rags. Always dispose of them carefully. The safest means is to burn them outdoors. You can also hang oil-soaked rags outdoors and allow the finish to harden completely. The rag is then safe.

WASH

A wash is a layer of thin paint that you brush on and wipe off in much the same way you would a stain. Its purpose is not to cover the figure of the wood but to give it a colored tint. Curiously, this technique was used in two very different ways on country woodworking. First, it was a quick and inexpensive way to finish utilitarian pieces. Second, it was a first step in finishing expensive pieces of furniture. Country woodworkers made furniture for their clients using native woods. In the city these pieces would have been made of mahogany, and, had they the choice, that is the wood most customers would have preferred. For that reason, country cabinetmakers often tinted native woods to resemble mahogany by giving them a red wash like that on the Ratchet Candle Stand (see the color photo on page 70). An expensive finish, such as shellac or varnish, was then applied over the wash. Today, antiques with an original wash are desirable and expensive.

A wash is nothing more than oil paint thinned to the consistency of water — about 2 parts paint to 1 part turpentine or paint thinner. You can also make a milk paint wash by doubling the manufacturer's recommended amount of water, as I did for the finish on the Windsor Stool (see the color photo on page 56).

Apply the thinned paint as you would a wiping stain. Brush it on quickly but uniformly all over a single surface or part. Unless the project is small, do not try to stain the entire piece at once. Before the wash has time to set, wipe it off with a rag. Because a wash has little body, it will not fill blemishes or cover glue spills or wood filler. Instead, a thin, translucent wash of color is left behind, through which the wood's grain and texture can be easily seen. Enough finish penetrates the wood to create a thin seal. You can make the wash more impervious by applying a layer of thinned boiled linseed oil or by applying shellac, varnish, or lacquer.

FALSE GRAINING

The Shakers were perhaps the only group that purposefully made their possessions plain. Country woodwork was simple and utilitarian out of necessity, not choice. If they had had their druthers, most country folk would have owned expensive furniture made of mahogany or covered with fancy veneers just like upscale city dwellers.

Instead, country woodworkers often simulated the grain of woods they could not afford or obtain for themselves or for their customers. They painted the grain onto the wood with a technique that is known by the general term "false graining." This technique is also sometimes called by the French *faux bois* (false wood), although in connection with country furniture, that seems a bit pretentious. The same impulse to imitate wood in other materials is still with us in the form of contact paper and kitchen countertops that are made to simulate the look of real wood.

You may be familiar with false graining in a commercialized form that was popular in the 1970s. It was called antiquing and was sold as a way to refinish old furniture. Paint and decorator stores carried antiquing kits.

There is currently a great deal of interest in these older and more creative ways of finishing wood, and for a good reason. These skills provide an opportunity for self-expression as well as some fun.

False graining is made up of at least two layers of contrasting oil paint colors. The base coat is called the ground and is usually a light red, yellow, or green. The second coat is called the glaze and is generally a darker color, such as black or brown. The brushed-on glaze is drawn out with a coarse object, generically referred to as the comb, so that the ground color can be seen (*Photo 4*). The result you obtain in false graining is determined by the type of comb you choose and how you manipulate it. The comb can be one of any number of special devices or tools. Several types of graining tools are available at paint and art supply stores. You can also use such everyday objects as a rag, a feather, a sponge, a crumpled wad of newspaper, or a corn cob. Your imagination is your only limit. Feel free to experiment. If you do not like the result, brush the glaze smooth and start again.

The most dramatic example of false graining in this book was used on the Child's Wing Chair (see the color photo on page 62). To create the grain, I first laid down a ground of red paint. When the red paint was dry, I spread on a black paint for the glaze. I purchased a comb from the hardware store and drew the glaze across the wood with it (*Photo 5*). The false graining on the child's wing chair illustrates an important idea—false graining can run in any direction. The false graining on the seat and back of the child's wing

Photo 4: This is my collection of false graining combs.

Photo 5: Drag the comb through the glaze to reveal the ground color underneath. The way in which you move the comb determines the shape of the false grain. "Dip" the comb (lean it forward or back) to create the look of wood figure.

chair runs *perpendicular* to the grain, and it really does fool the eye.

There is another form of false graining that makes no attempt to simulate wood. Sponge graining, like that used on the Doll Cradle (see the color photo on page 61), is an example. In this case, the glaze is not painted on with a brush. Rather, it is applied with a section of sponge that is used like an ink stamp. The sponge is dipped in paint and blotted on the ground coat. Several different colors of paint can be used to create patterns not only in texture but in color as well.

To false grain a project, prepare the surface of the wood by sanding it with 220-grit sandpaper, then wipe it clean with a tack rag. Apply the ground just as you would any normal painted finish. Apply two coats and allow the paint to dry.

Apply the glaze next, and while the paint is still wet, draw the comb through it to produce the grain. The comb pushes the wet glaze aside in some areas, exposing the dry ground coat. There is no limit to the grain patterns you can create. For this reason, I can give only a general description of a very creative process. Other examples of false graining in this book include the Cricket, the Footstool, and the Two-Shelf Bucket Bench (see the color photos on pages 62 and 63).

DECORATIVE PAINTING

Decorative painting is a distinctive form of folk art. Country woodwork is so simple and plain that often the only difference between one culture's products and those made by another is the style of decorative painting.

Like false graining, decorative painting is usually done with oil paint, which is applied over a ground coat. Rather than simulate another material such as marble or wood

grain, the decoration is made up of patterns and figures. The decorative painting done by the Pennsylvania Germans is perhaps the best known. Their work included people and animals (sometimes mythological) and painted plants, such as vines and flowers similar to those painted on the Bootjack (see the color photo on page 66). Geometric patterns similar to those found on their hex signs were favored as well.

In New England a distinctive type of decorative painting was taught to girls at private schools. This technique was usually done on a small tabletop or on drawer fronts. The girls painted scenes and landscapes, or objects such as flower arrangements. However, shellac was the preferred ground coat rather than paint.

The decorations you paint on your woodwork should be your personal expression or style. You can paint your designs freehand or

Photo 6: When applying decorations like leaves, flowers, or feathers, use a pointed brush like that used in Chinese calligraphy. This thin brush can be used to produce small, fine-lined details.

sketch the pattern on the wood with a pencil first. Apply the paint with a pointed brush like that used in Chinese calligraphy (*Photo 6*). The pointed end gives you more control over the direction of the paint, and it can also produce fine lines. If you haven't had much experience with this type of painting, practice on some paper or scraps of wood.

PRIMITIVE DECORATION

One other type of country decorative painting is appropriate for two of the projects in this book. The Toy Horse (see the color photo on page 61) and the Rocking Cat both have painted eyes, mouths, ears, and other typical animal features.

These toys were painted in a primitive style that demonstrates the simple, fun-loving spirit of country folk. The features were painted over a solid base color without referring to any predrawn pattern. You won't find any painting patterns in this book, either, because that would defeat the purpose of the primitive style. Don't simply copy the painting designs of these toys. Your design should come directly from your mind's eye.

AGING

This technique was not practiced by country folk, but the enduring interest in country woodworking has made it a popular finishing method. When wooden objects like the projects in this book are freshly finished, they appear brand new, but many people like their country woodworking to appear old. Objects that show their age seem comfortable and familiar.

Most country woodwork was used daily and became worn quickly. A piece soon looked

very different than when it left its maker's shop. You can achieve this appearance by accelerating the wear. Before starting, take a moment to think about wear. Some of it is predictable, as it results from actions that are repeated regularly. The cuts of a knife on a breadboard and the touch of fingers on the edges of a door or on a drawer's knob are predictable, repeated actions. The resulting wear patterns are also predictable.

Wear is also caused by less regular accidents. The Splay-Leg Table (see the color photo on page 56) is a small portable table. When it is moved from one place to another, it will, from time to time, bang against the doorway. The resulting dents will be random, so a convincing simulated old finish will be both predictable and random.

I usually simulate predictable wear with steel wool or sandpaper. With these, I can accomplish in minutes what it would take fingers years to do. As an example, I rubbed the mitered corners of the Octagonal Canister (see the color photo on page 58) with sandpaper. The sandpaper removed the paint from the corners and exposed the raw wood to make the piece look old.

Random wear is more difficult. Forget about beating the piece with chains. Those marks are quite predictable. I spend some time thinking about what accidents the piece might have. Then I may drop it or drop something on it. I look around the shop for various objects and make different-shaped dents here and there. The secret to successful aging is to not make too many marks of the same kind.

NATURAL OR CLEAR FINISH

If you want to put a natural finish on one of these projects, your best bet is to apply a tung oil and varnish mixture like Watco

Danish Oil. The oil brings out the depth in the wood grain that only oil can produce, and the varnish seals and protects the wood. Simply wipe the Watco Danish Oil on with a rag, following the directions on the container.

I have also finished some of my woodwork with boiled linseed oil because it is inexpensive and easy to apply. Spread out some newspapers to catch drips, then brush it on liberally. Allow the liquid oil to set on the surface for about a half-hour. Periodically examine the piece for dry spots where the oil has been completely absorbed and draw some more oil over those areas with the brush. When the half-hour is up, wipe the piece dry with a soft, absorbent rag. One coat of oil is sufficient for most projects. Use boiled linseed oil only on projects that won't take a lot of abuse. The oil alone can't prevent scratches as varnish can, but if necessary, you can rejuvenate the wood by simply applying another coat of oil.

SALAD BOWL OIL FINISH

Some pieces in this book come in contact with food and should not receive any of the finishes described above. Instead, use a nontoxic salad bowl oil. The Serving Tray and the Knife Box (see the color photos on page 59) are good candidates for salad bowl oil. Behlen Salad Bowl Oil can be obtained from the Olde Mill Cabinet Shoppe, R.D. 2, Box 577A, York, PA 17402. Directions for applying this finish are on the container.

IN THE WHITE

One final finishing option that is appropriate for several projects in this book is simply no finish at all. Country woodworkers referred to woodwork left unfinished as "in the white." Many wooden objects went out of their makers' shops in the white, and since country woodwork was utilitarian, many customers simply left them that way.

Some projects that are left in the white will develop a finish through use. Kitchen utensils such as the Breadboard, Spice Roller, and Pasta Roller (see the color photos on pages 55 and 57) will absorb oils from the food with which they come in contact. The oils from the food produce a light, natural finish that I find pleasing.

Raw wood that is not handled frequently will also change. The pine Hanging Quilt Rack and the Closed Shelf (see the color photos on pages 64 and 68) will take on a warm honey color as the wood ages. This natural color was referred to colloquially as pumpkin pine. Eventually, raw pine will become as dark as mahogany. My parents' farmhouse has unfinished feather-edge pine paneling put up by my grandfather. He sawed the wood from trees blown over by the great hurricane of 1938. The paneling has been a rich reddish brown for as long as I can remember.

TOOLS AND TECHNIQUES

In this chapter we will look at some of the less common or more specialized tools and techniques that are used in this book. You may already know a lot about the tools and techniques that follow, but everybody can use a refresher occasionally. And I'm sure you will also learn some things here. Perhaps you'll find a new way to cut a dado, or you might discover the convenience of using some old-time hand tool techniques. In any case, look over this chapter so that you'll understand what I'm talking about later in the book.

HAND PLANING

Basic hand planing. Hand planes are recommended frequently in this book. I joint edges on small parts with a hand plane be-cause it is safer than using the jointer. I also use a hand plane to remove all the machine marks from my work—from both seen and unseen surfaces. The resulting surfaces are much smoother than can be obtained by machines or sandpaper, and hand planes make curled shavings rather than dust.

Some shaping operations, such as tapering table legs, can be done easily with a hand plane. You can use a hand plane to flatten a board that is warped or cupped, and you can even use a hand plane to thickness plane small parts.

You will need to choose a plane that matches the operation. Smoothing is done with a steel smooth plane (10 inches long), thickness planing and leveling are done with a jack plane (14 inches long), and jointing is done with a jointer plane (22 inches long).

ANATOMY OF A HAND PLANE

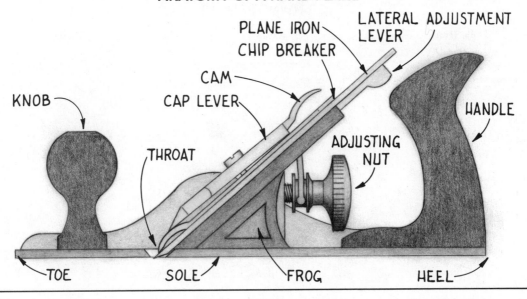

PLANE IRON
CHIP BREAKER
LATERAL ADJUSTMENT LEVER
CAM
CAP LEVER
KNOB
THROAT
ADJUSTING NUT
HANDLE
TOE
SOLE
FROG
HEEL

Tuning your hand plane. Before it will work right, a hand plane (new or old) must first be tuned, sharpened, and adjusted. The first step is to flatten the bottom, or sole, in a process called lapping. I flatten, or lap, the sole on a piece of 120-grit garnet paper (sandpaper) adhered to a strip of ⅜-inch-thick tempered glass 8 inches wide × 36 inches long. You can substitute the top of your table saw for the glass.

Hold the plane's sole perfectly flat on the garnet paper and slide it back and forth with even pressure. A few strokes will quickly reveal the high spots as the dulled metal is ground away to reveal the lighter metal underneath. Lap the sole until it is completely flat or until all the dulled metal has been ground away.

Honing the plane iron. Once the bottom of your plane is flat, you can turn your attention to the blade, or plane iron. The first step in sharpening a plane iron is to grind it to shape. The cutting edge on a blade used for smoothing should be very slightly crested; a jack plane's blade takes very heavy chips and should be ground to about an 8-inch radius; and the cutting edge on a plane that is used for jointing is ground straight across at a right angle to the blade's sides, as shown in the *Grinding Profiles.*

Next, flatten the back of the plane iron. Start by lapping the back of the plane iron in the same way that you lapped the bottom of the hand plane. Again, hold the plane iron perfectly flat and lap until the surface is all newly abraded metal. If the surface contains any scratches from surface grinding at the factory or pitting due to rust, completely remove these blemishes as well.

When the back of the plane iron has been thoroughly lapped, polish it to a mirror finish. I use a series of water stones, starting with 800-grit, then 1200-grit, and then 8000-grit. The 8000-grit stone creates a mirror polish so perfect I can clearly see my own eye in the steel. A surface that is less fine will not result in a razor-sharp cutting edge.

Turn the plane iron over and use the 1200-grit and 8000-grit stones to hone the bevel (*Photo 1*). If a slight burr remains, touch the cutting edge to a buffing wheel impreg-

GRINDING PROFILES

SLIGHTLY CRESTED

SMOOTH PLANE IRON

8" RAD.

JACK PLANE IRON

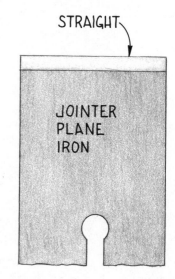

STRAIGHT

JOINTER PLANE IRON

Photo 1: Hold the plane iron so the bevel is flat on the sharpening stone and carefully move the plane iron back and forth to hone the edge.

Photo 2: Adjust the blade from side to side in the throat with the lateral adjustment lever. Check the adjustment by sighting down the sole of the plane or by lightly touching the edge of the blade with your fingertips.

nated with an abrasive compound. Test the sharpness of the edge by slicing the end grain of a piece of hardwood.

Attach the chip breaker to the plane iron and adjust it so its leading edge is about $\frac{1}{16}$ inch from the cutting edge of the plane iron. Put both in the plane and lock in place with the cap lever. Adjust the plane iron's side-to-side movement with the lateral adjustment lever and regulate the depth of the blade with the adjusting nut. You can adjust a plane by sighting down the sole and watching the cutting edge, but I prefer to feel the adjustment with my fingertips (*Photo 2*). Adjust the plane so the cut is even along the mouth. A smooth plane should take a shaving about the thickness of tissue paper; a jointing plane should take a chip about the thickness of writing paper; and a jack plane should take a cut about the thickness of posterboard.

Using the hand plane. To smooth a board, set the smooth plane on one corner of a board with the tool's body at a slight angle. Push the hand plane forward in a long, steady stroke from one end of the board to the other. Each stroke of the hand plane should overlap the preceding one as you move across the width of the board (*Photo 3*). If the machine marks are not completely removed, repeat the process a second time.

To joint an edge of a board with a jointer plane, clamp the board in your bench's side vise and place the plane at one end. Push the plane forward along the edge of the board using the fingers on your left hand as a guide (*Photo 4*). Make a complete pass from one end to the other. Make sure the edge is square by testing it with a try square. If you are making a glue joint, hold the two jointed boards together and check for gaps.

Photo 3: As you gradually plane a board, each stroke should slightly overlap the preceding one.

Photo 4: As you joint the edge of a board, keep the plane aligned with the edge of the board by guiding it with the fingers of your left hand.

To thickness a board or remove any cupping, use the jack plane. Push the plane across the board's surface at about a 45 degree angle (*Photo 5*). On the hollow side the blade will shave the raised edges. On the convex side it will shave the domed middle. The resulting surface is rough and should be surfaced with the smooth plane.

RABBETS AND DADOES

Different types of rabbets and dadoes. Rabbets and dadoes are used frequently in this book in a number of different ways. Rabbets join the ends of two boards, as shown in the Canted Display Shelf (page 231). Here, the rabbet is run across the grain. A rabbet can also secure the end of one board to the side of another, the way the back boards of the Bucket Bench (page 38) are joined to the sides. The back boards of the Keeping Bin (page 176) are joined along their edges

Photo 5: When thickness planing or flattening a board with a jack plane, hold the plane at a 45 degree angle to the edge of the board and slice across the grain.

with a shiplap (two overlapping rabbets). To make a tight rabbet joint, the edge or end of the mating board and the rabbet's shoulders have to be straight and square.

Dadoes come in a couple of different forms. A through dado runs all the way across the width of a board, like those used in the Egg Holder (page 145). Blind, or stopped, dadoes run only partway across the width of a board, like those in the top of the Bed Stair (page 48). Because stopped dadoes are generally cut with a cylindrical router bit, one or both ends of the dado are usually cut square with a chisel.

A dado, like a rabbet, must also have square sides and a smooth bottom. Since a dado encloses the end or edge of the part that it is joined to, the width is critical. A dado should form a friction fit with the part that fits into it. Dadoes also are often nailed.

Cutting rabbets and dadoes with a dado blade. Both rabbets and through dadoes can

Photo 6: The stacked dado blade is made up of two circular blades with several "chipper" blades sandwiched between them.

Photo 7: By raising the dado blade into a wooden auxiliary fence, you can cut to the very edge of the stock.

be cut with a stacked dado blade in a table saw. A stacked dado blade is made up of two circular saw blades with several "chippers" stacked between them (*Photo 6*). The number of chippers inserted between the blades determines the thickness of the dado cut. Raising or lowering the table saw's arbor controls the depth of the cut.

When cutting rabbets with a dado blade, I attach a wooden auxiliary fence to the table saw's rip fence to gauge the width of the cut. Using the wooden auxiliary fence allows me to raise the dado blade into the fence and cut to the very edge of the stock (*Photo 7*). Simply slide the stock along the fence to cut the rabbet.

To cut a dado, simply adjust the rip fence to guide the cut. When cutting dadoes in long and narrow pieces of wood, guide the stock with a miter gauge. Sometimes I even attach an auxiliary fence to the miter gauge to provide extra support (*Photo 8*).

Photo 8: An auxiliary fence can be attached to the miter gauge to help support longer boards.

Photo 9: You can clean up the edges, or shoulders, of a rabbet with a shoulder plane. The shoulder plane's blade can be sharpened just like that of a jointer plane.

A dado head leaves a rough surface on both dadoes and rabbets. I remove this roughness from both of a rabbet's surfaces with a shoulder plane (*Photo 9*). I smooth the bottom of rough dadoes with a router plane (*Photo 10*). You can also scrape the bottom of a dado smooth with a chisel.

Routing rabbets and dadoes. Rabbets and dadoes can also be cut with a router. You can rout rabbets with either a straight bit or a rabbeting bit with a ball-bearing guide. When using a straight bit to rout rabbets, guide the router with its removable edge guide (*Photo 11*). When using a rabbeting bit, simply guide the ball bearing against the edge of the stock.

Rabbets can be cut in small parts with a table-mounted router and either a straight bit or rabbeting bit. If you choose to cut rabbets with a straight bit in a table-mounted router, recess the bit as needed in a fence and guide the stock along the fence to make the rabbet.

Dadoes can be cut with a straight bit. To

Photo 10: A router plane equipped with a straight blade can smooth the bottom of rough dadoes.

Photo 11: When rabbeting with a straight bit, guide the router with its removable edge guide. Adjust the guide to determine the width of the rabbet.

Photo 12: When routing a dado with a straight bit, guide the router against a straightedge clamped to the stock.

Photo 13: Make repeated passes along the edge of the stock with the fillister plane to cut a rabbet. The plane will stop cutting when the depth stop hits the surface of the wood.

guide the router as you cut the dado, clamp a straightedge to the stock (*Photo 12*).

Cutting rabbets by hand. You can also cut rabbets by hand with a fillister plane. A fillister plane has a fence that slides across the sole to determine the width of the rabbet and an adjustable stop on the side of the plane to regulate the rabbet's depth.

Once the plane is adjusted, clamp the board to your workbench or secure it between bench dogs. Place the plane's fence against the board's edge. Make repeated passes with the fillister plane until the stop makes contact with the board's surface (*Photo 13*).

Cutting dadoes by hand. In pine, dadoes can be cut with a knife and chisel. Simply score the edges of the dado with a knife guided against a try square, then pare out the waste with a chisel.

Photo 14: Scribe around the ends of the parts to determine the length of the tails and pins.

Photo 15: Set a sliding T-bevel between 12 and 14 degrees and lay out the tails.

CUTTING DOVETAILS

Dovetail joints are strong and they look nice. For these reasons, dovetailing has always been considered an indication of good workmanship. The joint is made up of two parts, the tails and the pins. The tails are the flared parts that give the joint its name. Two basic types of dovetails are used in this book—open, or through, dovetails and half-blind dovetails. Open dovetailing joins boards with boxlike construction. Half-blind dovetails secure drawer sides to a drawer's front, but the tails are not visible from the front of the drawer. Instead, the tails fit into little pockets between the pins.

MAKING THROUGH DOVETAILS

Laying out through dovetails. Set a marking gauge to the thickness of the parts to be joined and scribe a line around each side (*Photo 14*). This scribe line is the base of the tails and pins.

> ### CONSTRUCTION TIP
>
> If your through dovetails are visible, as on the Serving Tray (page 189) and the Knife Box (page 181), make a dovetail template out of posterboard to ensure that the spacing of each row is even and identical on each corner.

Laying out the tails. Lay out the tails with a sliding T-bevel set between 12 and 14 degrees (*Photo 15*). Extend the layout lines across the end grain of the tail with a try square, then transfer the angle of the tails from the end grain down to the scribe line. To avoid mistakes, draw an X on the waste wood between the tails.

Cutting out the tails. Clamp the workpiece upright in a vise and cut along the waste side of the dovetail layout lines down to the scribe line with a dovetail saw (*Photo 16*).

Next, clamp the workpiece on the work

Photo 16: Define the tails by cutting along the layout lines down to the scribe line. As you cut, stay to the waste side of the lines.

Photo 18: Lay out the pins by tracing around the finished tails with a finely pointed scratch awl.

Photo 17: Remove the waste between the tails by driving a chisel into the waste along the scribe line. Pull back on the chisel to pop out the waste.

bench and use a chisel to cut the waste along the scribe line. Try to use a chisel with beveled edges that is as wide as the space between the tails. Drive the chisel with a mallet, then use the chisel as a lever to pop out the waste (*Photo 17*). Flip the part over and repeat the process to remove the second half of the waste. With a chisel, carefully remove any chips that remain in the corners.

Laying out the pins. Use the finished tails as a template to lay out the pins. It's best to trace the pins with a scratch awl rather than a pencil because the scratch awl's line is finer (*Photo 18*). Mark the waste between the pins with an X.

Cutting out the pins. Cut the pins the same way as the tails, cutting to the waste side of the lines. Remove the waste with a chisel (*Photo 19*).

Photo 19: Chisel away the waste between the pins after making the cuts.

Photo 20: Lay out blind dovetail pockets between the pins by tracing around the finished tails with a scratch awl.

Testing the fit. Clamp the board with the pins upright in a vise and place the tails over them. Tap the tails lightly with a mallet. If they do not slide easily into place, pare the pins to fit with a sharp chisel.

MAKING HALF-BLIND DOVETAILS

Modified procedure. When making half-blind dovetails in drawers, again lay out and cut the tails as described above. The tails should be as long as the drawer side is thick. Use the tails as a template to lay out the pins (*Photo 20*). Because the drawer front is thicker than the drawer sides, the pins are only open on one side, creating little dovetail pockets. Hold the dovetail saw at an angle as you cut out the pockets (*Photo 21*). Remove the waste between the pins with a chisel (*Photo 22*). Carefully pare away the waste on the sides of the pockets where the saw did not reach.

Photo 21: Cut along as much of the edge of the pins as possible by holding the dovetail saw at an angle and cutting across the corner of the stock. Country woodworkers often cut beyond the scribe lines on the inside of drawer fronts.

Photo 22: Cut and pare away the waste between the pins with a chisel. Tap the chisel into the waste with a mallet.

TURNING TOOLS AND ACCESSORIES

Turning tools are longer and heavier members of the chisel family. The extra strength helps resist shock and vibration. Turning tools also have longer handles to help prevent the tool from being knocked out of your hands and to provide greater control. The more you use the lathe, the more you are surprised how few turning tools you actually need. For most projects in this book, you will need only a ¾- and a ¼-inch standard flute spindle gouge, a ½-inch deep-flute spindle gouge, a ½- and a ¾-inch skew, a ³⁄₁₆-inch parting tool, and a ½-inch roundnose scraper (*Photo 23*). I generally don't use a large roughing gouge. I round a blank and shape its elements with the same gouge. Of course, I round larger blanks with the larger gouges.

If you enjoy wood turning and would like

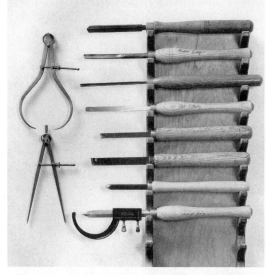

Photo 23: Here are my basic turning tools. *Left top:* pair of calipers; *left bottom:* pair of dividers; *right, top to bottom:* ¾-inch standard flute spindle gouge; ½-inch deep-flute spindle gouge; ¼-inch standard flute spindle gouge; ½-inch roundnose scraper; ½-inch skew; ¾-inch skew; diamond point; and ³⁄₁₆-inch parting tool.

more information on the subject, look for my book *Woodturning for Cabinetmakers*. I go into much greater detail on the subject than is possible here.

Spindle gouges. Spindle gouges are the tools most people think of when turning tools are mentioned. Spindle gouges are made with two different curves called flutes. These are designated as standard-flute (also called shallow-flute) and deep-flute gouges.

There is no single purpose for any individual spindle gouge. Use each where and when it feels the most comfortable. A spindle gouge's cutting edge is rounded so that it looks like one of your fingernails. In fact, the colloquial name for the ¼-inch spindle gouge is a lady finger.

SKEW DETAIL

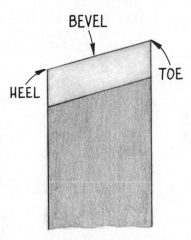

Skews. Skews are flat chisels with bevels ground on each side of the blade. The cutting edge is formed by the intersection of the bevels and is centered on the thickness of the skew. The edge is angled at about 75 degrees to the blade's edges.

The edges form two angles. The acute angle is called the toe and is generally considered the upper end of the cutting edge, while the obtuse angle is known as the heel, as shown in the *Skew Detail*.

The skew is perhaps the most difficult turning tool to learn to use properly, but it is also the most versatile. The more accomplished the wood turner, the more he relies on his skews for shaping and smoothing.

To cut shapes with the skew, place the blade's narrow lower edge on the rest and cut with the heel. A rolling motion creates a round surface (*Photo 24*), a sideways motion will cut a bevel (*Photo 25*), and pushing the tool straight into the wood will score it (*Photo 26*).

To plane with the skew, lay it on one of its wide sides and touch only the center portion of the cutting edge to the wood (*Photo 27*). Slowly slide the skew along the stock, removing small curls of wood. If the toe makes contact, the tool will be pulled out of control. If the heel makes contact, the tool will dig into the wood.

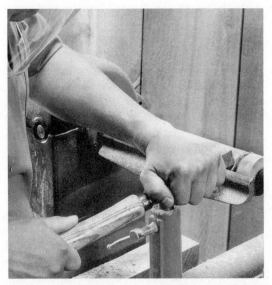

Photo 24: Rolling the skew up and to the side creates a round-over in the spinning stock.

Photo 25: Pushing the skew sideways and down creates a bevel.

Photo 26: Pushing the skew's heel straight into the wood creates a score line.

Photo 28: Push the parting tool straight into the spinning stock to cut a groove.

Parting tool. Like the skew, the parting tool also has two bevels, but they are ground on the blade's narrow edges. The cutting edge is created by their intersection and is centered on the width of the tool. Parting tools specialize in making plunge cuts and laying out the different sections of a turning.

To use a parting tool, set it on the tool rest and slowly push it forward into the wood at a right angle (*Photo 28*). Experienced turners can use a parting tool for parting (cutting) the stock off the lathe.

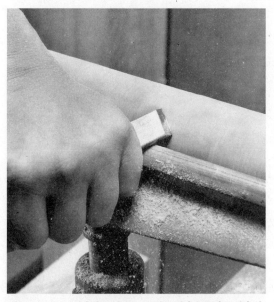

Photo 27: Hold the skew on its side and guide it slowly along the stock to plane the wood. Only the center portion of the cutting edge should slice into the wood.

Diamond point. Like the skew and parting tool, a diamond point also has two bevels. However, both are ground onto the same surface of the blade and placed at 90 degrees from each other, producing a pointed end. Unlike the skew and parting tool, a diamond point has two cutting edges.

Like the skew, the diamond point is a very versatile tool. It will take a clean slice off the end of a turning, leaving a glassy, smooth

CENTER SCRIBE OVERVIEW

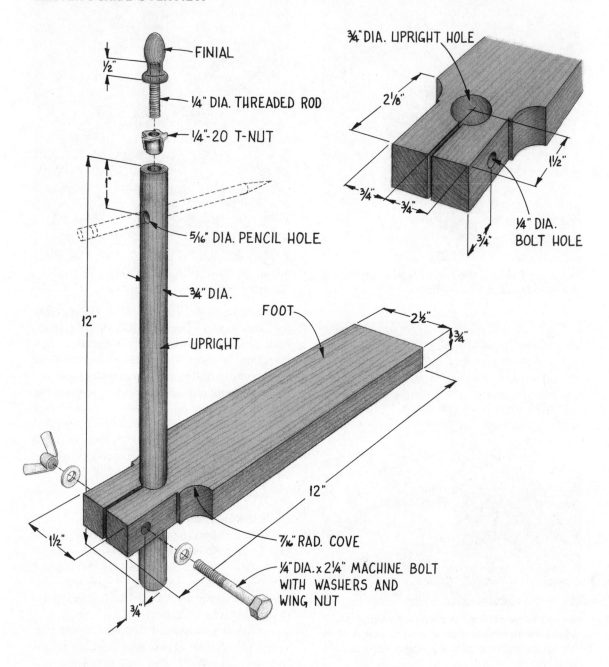

FINIAL

½"

¼" DIA. THREADED ROD

¼"-20 T-NUT

¾" DIA. UPRIGHT HOLE

2⅛"

1½"

¾"   ¾"

¾"

¼" DIA. BOLT HOLE

1"

5⁄16" DIA. PENCIL HOLE

¾" DIA.

12"

UPRIGHT

FOOT

2½"

¾"

12"

7⁄16" RAD. COVE

1½"

¾"

¼" DIA. x 2¼" MACHINE BOLT WITH WASHERS AND WING NUT

surface on the end grain. I used a diamond point to smooth and hollow the bottom of the Mortar (page 123). It can also be used like a small skew to plane small surfaces, and its pointed end can make V-grooves.

LATHE CENTER SCRIBE

A center scribe is used for drawing a horizontal line along a turning. The jig is handy for laying out details that are equally spaced around the turning, like the square designs of the Spinning Top (page 270) or the mortises in the handle of the Knife Box (page 181).

The dimensions given in the *Center Scribe Overview* are for a scribe that will work well on most big lathes. If it doesn't seem right for your machine, you will have to modify the dimensions to suit. Make the center scribe from a good close-grained hardwood like maple or cherry.

First, make the foot. Cut stock for the foot to size. The coved corners on the foot are not necessary for function; they just dress up the scribe a bit. If you choose to cut the coves, cut them on the band saw, as shown in the *Foot Detail*. Drill holes for the upright and the hexhead bolt, as shown. Use the band saw to cut the saw kerf.

Next, make the upright. Cut a length of ¾-inch-diameter dowel to the size shown in the *Center Scribe Overview*. Drill a ⁵⁄₁₆-inch-diameter pencil hole through the upright, as shown. Drill a centered hole through the top of the upright for the T-nut. The T-nut houses a threaded rod, which tightens against the pencil to hold it in place. Stop drilling when the T-nut hole meets the pencil hole. Coat the T-nut's shaft with epoxy and drive it into the hole. Be careful not to get epoxy on the threads.

When the upright is complete, turn a finial for the top of the scribe. The threaded rod fits into the finial, which acts like a knob when tightening the pencil. The exact profile is up to you. Drill a ¼-inch-diameter × ½-inch-deep hole in the bottom of the finial for the threaded rod. Epoxy the threaded rod in place. Be careful not to get epoxy on the exposed threads.

Finally, assemble the scribe. Put a washer on the bolt, slide the bolt through the hole in the foot, add another washer, and thread on the wing nut. Put the upright in its hole and tighten the wing nut to hold it in place. Slip the pencil through the pencil hole until the point protrudes 2 to 3 inches. Tighten the finial to hold the pencil in place. There should be just a small gap between the finial and the upright when the pencil is in place. If the gap is too big, grind a little off the bottom of the threaded rod.

To use the center scribe, place the foot of the scribe on the lathe bed and adjust the upright until the pencil point aligns with the point in the drive center. Tighten the wing nut to retain this setting. Mount the piece to be scribed on the lathe. Hold the foot flush on the bed and slide the center scribe along, allowing the pencil to draw a line on your work (*Photo 29*). The scribe can be used in conjunction with an indexing head if you need to draw lines that are evenly spaced around the turning.

HANDLING HANDSAWS

These days when a woodworker wants to cut a board he or she generally heads for the table saw or band saw; I will also often send you there in the pages of this book. You should be aware, however, of the lowly handsaws, which have many virtues that sometimes make them the better choice (*Photo 30*). These tools are very versatile, and I often find it handier to use a handsaw than its electrified cousin.

Photo 29: Slide the center scribe along the bed of the lathe to draw a line along the length of the turning.

Photo 30: Here are my basic handsaws. *Left to right*: Coping saw; bow saw; dovetail saw; backsaw; crosscut saw; rip saw.

Cutting and ripping with handsaws. When a woodworker begins a project, the first step is to cut out the stock. It has to be cut from the board to roughly its finished length and width. There are two types of handsaws for these purposes—the crosscut saw and the rip saw. The crosscut saw cuts across the grain; a rip saw cuts with the grain. I own two of each, one coarse (a small number of teeth per inch) and one fine (a large number of teeth per inch). The coarse saw is used for quick work in softwood. The fine saw is used for finish work in softwood and for hardwood cuts.

Sawing around curves. For larger curved work, I use a bow saw. A bow saw is similar to a band saw in that it has a thin, narrow blade, but instead of being a continuous loop, the blade is a single length stretched taut in a wooden frame. Traditionally, the frame was tightened by a tourniquet arrangement of waxed cobbler's twine and a toggle. Today,

this is often replaced with a length of wire and a bolt and a wing nut.

I cut small curved parts from thin stock with a coping saw. The coping saw is the only saw I own that cuts on the pull stroke, and I find that it gives me more control.

Fine cutting and trimming. I cut tenons and do a variety of trimming with a backsaw, and I cut dovetails with a dovetail saw. The blades on these saws are so thin that they are supported by metal spines that keep them from buckling. Like coping saws, dozuki (Japanese dovetail) saws cut on the pull stroke. The American/European variety that I use cuts on the push stroke.

Accurate hand sawing. When starting a cut with any saw, I place the saw on the mark and tilt it so its corner enters the wood first. Place your thumb close to the mark and use it to steady the blade (*Photo 31*). Although most

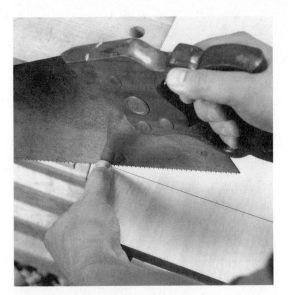

Photo 31: Guide the blade with your thumb as you cut the guide kerf.

Photo 32: You can protect the teeth of your handsaws with plastic notepaper binders.

saws cut on the push stroke, begin a cut by drawing the saw toward you to create a shallow kerf to guide the saw. Then you can move your thumb away from the blade.

Try to keep the saw on the line. If it should wander during a stroke, return it with the next. As you cut, the line you are following should disappear into sawdust. The exception to this rule is in cutting tenons and dovetail pins, when you cut outside the line.

Healthy handsaws. Treat your handsaws with the same respect you would a table saw blade. Do not leave saws lying on the bench after use. To protect mine from accidental damage, I hang them on a wall behind the bench. I further protect the teeth on my rip saw, crosscut saw, backsaw, and dovetail saw with inexpensive plastic notepaper binders available at any stationery store (*Photo 32*).

SELLING YOUR CRAFT

Most woodworkers obtain so much pleasure from their hobby that they occasionally dream of quitting their day jobs and earning a living from their craft. I understand that dream. For me it came true. I ran my own furniture-making business for 15 years.

The biggest obstacles to starting your own business are lack of confidence and fear of the unknown. You do not know what to expect, where to begin, what to make, or how to go about selling your work.

Before handing in your notice, talk to some self-employed people and find out what their life is like. You will discover that these folks are the last remnant of America's pioneer spirit. Most are fiercely independent and could not imagine ever again working for a boss.

Working for yourself has some very important benefits. You answer to yourself. You do not have to tolerate arbitrary authority or a boss's neuroses. Although you have a schedule, it is more flexible. If you decide to go fishing during the week, you can make it up by working on the weekend.

When you work for yourself, your accomplishments belong only to you. You are someone. You have a reputation and an identity. You are more than a cog in the wheel of life. However, working for yourself is hardly a bed of roses. There are serious drawbacks that most people cannot accept. Answer the following questions honestly to determine whether you have the temperament to be in business for yourself.

Can you handle risk and uncertainty? While working for yourself is rewarding, it is also frightening. There is no safety net. If you fall, you land hard. You receive none of the benefits provided by an employer. You buy your own insurance. There are no paid vacations. If you get behind schedule and have to work longer hours, there is no overtime.

Do you have the discipline? When you are self-employed, the boss has to be a son-of-a-gun. No money is being earned unless you're working, and no one is looking over your shoulder. You are responsible for maintaining good records, paying the bills on time, and meeting deadlines. Since you do not receive a weekly paycheck, you have to save money to get through the lean times.

Are you thick skinned? When you offer your products for sale, they will be critiqued. Can you handle the criticism, especially when it is often gratuitous? You will discover that everyone fancies him or herself an expert. Many of the comments you receive will be thoughtless and some will be downright hurtful.

If you can say yes to all these questions, you may be ready to go into business. Here's some general advice: Keep your costs low. Start in your garage or basement, if zoning allows. Have a cushion to fall back on. Have some savings, or a spouse who will carry you for a while. Better yet, have a spouse with health insurance who will carry you for a while.

I've found that people who do the best in the woodworking business don't just make anything that comes along. They minimize their risk by having a line of products they make time after time. The projects in this book, for example, might be considered a line of products. But it's a pretty big line. Why not confine yourself to some of the boxes and joinery projects? Leave the turning projects to somebody else. By confining your work to certain areas, you'll avoid the number one pitfall in woodworking as a business: estimating the time involved. Very few woodworkers can accurately predict just how much time it's going to take to make something, and the rest end up losing money. If you're building the same sort of thing repeatedly, you won't have to estimate. You'll know. And once you know how long it takes to build something, you're halfway to knowing how much to charge.

SETTING THE PRICE

In theory, the price you charge equals the cost of producing an object. This is true, as far as it goes. But you're really going to have to consider four things when you set your price. The first, cost of materials, is easily ascertainable, and I won't go into it here. The second cost is your labor; the third cost is your overhead. Finally, you have to consider the price the market will bear. If, when all is said and done, it's going to cost you more to produce the piece than people are willing to pay, you're going to make more money by staying home and taking a nap.

Labor costs. What are they? Begin by figuring out how much you earn per year at your current job. Figure in at least some of your current benefits—allow yourself some vacation and, at the very least, figure in the cost of health insurance. Divide the total by the number of hours you want to spend working as a craftsman. The result is the hourly rate you'll have to charge to maintain your current standard of living.

If, despite my earlier advice, you're making a one-of-a-kind item, estimate your time—

and double it. You're never going to get paid again for the item, so your price has to account for making patterns, doing drawings, figuring out joinery, and making mistakes. And no matter how long you've been in the business, you make mistakes. Despite many years of experience, I made a lot of mistakes building projects for this book. If you're in the business, that's profit that's gone right out the window.

Overhead. The most obvious overhead cost is your rent. If you pay $350 per month in rent, you're probably getting a deal. But if you work a 40-hour week, that place is costing you over $2 an hour, a cost you're going to have to add to your hourly cost. Add to that heat, electricity, and insurance—it may cost you $5 to $10 an hour just to have a shop.

On the other hand, when I moved from a rented shop to my basement, I applied my rent directly to my mortgage payment. I not only saved money, but was able to write off part of the building. There aren't any hard-and-fast rules. No one can tell you that overhead should be a certain percentage of income. The best advice I can give you is to keep your costs low.

Production costs. To determine what it costs to produce a project, add the materials cost and your hourly labor costs (including vacation and fringe benefits) to your hourly overhead, and multiply the result by the hours it takes to make something. That's your price. Once you've set it, stick with it: It's what you need to make a living. Now, some people aren't going to want to buy at that price and you're going to lose a customer or two. Fine. When it comes to losing a customer or losing my shirt, I'd rather lose a customer.

Market constraints. Finally, accept the fact that there are market constraints. You can't charge $1,000 for a rolling pin no matter how good it is. Probably the best thing you can do is to test the waters by doing a few craft shows or putting your work in a consignment shop. Make sure you've chosen the right shows or stores. When I first started, I was making exact reproductions of Windsor chairs. It was crazy for me to try to compete with J. C. Penney. I couldn't match them on price, and those people didn't want a handmade chair anyway. My place to go was the museum area. To succeed, your product has to connect with your customer. Go to the sorts of places you expect to find your customer. There are more than you think.

MARKETING YOUR WOODWORK

There are countless ways to sell your work. The one you settle on will depend on your personality, your method of doing business, and your product. Perhaps the most obvious is retail.

Retail. The ideal situation is to sell directly from your own space, in or adjacent to your workshop. This gives you the greatest amount of independence and eliminates the largest number of headaches. Catering to a walk-in clientele avoids problems like packing and shipping. You must attract customers to your shop, however. Put up a sign large enough to be seen from the road. The sign should also relate to your work. If you do country woodworking, a neon or a plastic sign would be inappropriate. Go with a wooden sign and carved letters.

Set up a display area separate from your work area. Consider using your house as a showroom so that you can live with your display samples. It's great as long as you can tolerate a stream of strangers through your home. If you'd prefer your privacy, set up the show-room somewhere else. It doesn't have to be big—it can be no more than a corner—but it should be tasteful and interesting. Many woodworkers are far more accomplished at making objects than at displaying them. Seek help from someone who has the talents you lack. Wherever it is, and however you set it up, keep the display area clean.

If your line of products is limited, display an example of each for customers to examine. If you take custom orders, maintain a portfolio of your past work. This can be as simple as a notebook of photographs. You can also mount these photos on the wall. Invest the money required to have the pictures done by a professional. Provide a free brochure, price list, or business card so people who want to contact you later can do so easily.

When you run your own shop and display room, browsers are a fact of life. If you ignore them, you risk developing a reputation for being inhospitable and you may lose sales. But if you are too attentive, they will eat up a lot of your time and give you nothing in return. I recommend greeting each person that arrives and exchanging a few pleasantries. Then, explain that you are working but will gladly stop to answer any questions. This lets people know you are approachable, and by stating that you are working, you eliminate many routine questions.

Advertise, but advertise locally. Instead of blanketing the general population, try to target potential customers. For example, advertise in the home and garden section of your newspaper's Sunday edition. In fact, call the home and garden editor and suggest yourself as the subject of an article. It's free (and compelling) advertising.

When your business becomes large enough, you can hire a salesperson who can also double as a secretary, bookkeeper, manager, and jack-of-all-trades. You may also find a family member who is willing to take on these duties—a spouse, a parent, or an older child. Still, you will find that most customers will want to spend some time talking with you before they place an order.

Before hanging out a sign, check with your community to be sure you are not violating any zoning laws or fire and safety codes. Check with your insurance agent to make sure your policy gives you ample protection.

Mail order. You can sell your woodworking exclusively by mail or operate a mail-order business adjacent to your showroom. You will still have to spend time with customers, but now you do it on the phone rather than in person. In fact, you will spend even more time with the average caller than with a customer in your shop. You cannot tell the person on the other end of the line to browse while you work and to interrupt when he has a question. On the other hand, most people who bother to call are primed to buy. You will sell to a higher percentage of callers than to walk-ins.

When you sell mail order, you are not limited to a local clientele. You can advertise regionally or nationally. This allows you to target your customers more effectively by placing ads in special-interest magazines. For example, if you do country woodworking, advertise in country decorating magazines. Also consider magazines that specialize in Americana. Buy copies at a newsstand and get the addresses and phone numbers from the masthead.

Magazine advertisements are usually more expensive than newspaper advertisements. Because they are targeted, however, the response rate is higher. Being featured in an article in one of these publications is a bonanza—the subscribers are already predisposed to the type of work you do.

When you place an advertisement, ask the sales representative to give you the names of the writers and editors. Call these people and tell them what skills and knowledge you have. Offer to be a resource when they have questions in your field. Time spent with people in the editorial department can be an excellent investment in future sales.

Develop a brochure that you can mail to the people who contact you. A brochure is expensive and preparing one is full of risk. You can make dozens of little mistakes that you will have to live with for some time. Avoid these problems by paying a professional to prepare a brochure for you. At a minimum, the brochure should list your products, their prices, and your terms.

Develop a sales form, too. This is largely for your own purposes. It helps avoid mistakes and keeps your work better organized.

Keep a mailing list. Retain the name, address, and phone number of each person who contacts you. In the future you may want to do a targeted mailing to the list. A computer makes it much easier to maintain and use a mailing list.

You will need a packing area. Stock shipping boxes, packing materials, labels, and other supplies. Lost or damaged products are a major headache. Find a shipper you can trust and develop a close working relationship.

Craft shows. You can sell your woodworking exclusively through craft shows or as an addition to your other business. Craft shows are an especially good way to sell your work if it's only a part-time business.

Craft shows take place in a large hall or outdoors. The management provides a display space, eliminating your need to maintain a showroom. The management also takes responsibility for advertising and attracting customers.

You will have to pay a booth fee, however,

and you make no profit on the show until you have cracked this nut. Unlike your own showroom, craft shows are only open for a limited number of days. You have to get to the show and set up your own display. You also have to deal directly with a crowd. Having paid admission, these people often feel you are obligated to entertain them.

Before renting a booth, become familiar with the management's terms. Some shows will allow you to bring only a display of your wares and to take orders that you fill later. Others require you to bring an inventory. This requires a substantial investment in time, and the income to offset it is deferred until the show. If you do not do well at the show or if attendance is affected by bad weather, you could face a financial squeeze.

Each show targets an audience. Only participate in shows that suit your products. For example, if you make country reproductions, don't bother with shows that attract an avant-garde crowd. If you make expensive wares, don't bother with low-end shows.

Some shows are run by the exhibitors themselves rather than a company. I used to participate in one of these along with a group of other craftspeople who made Early American reproductions in wood, metal, cloth, and paper. Each year, we had our show one Sunday in May. To find such a group, make inquiries, or take the initiative and form your own group.

As part of such a group, you may be asked to contribute to the costs and will be expected to help set up, break down, and so forth. You will also have to take more responsibility for advertising. The show should mail notices to potential customers. You should be willing to provide a list of your customers or to mail to them yourself.

Cooperatives. A cooperative is a store in which the management rents space where individual craftsmen display their work. Some woodworkers sell through a cooperative to avoid the problems of maintaining a showroom. Others sell through a cooperative as an extension of their own showroom. It allows them to make sales to people they might not otherwise see. Like craft shows, cooperatives are a good outlet for part-time woodworkers.

Like craft show management, the cooperative's management takes care of many responsibilities for you. For example, the management staffs the store and does its own advertising. You are responsible only for keeping your display area stocked. You are given an accounting of your sales once a month— usually when your rent is due.

There are several drawbacks to cooperatives. You have to pay rent and you have to maintain an inventory. Your wares must sell themselves, as there is little personal contact. You cannot be there to sell and the salespeople cannot do the job as well as you can. Damage and theft are ever-present risks.

Consignment. Consignment shops are similar to cooperatives. Here, however, you do not pay rent. Instead, the management takes a percentage of every item you sell. This arrangement creates an incentive for management to actively sell. The percentage does lower your profit, however.

Wholesale. Some woodworkers wholesale their wares to a company or store that then sells directly to its customers. Your only customers are those shops to whom you wholesale. This frees you to do more woodworking—the reason you wanted to be in business for yourself.

As nice as this sounds, there are drawbacks. You make a lot less profit—the wholesale price of your products is as low as 50 percent of the retail price. Usually, you make your money on volume. This means your woodwork may be limited to large production runs. Instead of being a craftsperson, you may find yourself reduced to a self-employed factory laborer.

You also lose some of the independence that makes being self-employed worthwhile. A wholesaler who buys a large percentage of your production can force you to accept terms and conditions you might resent. If one of your wholesalers drops your products or goes bankrupt, you can face hard times and even financial ruin.

Whatever method you choose to market and sell your wares, keep in mind that you are selling your craft. Make sure that you are getting out of your sales all the time, sweat, and personal attention you put in.

STANDS
AND
STOOLS

BUCKET BENCH

Families living in early America did not have access to many of the amenities that we take for granted today. They didn't draw water from the tap or get milk from the convenience store. They drew water from a well and kept it handy—in wooden buckets—for cooking or cleaning. They got milk from the family cow and stored it in buckets, too, until they drank it, cooked with it, or made it into cheese or butter.

Thus, a family's daily life required a number of buckets kept continually near the kitchen—usually in the scullery, a room just inside the back door. Near the door, a very utilitarian bench provided a handy surface for storing milk and water buckets. Today, a bucket bench is still a useful item to have in the same location, although for different purposes. Family members can sit on it while pulling on boots, and the space underneath is handy storage. The bucket bench can also hold gardening equipment or potted flowers.

This simple, backless bucket bench can be made to any length you need. The original bench was 6 feet long, which is the maximum length appropriate for ¾-inch pine. If you make the bench any longer, use full 1-inch pine. I made my top from a 40½-inch-long piece of wood I had on hand. Make your bench no shorter than this, as the legs would

CONSTRUCTION OVERVIEW

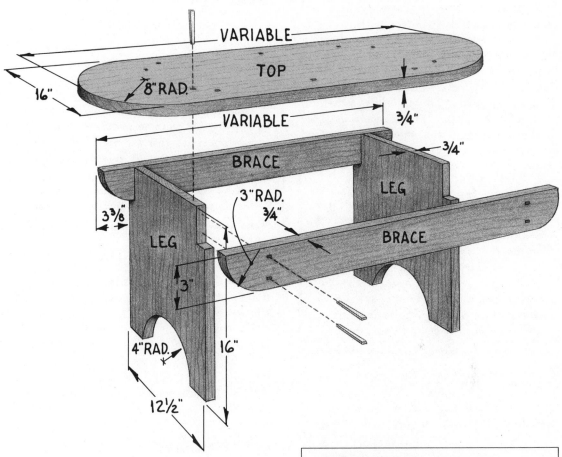

be too close to provide stability. If you lengthen the bench, leave the legs the same distance from the ends. Just expand the bench from the middle. Only the top and brace lengths will change: Add an inch to each brace for each inch you add to the top. The leg dimensions are constant no matter what length the bench is.

The original bench had been painted many times in many different colors. I painted mine with red milk paint. Because I used paint, I didn't need to sand away penciled layout lines.

MATERIALS LIST

PART	DIMENSIONS
Legs (2)	¾" × 12½" × 16"
Braces (2)	¾" × 3" × 33"
Top	¾" × 16" × 40½"

HARDWARE AND SUPPLIES

6d cut nails (as needed). Available from Tremont Nail Company, 8 Elm Street, P.O. Box 111, Wareham, MA 02571. Part # N-21 Std.

MAKE THE PARTS.

1. Prepare the stock. If necessary, joint and plane all materials to ¾ inch. (If you buy 1-inch boards at a lumberyard, they are actually ¾ inch thick.) Glue up boards as needed to obtain the width for the top and legs. When the glue is dry, rip and cut the stock to the dimensions given in the Materials List. Hand plane all visible surfaces to remove any machine marks and any glue that may have squeezed out.

> **TECHNIQUE TIP**
>
> When working on identical parts, perform one step on all the parts and then move on to the next step. In this case, joint a face on each part and then plane the parts all at once. If you make one part from start to finish and then make an identical part, you have to keep switching tools and changing workstations. Not only is this less efficient, but you're more likely to make a mistake.

2. Cut out the parts. Cut the legs, braces, and top to the shapes shown in the *Construction Overview* with a band saw or bow saw. Make the cutouts that hold the braces in the legs.

Clean up all curved areas with either a drum sander or a spokeshave and sandpaper.

> **TECHNIQUE TIP**
>
> You can run a grinding tool, such as a drum sander, in either direction along a curved edge without worrying about the grain. However, a cutting tool, such as a spokeshave, has to be worked in the direction of the grain to avoid digging and tearing, as shown in *Trimming Curves with a Spokeshave*. On the curve in the legs, start at the bottom of the curve and work up the sides. On a convex curve, start at the bottom and cut up toward the apex.

ASSEMBLE THE PARTS.

1. Nail the legs to the braces. Lay out the nail locations on the braces, as shown in the *Construction Overview*. To avoid splitting the stock, drill ⅛-inch pilot holes for the nails. Position the braces against the legs, centering the nail holes on the legs. Square the legs to the braces and extend the pilot holes into the legs. Nail one brace to the pair of legs, flip the assembly, and nail the other brace in place (*Photo 1*).

TRIMMING CURVES WITH A SPOKESHAVE

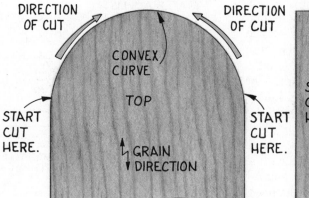

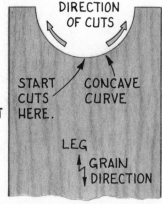

If any of the legs' edges stand slightly proud of the brace's surface, trim them flush with a block plane. Be careful to avoid the nail heads.

2. **Lay out the nail holes in the top.** Lay out the nail locations on the top, as shown in the *Construction Overview*. Lay the top on the legs and make sure the layout lines are centered on the legs. Make any necessary adjustments.

3. **Nail the top to the legs.** Position the edges of the top to overhang each brace by 1¾ inches. Drill a pilot hole and drive the first nail. The top will now pivot slightly should you need to make any adjustment. Drill and nail the opposing corner. This will fix the top in place. Drive the rest of the nails into the legs, then nail the top to the braces (*Photo 2*). Three nails per brace are sufficient for a short bench. More will be required for a long bench.

TECHNIQUE TIP

When nailing the top to the braces, lay the bucket bench diagonally across a corner of the workbench so it is resting on the braces. The braces will be supported by the bench and will not flex as you nail the top to them.

Photo 1: Square the leg to the brace and drive the nails into the pilot holes.

Photo 2: Center the nailing layout lines on the thickness of the legs and drive the nails through the pilot holes in the top and into the legs.

TWO-SHELF BUCKET BENCH

This bucket bench is a further evolution of the one shown on page 38. Most bucket benches are a simple, wide, open shelf. This bench has a back and an additional, smaller shelf for storing other objects. Like earlier bucket benches, the lower shelf is high enough so that objects placed on the floor can be pushed under it for protection.

Like many projects in this book, this bucket bench makes use of circles to add decorative interest to an otherwise utilitarian piece of furniture. The cutouts in the back and sides of this bench are arcs, which create a theme that cascades gently along the bench's outline.

The effect is sophisticated for such a simple, utilitarian piece.

The bucket bench's shelves are held in place with nailed butt joints, while the back boards are nailed into rabbets in the sides. Notice that the rabbets extend all the way to the floor, while the back boards end just below the bottom shelf. In the completed piece this extra length of rabbet is not noticeable.

The edges of the back boards are joined with lapping rabbets, a type of joint called a shiplap. Like any boards, those in the back of this piece expand and contract in relation to the humidity. Without the shiplap joint,

CONSTRUCTION OVERVIEW

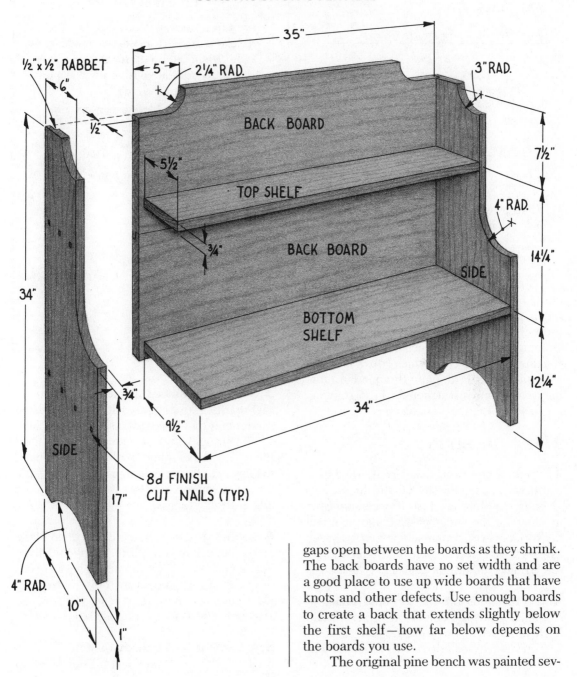

35"

½" x ½" RABBET

5"

6"

2¼" RAD.

½"

3" RAD.

BACK BOARD

7½"

5½"

TOP SHELF

4" RAD.

¾"

BACK BOARD

14¼"

SIDE

34"

BOTTOM SHELF

¾"

12¼"

9½"

34"

8d FINISH CUT NAILS (TYP.)

SIDE

17"

4" RAD.

10"

1"

gaps open between the boards as they shrink. The back boards have no set width and are a good place to use up wide boards that have knots and other defects. Use enough boards to create a back that extends slightly below the first shelf—how far below depends on the boards you use.

The original pine bench was painted sev-

MATERIALS LIST

PART	DIMENSIONS
Sides (2)	¾″ × 10″ × 34″
Back boards (as needed)	½″ × (variable) × 35″
Bottom shelf	¾″ × 9½″ × 34″
Top shelf	¾″ × 5½″ × 34″

HARDWARE AND SUPPLIES

6d finish cut nails (as needed). Available from Tremont Nail Company, 8 Elm Street, P.O. Box 111, Wareham, MA 02571. Part #N-19 Std.

1½″ finishing nails (as needed)

eral times, the final coat being white. Because the bench has numerous broad surfaces, it presents a good opportunity to do some false graining. I grained this bench with a red ground coat and black top coat, which I drew out with a rag moistened with paint thinner. For more information and instructions on false graining, see "False Graining" on page 8.

MAKE THE PARTS.

1. Prepare the materials. Joint, thickness plane, rip, and cut the stock to the dimensions given in the Materials List. If necessary, glue up stock for the wider parts. Hand plane all the surfaces to remove machine marks as well as any excess glue. For more on this technique, see "Hand Planing" on page 13.

2. Cut the sides and the top back board to shape. Lay out the curves on the sides and back, as shown in the *Construction Overview.* Cut out the curved edges with a bow saw or band saw.

CONSTRUCTION TIP

The top portion of each side is 6 inches wide and the bottom portion is 10 inches wide. When gluing up for the sides, save lumber by adding width only to the bottom 21 inches of the side.

3. Smooth the sawed surfaces. Clean up the saw marks in the curves with either a drum sander or a spokeshave and sandpaper. Clean up the straight part of the cuts with a block plane. The block plane's sole is short enough to allow you to start planing very close to the curves as you remove the saw marks from the edges' straight areas.

4. Rabbet the sides. Use either a dado blade on the table saw or a fillister plane to make a ½ × ½-inch rabbet on the inside back corner of each side, as shown in the *Construction Overview.* For more on cutting rabbets, see "Rabbets and Dadoes" on page 16.

5. Rabbet the back boards. Use either a dado blade on the table saw or a fillister plane to

TECHNIQUE TIP

Hold the block plane at an angle to the edge. This shortens the sole's length, allowing you to reach further into a tight spot such as a curve. It also skews the blade, which helps it cut more cleanly.

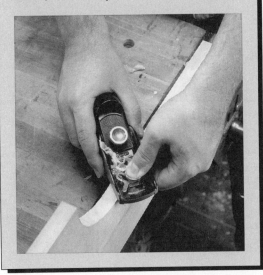

SHIPLAP DETAIL

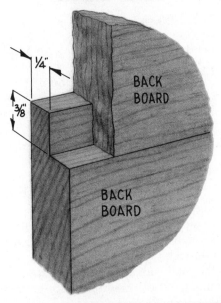

make ¼ × ⅜-inch rabbets on the edges of the back boards, as shown in the *Shiplap Detail*. As shown in the *Construction Overview*, only the bottom edge of the top back board is rabbeted, and only the upper edge of the bottom back board is rabbetted. The other back boards are rabbeted on both edges.

CONSTRUCTION TIP

Be sure to cut the rabbets in the sides on surfaces that face each other. To lay out the rabbets, hold the two sides together and mark the wood to be removed for the rabbets. If the rabbets don't face each other, you'll be unable to assemble the bench because one side will face forward and the other backward.

TOOL TIP

If there is any roughness along the rabbet's visible edge, this will show in the joint. Remove any roughness with a shoulder rabbet plane, sometimes called a shoulder plane.

ASSEMBLE THE SHELVES AND SIDES.

1. Nail the shelves and sides. With a square, lay out the nail holes for the shelves on the outside surface of each side. These holes will be centered on the thickness of the shelves. I recommend 6d finish cut nails for fastening the shelves to the sides. Drive two nails in each joint. Once the bench is assembled, you'll drive additional nails to secure it.

Begin by drilling pilot holes in one of the sides. Drill two pilot holes with a ⅛-inch bit. Holding the bottom shelf upright in your vise, lay the side on the shelf end. Align the center of the shelf's thickness with the layout line. Drill through the pilot holes, extending them into the shelf end. Drive the nails through the side into the shelf, and repeat the process for the top shelf (*Photo 1*).

Photo 1: Clamp the shelf upright in a bench vise, extend the pilot holes, and drive the nails.

2. Nail the other side. Rest the first side on the floor so that the unnailed shelf ends face up. Drill pilot holes in the side and shelf, as above, and drive the nails.

TECHNIQUE TIP

Place a clean board or piece of plywood under the first side to protect it from being dented or scratched while nailing the second.

---

3. Complete the nailing. Although the bench is now assembled, a few more nails will give it added strength. Drill additional pilot holes and drive nails to provide four nails per side to hold the bottom shelf. Drill pilot holes and drive nails to provide three per side for the top shelf.

ASSEMBLE THE BACK BOARDS.

1. Attach the top back board. Place the top back board in the rabbets and align it with the top of each side. At the same time, ensure the piece is square by laying a square on the lower shelf and against the side. (It's nice to have an extra pair of hands for this job, but you can do it yourself.) The nailed shelf joints are flexible enough to be pulled or pushed into square.

When you have the sides square to the shelves, nail the top back board in place (*Photo 2*). The board is only ½ inch thick and the rabbet is only ½ inch wide. I recommend nailing it with 1½-inch finishing nails. Once the top back board is nailed in place, it will hold the bucket bench square while you finish nailing.

Photo 2: Make sure the sides are square to the shelves and nail the top back board into place.

2. Attach the remaining back boards. One at a time, place the remaining back boards in the rabbets and nail them in place. Before nailing, pull the shiplap joint together tightly with a pair of lightweight bar clamps.

BED STAIR

Many different types of beds were used in early rural America, but the high-post canopy bed is the one most of us think of first. This type of bed is surprisingly high by modern standards, with the top of the mattress often as much as 28 inches from the floor.

Such a height was difficult to manage for children, the elderly, and the infirm. The solution was to keep a bed stair nearby. A bed stair is a step stool with one or two levels that was originally designed for getting in and out of a high-post bed.

Canopy beds are still reproduced today,

and if you have one, you may find a bed stair helpful. I have a friend who keeps a bed stair by the bed to help an elderly dog get up and down. More than likely, the bed stair you make will be used as a step stool. Children especially will find the bed stair helpful in dealing with adult-size fixtures, such as kitchen counters and bathroom sinks. If placed on a table or bureau, this bed stair could also function very nicely as a display shelf.

Canopy beds were very expensive, and their designs were usually quite formal. Many old bed stairs are also formal pieces of furni-

CONSTRUCTION OVERVIEW

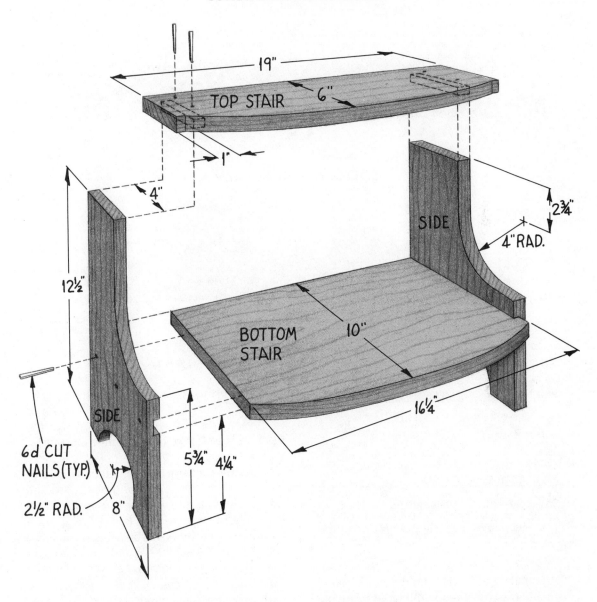

TOP STAIR

19"

6"

1"

4"

SIDE

2¾"

4"RAD.

12½"

BOTTOM
STAIR

10"

16¼"

SIDE

6d CUT
NAILS (TYP.)

2½" RAD.

8"

5¾"

4¼"

ture made to match the formal beds. This example, on the other hand, is a country bed stair. Instead of relying on reeding or inlay, its visual interest is provided by curves that are

laid out with a compass. Country cabinetmakers usually had a solid grounding in geometry and often used geometric shapes in their work.

This bed stair has to support as much as

TOP STAIR PATTERN

ONE SQUARE = ½"

TOP STAIR

BOTTOM STAIR PATTERN

ONE SQUARE = ½"

BOTTOM STAIR

MATERIALS LIST

PART	DIMENSIONS
Top stair	¾" × 6" × 19"
Bottom stair	¾" × 10" × 16¼"
Sides (2)	¾" × 8" × 12½"

HARDWARE AND SUPPLIES

6d cut nails (10). Available from Tremont Nail Company, 8 Elm Street, P.O. Box 111, Wareham, MA 02571. Part # N-21 Std.

250 pounds and should therefore be made from a hardwood. I made mine out of maple and painted it red, like the original. However, if your bed has a natural finish, you might want to make your bed stair out of the same wood species to match.

MAKE THE PARTS.

1. Prepare the stock. Joint, thickness plane, rip, and cut the stock to the dimensions given in the Materials List. Hand plane all the surfaces and edges to remove any machine marks.

2. Cut the parts to shape. Make a grid of ½-inch squares on a piece of posterboard and transfer the shapes shown in the *Top Stair Pattern* and *Bottom Stair Pattern.* Cut out a template from the posterboard and trace the curves onto the stock. Lay out the curves on the sides with a compass, as shown in the *Construction Overview.* Cut the parts to shape with a coping saw, band saw, or scroll saw. Clean up the sawed edges with a spokeshave and sandpaper.

3. Make the dadoes. Cut the dadoes in the

Photo 1: Clamp the parts to your workbench, then clamp a straightedge to the stock to guide the router as you cut the dadoes.

sides and the stopped dadoes in the top stair with a ¾-inch-diameter straight bit in your router. Set the bit to a depth of ⅜ inch. Clamp the parts to your bench and clamp a straight-edge to the stock to guide the router (*Photo 1*). Square up the ends of the stopped dadoes in the top stair with a chisel.

ASSEMBLE THE BED STAIR.

1. Attach the bottom stair. Slip the bottom stair into one of the side dadoes and drill three ⅛-inch-diameter pilot holes through the side and into the stair. Make sure the side and stair are square, then drive 6d cut nails into the pilot holes, as shown in the *Construction Overview.* Repeat the process to attach the second side.

2. Attach the top stair. Place the top stair dadoes over the top ends of the sides. Drill pilot holes for the 6d nails. Make sure the sides and top stair are square and nail the top stair in place.

Finish sand the assembled bed stair.

FOOTSTOOL

The footstool served the same purpose as a cricket (see page 71) in a country home, but it is more sophisticated in several ways. Instead of four plain legs, its two solid ends are decorated with what are colloquially known as bootjack cutouts. The stool is joined with nailed lap joints rather than drilled holes.

The footstool's tilted top also adds to its sophistication. When you want to elevate your tired, aching feet, the footstool's tilted top holds your feet in a more relaxed position than the flat-topped cricket.

Because the stool is more sophisticated, you might want to make it out of a figured

wood, such as curly maple or even walnut. You could also simulate these woods or others, as I have, with a false grain finish. For an explanation of how to apply a false grain finish, see "False Graining" on page 8.

MAKE THE PARTS.

1. Cut the stock to size. Joint and thickness plane the stock. Rip and cut the ends to the dimensions given in the Materials List. Cut the angle at the top of each end, as shown in the *End View*, on the table saw with the miter gauge set at 70 degrees.

CONSTRUCTION OVERVIEW

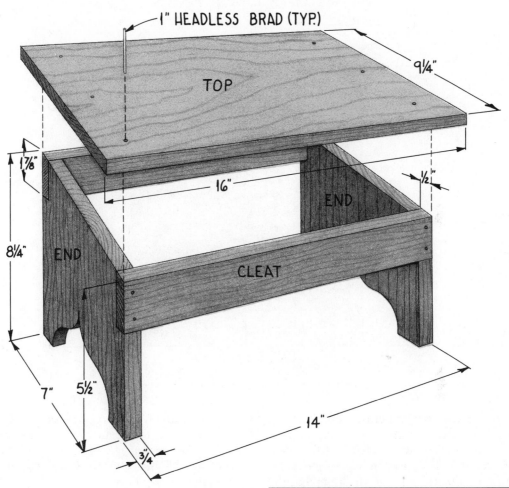

1" HEADLESS BRAD (TYP.)

9¼"

TOP

1⅞"

16"

½"

END

8¼"

END

CLEAT

7"

5½"

14"

¾"

Set your table saw's arbor to 20 degrees and bevel the upper edges of the cleats as you rip them to width. Also bevel the edges of the top while you rip it to width. Orient the bevels as shown in the *End View.* Cut the top and cleats to length.

Hand plane all surfaces to remove any machine marks.

MATERIALS LIST

PART	DIMENSIONS
Top	½" × 9¼" × 16"
Cleats (2)	½" × 1⅞" × 14"
Ends (2)	¾" × 7" × 8¼"

HARDWARE AND SUPPLIES

1" headless brads (as needed)

END VIEW

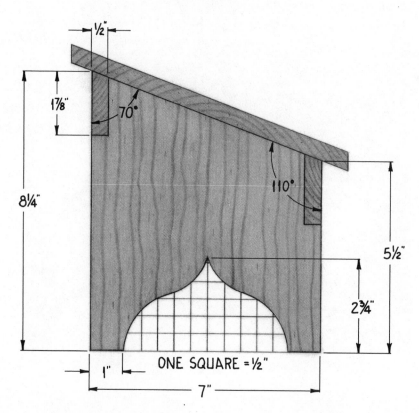

ONE SQUARE = ½"

2. Cut out the bootjack ends. Make a grid of ½-inch squares on a piece of posterboard or cardboard, and draw the shape of the boot-jack cutout on it, as shown in the *End View.* Transfer the pattern to the stock and cut the ends to shape with a band saw, scroll saw, or coping saw. Clean up the saw marks with a spokeshave or rasp. Sand the cut smooth.

MAKE THE JOINTS AND ASSEMBLE THE PARTS.

1. Make the joints. The edges of the ends are cut out to accept the cleats, as shown in the *End View* and *Construction Overview.* Guide the ends against the band saw rip fence (clamp a fence in place if necessary) as you cut the joint to its ½-inch width. Carefully cut the shoulders with a dovetail saw and remove the waste.

2. Assemble the footstool. Spread glue in the cleat cutouts. Put the cleats in place and nail each joint with two headless brads.

Nail the top to the base with headless brads. Use three per side, as shown in the *Construction Overview.*

From a Turned Breadboard (page 111) to an Egg Holder (page 145), the essence of country woodworking is simple, functional beauty.

This Windsor Stool (page 75) and the simple, elegant Splay-Leg Table (page 84) could fit into a modern setting, but the designs are nearly 200 years old.

Simple, turned "treen" items, like the Pasta Roller (*top*), page 118, the Spice Roller (*left*), page 137, and the Clothespins, (*right*), page 128, were used every day in early homes.

Country woodworkers often used simple geometric shapes in their designs as seen in this Hexagonal Candle Box (*left*), page 164, and the Octagonal Canister (*right*), page 194. The original design of these canisters was influenced by the Chinese.

If you keep your wits about you, you'll find that the angled dovetail joinery that holds together this Knife Box (page 181) and Serving Tray (page 189) isn't really much more challenging than cutting regular dovetails, but the joints look very impressive.

Make the Spinning Top (page 270) for your child or grandchild, but make the Noisemaker (page 276) for a *distant* relative.

Nothing brings a smile to a child's face like miniature furniture. Perhaps kid-sized stuff such as this Doll Cradle (page 286) and Child's Hutch Table (page 290) will help them feel grown up as they play house. The Toy Horse (page 280) will carry them off to unknown adventures, riding bucking broncos or roping cattle.

Country woodworkers had a handful of local woods to choose from, so they often simulated the grain and color of exotic woods. False painted grain could be bold as on the Child's Wing Chair (*left*), page 295, or it could be subtle as on the Cricket (*top*), page 71, or the Footstool (*bottom*), page 52.

Before the advent of indoor plumbing, water for cooking or washing was kept by the back door in buckets. To keep dirt and pets from getting into the water, the buckets were stowed under a Bucket Bench (*left*), page 38. Later, extra shelves were added to make the Two-Shelf Bucket Bench (*right*), page 42.

Today, we mainly use quilt racks for display, but in country houses with few closets they were used for storage. While the Standing Quilt Rack (page 91) could store quilts for one bed, the in-and-out rack design of the Hanging Quilt Rack (page 241) could store quilts and blankets for an entire household.

The Open Wall Box (*top left*), page 168, and the Two-Drawer Hanging Shelf (*bottom left*), page 209, added valuable wall storage space to small country homes. A heavy bulk item such as flour was kept in a Keeping Bin (*top right*), page 176. The bin's lid kept out dampness and rodents.

Fall and winter were muddy times for country folk, so muddied boots were removed at the door with the aid of a Bootjack (*bottom*), page 148. Bootjacks were decorated on the bottom since boots scuffed the top. Wet hats and jackets were hung on homemade coat racks such as this Lord Coatrack (*top left*), page 222, or Primitive Coatrack (*top right*), page 218.

Few country folk could afford a tall clock, but this Watch Hutch (page 96) was an elegant place for a pocket watch.

Country wood-working was rich with clever shelving ideas. The Closed Shelf (*left*), page 172, provided a place to hide a pair of reading glasses or the trinkets that collected in pockets, and the Corner Shelf (*right*), page 264, furnished an opportunity to display a few cherished belongings in an unused corner.

Here are some more examples of geometric shapes used by country woodworkers. The Pipe Box (*top left*), page 159, and the Spoon Rack (*top right*), page 255, make use of bold arcs and circles, while the cleverly designed rawhide strings of the Pyramid Shelf (*bottom left*), page 250, converge through the shelves to form a pyramid.

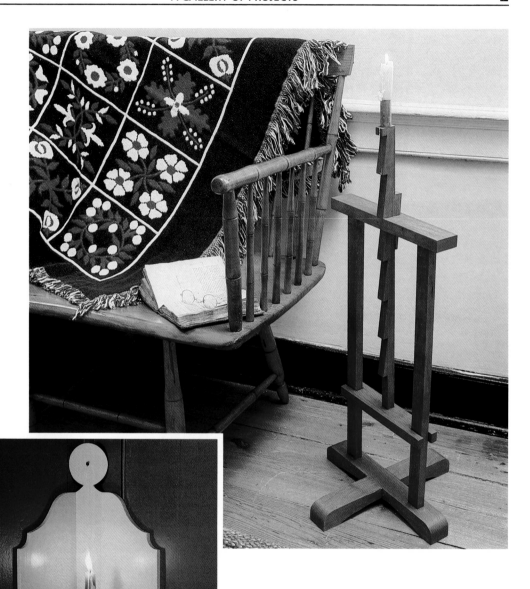

In pre-electric days, country folk made the most of candlepower. The Corner Candle Shelf (*bottom left*), page 214, was designed to fit easily into a corner so the candlelight could reflect off the shelf back and walls. With the Ratchet Candle Stand (*top right*), page 102, one could raise or lower the flame to suit a particular need.

CRICKET

This very basic four-legged footstool is known colloquially as a cricket. Small pieces of furniture like this were common in country houses; they made living a little more comfortable in two important ways. First, in an era before the reclining easy chair, a footstool was a way to elevate your tired, swollen feet. Second, before the development of central heating, homes were heated with fireplaces or stoves. These drew air out of the room and sent it up the chimney, requiring that it be replaced by air from outside. The result was a steady cold draft flowing across the floor of a country house. A cricket was used to keep feet up off the cold floor.

When I first began woodworking, I made lots of crickets like the one shown here, and I sold them at craft fairs. I made and painted the crickets, and my wife decorated them. My production crickets were primitives left purposefully rough. The legs and chamfering were done quickly with a drawknife, the top surfaced with just a jack plane. You can make yours more precisely and with a more finished look if you like. You can even substitute the rough whittled legs with turned legs of your own design.

The cricket's top is made from a workable wood such as pine or poplar. The legs are made from a hardwood. In the days when I

CONSTRUCTION OVERVIEW

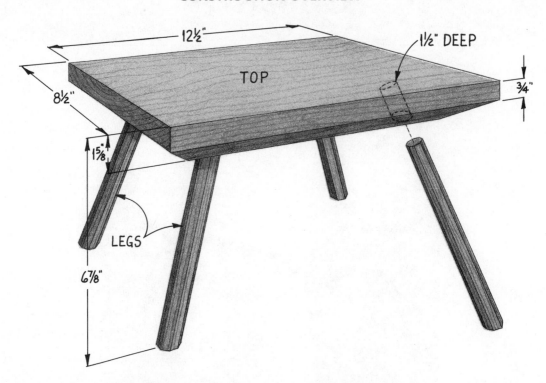

made crickets, I would begin a production run by cutting a bundle of saplings and shoots. I cut these into short sections that still contained the pith. If you prefer, you can saw scrap hardwood into leg blanks. I applied a false grain finish to my cricket (for instructions for applying a false grain finish, see "False Graining" on page 8). Finish yours in any way that suits you.

MAKE THE TOP.

1. Prepare and lay out the material. Joint and plane the top, and cut it to the dimensions given in the Materials List.

The underside of the top is beveled, as shown in the *Construction Overview.* To lay out the bevel, set a marking gauge to ¾ inch

MATERIALS LIST

PART	DIMENSIONS
Top	1⅝″ × 8½″ × 12½″
Legs (4)	⅞″ × ⅞″ × 7½″

and scribe a line along the top's four edges. Reset the marking gauge to 1¼ inch and scribe a line around the bottom, as shown in the *Bottom View.* The result is a smaller rectangle on the underside.

2. Lay out the leg joints. Scribe an X that connects the four corners of the bevel layout lines on the underside of the top, as shown in the *Bottom View.* The resulting intersecting lines are called sight lines.

BOTTOM VIEW   **LEG CROSS SECTION**

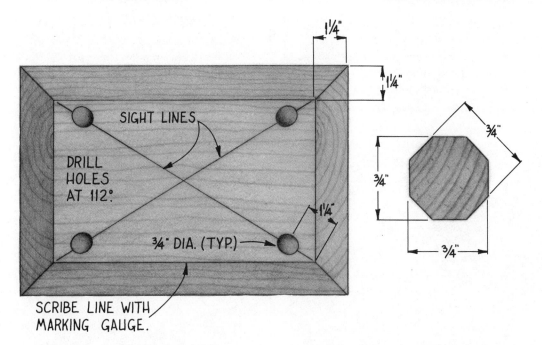

SIGHT LINES

DRILL
HOLES
AT 112°.

¾" DIA. (TYP.)

SCRIBE LINE WITH
MARKING GAUGE.

1¼"

1¼"

1¼"

¾"

¾"

¾"

3. Bevel the edges. Using either a bench plane or a drawknife, chamfer the edges by removing all the wood between the scribe lines on the edges and those on the underside of the top. As shown in the *Bottom View,* the mitered corners created by the chamfered edges will not align with the sight lines.

MAKE THE LEGS.

1. Prepare the leg stock. Rip and cut the leg stock to the dimensions given in the Materials List.

2. Shape the legs. With a spokeshave or drawknife, shape the legs to a rough ¾-inch octagon, as shown in the *Leg Cross Section,* or if you prefer, turn the legs to your own pattern. If you choose to turn the legs, make a ¾-inch-diameter × 1½-inch-long tenon on the top of each leg.

ASSEMBLE THE PARTS.

1. Make the joints. Set a sliding T-bevel to 112 degrees. Clamp the top between bench dogs with its underside facing up. Set the T-bevel on the underside, parallel to a sight line.

Drill the leg holes with a ¾-inch-diameter bit. To establish the correct angle, line up the bit with both the sight line and the T-bevel (*Photo 1*).

2. Attach the legs. Swab glue in the four holes. Set the end of a leg in a hole and drive it in with a hammer. The leg hole, drilled into softwood, will conform to the faceted hardwood leg. Do the same with the other three legs.

Photo 1: Align the drill bit with the sight lines and the sliding T-bevel when drilling the leg holes.

3. Trim the legs. Measure the height of your cricket to determine how much of the legs you will need to remove. The finished height is 6⅞ inches. Hold a backsaw parallel to the bench top and cut off the excess from the legs.

WINDSOR STOOL

Judging from its simple double-bobbin legs, the original Windsor stool was made around 1810. At that time, the Windsor chair was the most popular form of seating in America. While Windsor stools were never as common as Windsor chairs, there were many made. One of these could be found in almost every country home. Windsor stools came in many heights—from footstools to desk stools. They were used for occasional seating because they're easy to move about. Their splayed legs also make them stable enough to stand on.

Windsor stools are made with the same construction methods used in Windsor chairs. The four turned legs are braced by an H-stretcher and are anchored to a solid wooden seat that is dished out for more comfort. Like many Windsor chairs, the legs on the original stool were joined to the seat with locking tapered tenons. This unusual joint has cone-shaped tenons that fit into similarly shaped mortises. With this construction, the weight of someone sitting on the stool tightens the joints.

Windsor chairs earned their reputation for durability thanks, in part, to the unusual way in which the stretchers work. Instead of holding the legs together, the stretchers on a Windsor push the legs apart. This force puts the joints under compression. In the event that the glue joint fails, the tenon still cannot separate from its mortise.

The stool's seat is faceplate turned. To

CONSTRUCTION OVERVIEW

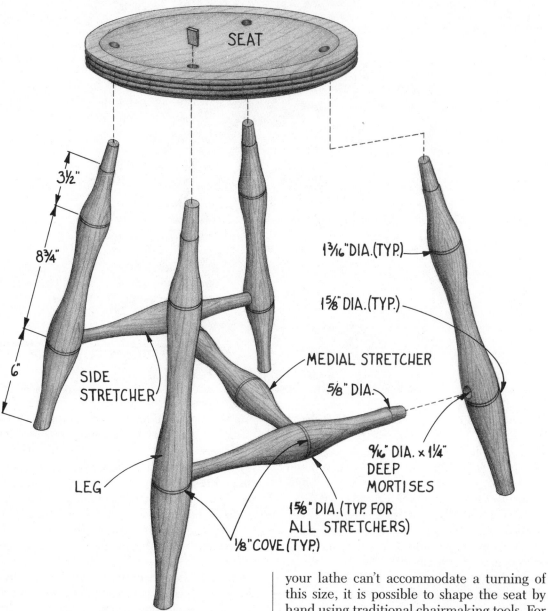

SEAT

3½"

8¾"

6"

SIDE
STRETCHER

LEG

1³⁄₁₆"DIA.(TYP.)

1⅝"DIA.(TYP.)

MEDIAL STRETCHER

⅝" DIA.

⁹⁄₁₆" DIA. × 1¼"
DEEP
MORTISES

1⅝"DIA.(TYP. FOR
ALL STRETCHERS)

⅛"COVE (TYP.)

turn the seat, your lathe must either have a 7-inch swing or allow you to turn outboard. If your lathe can't accommodate a turning of this size, it is possible to shape the seat by hand using traditional chairmaking tools. For a more involved explanation of Windsor construction, I recommend my book *Make a Windsor Chair with Michael Dunbar.*

MATERIALS LIST

PART	DIMENSIONS
Seat blank	1½″ × 14″ × 14″
Leg blanks (4)	1⅝″ × 1⅝″ × 21″
Side stretcher blanks (2)	1⅝″ × 1⅝″ × 16½″
Medial stretcher blank	1⅝″ × 1⅝″ × 16½″

Like Windsor chairs, this stool is made with more than one type of wood. The original stool's legs and stretchers are made of an even-grained hardwood. The simple double-bobbin shape has no fragile details, so any hardwood can be used. On the copy shown here, I used birch for the legs and stretchers.

As on Windsor chairs, Windsor stool seats were made of a softwood. The original stool has a pine seat, but my copies have tulip (yellow poplar) seats. Tulip turns more cleanly than pine, especially on the end grain.

Like Windsor chairs, stools were always painted. The original has a tortoiseshell finish on the seat done with random sponge graining. Red and black were used over a white background. The legs are white with green striping in the coves and simple painted sprigs for decoration.

You can finish your stool in any way you choose. If it is going to see rough or frequent wear and you want a natural finish, I recommend oil. An oil finish can be periodically renewed to hide scratches and scuff marks.

PREPARE THE MATERIALS.

1. Make the seat blank. Thickness plane the stock to 1½ inches. If necessary, glue up several boards to get the necessary width. Hand plane the bottom surface to remove any machine marks and excess glue.

2. Make the leg and stretcher blanks. Thickness plane the stock to 1⅝ inches. Rip the material to 1⅝ inches wide and cut it to the lengths shown in the Materials List. The listed leg lengths include 1½ inches of trim length—½ inch from the tenon end and 1 inch from the foot end. The stretcher lengths also include ½ inch of waste on each end. Because of this, the leg and stretcher lengths may vary slightly from the drawing.

TECHNIQUE TIP

The legs and stretchers can also be split, or riven, directly from a log. Choose a straight-grained log with no knots, and cut the log to the lengths needed for the blanks. Split the log in half by driving one or two wedges down into its end. Lay out as many 2-inch-square blanks on each half of the log as possible, and rive the blanks from the log with a heavy mallet, or maul, and a hatchet.

MAKE THE SEAT.

1. Prepare the seat blank. Use a large compass or a pair of dividers to trace a 7-inch-radius circle on the seat blank. Make sure that the fixed leg of the dividers creates a well-defined center mark because you will need to refer to this mark when laying out the joints.

Cut out the circular seat blank with a band saw or bow saw.

2. Turn the edge of the seat. Center the lathe's faceplate on the bottom of the seat blank and screw it in place. Mount the seat blank on the lathe. Position the tool rest along the edge of the seat blank, turn on the lathe, and round the outer edge of the blank with a gouge until all the band saw marks are removed (*Photo 1*). Turn the bead, as shown in the *Seat Cross*

Photo 1: Remove the saw marks from the edge of the seat blank with a sweeping gouge cut.

Section, with a skew (*Photo 2*). Bevel the top and bottom edges of the seat blank, as shown in the *Seat Cross Section,* with a gouge.

Photo 2: Cut the bead in the edge of the seat blank with a swinging skew cut.

TOOL TIP

If you choose to shape the seat by hand rather than turning it on the lathe, you will need to use some specialized chair-making tools. First, scribe an 11½-inch-diameter circle centered on the top of the seat blank with a pair of dividers. Clamp the blank to the top of your workbench and hollow out the top of the seat with a scorp. Hollow the seat to approximate the depth shown in the *Seat Cross Section.* Hold the scorp as shown in the photo, and draw it toward the center of the chair as you remove the waste. Sand the hollowed seat.

Next, bevel the top and bottom edges of the seat with a spokeshave and draw-knife. When shaping the seat by hand, simply omit the bead.

3. Hollow out the seat. The seat is hollowed for comfortable sitting, as shown in the *Seat Cross Section.* First, move the tool rest from the edge of the seat blank to the top of the seat blank. Measure out 5¾ inches from the center of the spinning seat, and hold a pencil against the seat to draw a 5¾-inch-radius circle.

SEET CROSS SECTION

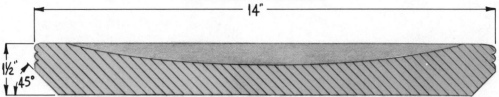

14"

1½" 45°

TECHNIQUE TIP

The bottom edge of the seat is beveled at 45 degrees. Lay out the bevel with a pencil while the blank is spinning. First, draw two lines on the seat blank—one on the bottom that is ¾ inch from the edge, and another on the edge that is ¾ inch from the bottom.

When the layout lines have been drawn, remove the wood between them with a gouge.

Photo 3: Move the gouge from the layout line to the center of the seat blank as you hollow the seat. Increase the depth of the cut as you move toward the center of the seat blank.

Next, hollow the seat with a gouge. Make several shallow cuts with the gouge, moving from the layout line toward the center of the seat blank (*Photo 3*). The gouge should cut deeper as you near the center of the seat blank, as shown in the *Seat Cross Section.*

Sand the seat as needed, then remove it from the lathe and faceplate.

TURN THE LEGS AND STRETCHERS AND DRILL THE MORTISES.

1. Turn the legs. One at a time, mount the leg blanks between centers on the lathe. First, turn the leg blanks round with a gouge, then turn the legs to the shape and thickness shown in the *Construction Overview.* Cut the decorative coves on the legs with a ¼-inch lady finger gouge (*Photo 4*).

Next, you must decide what kind of leg tenons you want to use—simple straight or traditional tapered. The mortises for straight tenons can be cut with an ordinary ⅝-inch-diameter drill bit, but the mortises for the more traditional tapered tenons must be cut with a special tool called a reamer. A reamer (available from Olde Mill Cabinet Shoppe, R.D. 2, Box 577A, York, PA 17402) looks like a cone of steel that has been sliced down the middle (*Photo 5*).

If you decide to use locking taper tenons similar to the one shown in the *Locking Taper Leg Tenon Detail,* you must turn tenons on the top end of your stool's legs that match the

LOCKING TAPER LEG TENON DETAIL

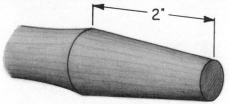

← 2" →

STRAIGHT LEG TENON DETAIL

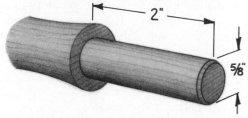

← 2" →

⅝"

STRETCHER TENON DETAIL

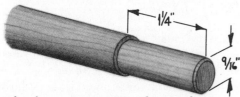

← 1¼" →

⁹⁄₁₆"

Photo 4: Push the ¼-inch gouge into the leg to create the decorative coves.

angle of your reamer. Simply turn the tapered tenons to shape with a gouge.

If you decide to make straight tenons, turn the tenons to the dimensions shown in the *Straight Leg Tenon Detail.* First, define the base of the tenon with a parting tool (*Photo 6*), then shape the tenon with a gouge or skew. Round the end of the straight tenon so that it will start easily into its mortise.

2. Lay out the mortises. Using the original center mark on the bottom of the seat, scribe a 5¹⁄₁₆-inch-radius circle. Draw a diameter line across the seat bottom and, with a square, draw a second diameter line at a right angle to the first. The points at which the diameter lines intersect the circle mark the centers of the four leg mortises.

3. Drill the leg holes. Put a ⅝-inch drill bit in a hand-held electric drill or hand-turned brace and clamp the seat in your bench vise.

Set a sliding T-bevel to 18 degrees and rest it on the seat, parallel to one diameter line. Refer to the angle of the sliding T-bevel and diameter lines as you drill the holes (*Photo 7*).

4. Ream the holes (optional). If you chose to turn straight tenons on your stool's legs, you can skip this step.

If you chose to use traditional tapered tenons, put a reamer in your brace (*Photo 5*). Slowly taper, or ream, a hole by holding the brace and reamer at the same angle as the hole and in line with the diameter line. A reamer can wander and, in the process, change the hole's angle, so check the angle frequently by placing a leg in the partially reamed hole and comparing its angle with that of the sliding T-bevel (*Photo 8*). You can correct any deviation in the angle by gently leaning the brace

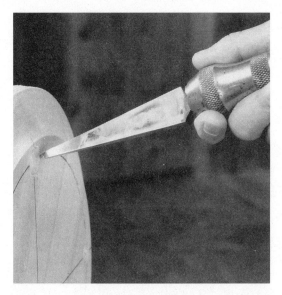

Photo 5: The reamer fits into the end of a brace and is used to taper the edges of a cylindrical mortise.

Photo 7: Align the drill bit with the angle of the sliding T-bevel and the diameter lines to drill at the proper angle. Notice the orientation of the mortises. The legs must flare out below the seat.

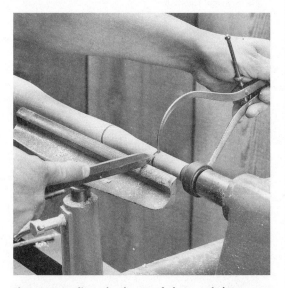

Photo 6: Define the base of the straight tenon with a parting tool. Push the parting tool into the wood until the base of the tenon has a ⅝-inch diameter.

Photo 8: To determine whether you are reaming at the correct angle, put a leg in the partially reamed hole and compare its angle with that of the sliding T-bevel.

and reamer in the desired direction. Ream the hole until the cone-shaped tenon's wide lower end is even with the bottom of the seat.

5. Make the side stretchers. Set the stool upright and measure the distance between the mortises in both pairs of legs (it does not matter which you choose to pair). The distance between each pair should be the same. Add 2½ inches to the distance between the legs (1¼ inches for each stretcher tenon), then place the joints under compression by adding on another ¼ inch. Turn the side stretchers on the lathe to your determined length and to the shape shown in the *Construction Overview.* Turn tenons on the ends of the side stretchers, as shown in the *Stretcher Tenon Detail.*

6. Drill the stretcher mortises. Put a ⁹⁄₁₆-inch-diameter drill bit in your hand-held electric drill. To drill the side stretcher mortises in the legs, set a sliding T-bevel to 11 degrees and sight across it to guide the angle of the bit. The base of the sliding T-bevel should align with the leg's axis. Tape a flag of masking tape to the drill bit 1¼ inch above its point. When the drill has penetrated the wood up to the flag, the hole is 1¼ inches deep.

The side stretchers are also mortised to accept the medial stretcher, as shown in the *Construction Overview.* To drill these mortises, set the sliding T-bevel to 90 degrees and sight across it to align the drill bit.

7. Turn the medial stretcher. Put the side stretchers between their leg pairs and put the legs into the mortises in the seat. Measure the distance between the mortises in the side stretchers and add 2½ inches (1¼ inches for each tenon) plus ¼ inch for compression. Turn the medial stretcher to the determined length and to the shape shown in the *Construction*

Overview. Turn tenons on the ends of the medial stretcher, as shown in the *Stretcher Tenon Detail.*

ASSEMBLE THE STOOL.

1. Assemble the legs and stretchers. Assemble the stretcher joints one at a time. Before you secure the joints, swab them with a light layer of white glue. Begin by joining the side stretchers to the medial stretcher. Drive the medial stretcher with a mallet if necessary to completely seat the tenons. Lay the "H" made from the stretchers on your workbench to make sure the stretchers are parallel and on the same plane.

Glue one leg to the H and place its tenon in a seat hole. Pivot the stretcher assembly until the H is parallel to the seat bottom. Add the other three legs one at a time. After each joint is assembled, pivot the leg on the stretcher tenon until the leg tenon aligns with its seat hole.

2. Assemble the top and legs. Swab glue in each of the seat holes. Insert the legs and tap them in place to be sure the tenons are completely seated. The leg tenons will protrude through the top of the seat.

Set the stool upright, then split and wedge the ends of the tenons. To avoid splitting the seat, make sure each wedge is placed at a right angle to the grain of the seat. Trim the leg tenon ends flush with the seat's surface.

3. Level the stool. Place the stool on the table saw table and fit shims under the four feet until the seat is level.

Measure the height from the seat to the table and subtract 19½ inches from this measurement. Set a compass to the difference. For example: If the stool height is 20¾ inches,

---

TOOL TIP

Rather than cutting wedge slots in the tenons with a saw, simply make a split with a ⅝-inch chisel. Drive the chisel into the end of the tenon with a mallet, making sure the split is at a right angle to the grain of the seat.

Drive the wedges into the tenons with a metal hammer rather than a light wooden mallet.

---

subtract 19½ inches and set the compass to 1¼ inches.

Trace a pencil line around the bottom of all four feet with the compass. Cut the feet at the pencil lines with a fine-tooth backsaw or dovetail saw. Round the edges on the bottom of the legs with sandpaper.

SPLAY-LEG TABLE

I have had this table around my house for about ten years now. It's a copy of a nearly 200-year-old piece. The table is small: It is most comfortable for two, but it will seat four. Made of pine, it's very lightweight. This, coupled with its size, makes it the ideal occasional table—useful for numerous light-duty, utilitarian tasks. In this way it serves me much as the original served its owners.

We keep the table against a wall in the den and move it out when we want to eat in front of the television. It acts as a serving table when we have a large number of guests and as a work table when I pay the monthly bills;

in the summer it is easily carried outside when we are entertaining in the backyard.

The legs on this table are canted, or splayed, which gives the form its name. Though they are splayed at only 99 degrees, the legs' cant is exaggerated because only their two inside surfaces are tapered. This makes the angle formed between the bottom of the skirt and the leg's surface 101 degrees.

I used this table as a project for a class I once taught on basic hand tools, particularly the hand plane. Therefore, the table shown was made using hand tools exclusively. You, however, will most likely use some machinery

CONSTRUCTION OVERVIEW

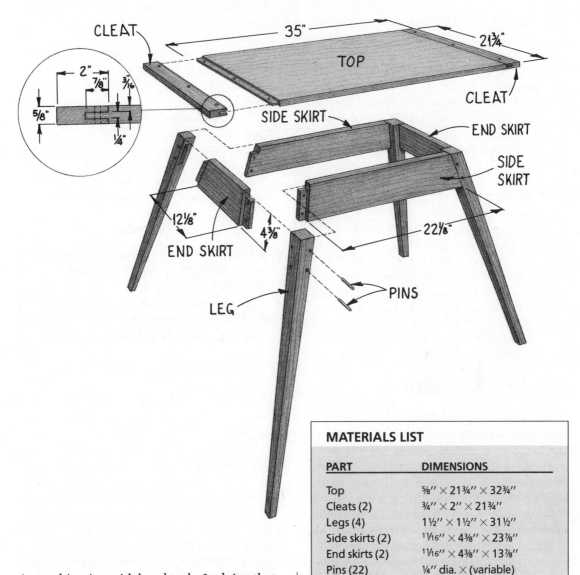

CLEAT

35"

TOP

21¾"

CLEAT

2"

7/8"

3/16"

5/8"

¼"

SIDE SKIRT

END SKIRT

SIDE SKIRT

12⅛"

4⅜"

END SKIRT

22⅛"

PINS

LEG

MATERIALS LIST

PART	DIMENSIONS
Top	5/8″ × 21¾″ × 32¾″
Cleats (2)	¾″ × 2″ × 21¾″
Legs (4)	1½″ × 1½″ × 31½″
Side skirts (2)	1¹/16″ × 4⅜″ × 23⅞″
End skirts (2)	1¹/16″ × 4⅜″ × 13⅞″
Pins (22)	¼″ dia. × (variable)

HARDWARE AND SUPPLIES

6d finish cut nails (4). Available from Tremont Nail Company, 8 Elm Street, P.O. Box 111, Wareham, MA 02571. Part # N-21 Std.

in combination with hand tools. In doing that, don't completely surrender the details that portray the handmade character of the table. Among these are the whittled pins that secure the joints and the cut nails that attach the top to the leg assembly. They may not seem very important, but small details often make the piece.

I painted my table with blue milk paint, then oiled it, turning the color a green-blue. The original had a scrubbed top, a feature collectors consider very desirable and for which they pay lots of money. A genuine scrubbed top results only from many years of frequent cleaning with harsh soaps (made of lye), which slowly wear away the finish and bleach the top the color of an old bone. The process also rounds the edges and wears away the grain's softer late wood. As a result, the denser early wood stands slightly proud.

If you want to create a scrubbed top in far less time, apply a finish to only the legs and skirts. Dilute 1 part liquid laundry bleach in about 3 parts water. Immerse a #3 steel wool pad in the solution, and without squeezing out any of the liquid, scrub the top vigorously. The steel wool is very coarse and will gently round the soft pine edges and will wear away the late wood. Meanwhile, the bleach whitens the surface.

MAKE THE TABLETOP.

1. Make the top panel. The table has what is known colloquially as a breadboard top. It has a cleat on either end to keep it from warping, as shown in the *Construction Overview.* Each cleat is joined to the top panel with a deep tongue-and-groove joint, pinned in three places, which allows for seasonal movement. The top is 21¾ inches wide. Although it is possible to find boards that wide in some parts of the country, most woodworkers will have to glue up several boards to achieve the width. To allow for truing and squaring the top, the boards' total width should be slightly more than the finished width specified in the Materials List. Joint the edges of the boards, then glue and clamp them together.

After the glue has dried, plane or sand the top to achieve a truly flat surface with no irregularities. Then cut the top to size. Without the cleats, the length is 32¾ inches. Joint one edge to be sure it is straight and to remove any dents made by the clamps. Square the two ends with this edge. Cut the second edge parallel to the first.

Cut the tongues next. The tongues are formed by cutting a ⅞-inch-wide × ³⁄₁₆-inch-deep rabbet in each face of each end of the top, as shown in the *Construction Overview.* Use a router with a straight bit and fence attachment to cut these wide rabbets.

CONSTRUCTION TIP

To counter a wide surface's tendency to warp, alternate the grain orientation of the boards composing the panel. If the first is heart-side up, place the second heart-side down, and so forth.

2. Make and attach the cleats. Cut the cleats to length, width, and thickness. Rout the ¼-inch-wide × ⅞-inch-deep groove along the edge of each cleat, as shown in the *Construction Overview.*

Because the grain in the cleats runs opposite to the grain in the top, you may experience an interesting phenomenon. If you make the top in the summer and the humidity is high, the top will shrink in the winter when your house is full of very dry air and be more narrow than the cleats are long. On the other hand, if you make the top in the winter, it will swell wider than the cleats in the summer. For this reason, you should fasten it only with wooden pins, as shown in the *Construction Overview. Do not* glue these joints, as the top will tear itself apart if not allowed to move freely.

Slide each cleat over its tongue and hold the parts tightly in place with a pair of bar clamps. Drill three ¼-inch holes that are centered on the tongue's width. Position the end holes about 1¾ inches from the edges, and center the third hole on the top's width. Drill from the top side so any problems with tear-out will occur on the underside.

Whittle a pin that will fit snugly into a drilled hole. Tap it through the hole with a light hammer until it is flush with the top. Cut the waste off with a backsaw and pare it flush with a chisel. Repeat for all the holes.

TECHNIQUE TIP

If you cut the cleat to length and thickness before routing the groove, you have to be very exact, as the slightest error will result in the cleat being offset from the upper surface. I made the cleats overlong and out of ¾-inch stock. After routing the grooves, I cut the cleats to length and attached them. Finally, I hand planed them flush with the top's upper and lower surfaces.

MAKE AND ATTACH THE BASE.

1. Make the legs. Prepare the stock. The lengths given for the legs in the Materials List are two inches longer than the legs' finished dimension. This is excess that will be cut off when the joinery is complete. Thickness plane the stock and joint one edge. Rip four legs to 1½ inches square and hand plane all four surfaces to remove the tool marks.

Lay out the mortises, as shown in the *Joinery Detail*, leaving an inch of each leg's extra length above the skirt's upper edge. Cut the mortises with a straight bit in a plunge router or by drilling a series of holes within

the layout lines. Square the ends of the mortises with a sharp chisel. At the same time, use the chisel to angle each mortise's lower edge toward the foot. This will accommodate the lower edge of the tenon, which is not at a right angle to the shoulder.

2. Make the skirts. The tenons that join the skirts to the legs have only one shoulder and one haunch, a form traditionally used in table and chair construction. With no shoulder on the back surface, the front shoulder becomes deeper, resulting in a thicker mortise wall— important on a long-legged piece of furniture. While glue blocks usually back up this single-shoulder-type of tenon, no glue blocks were

JOINERY DETAIL

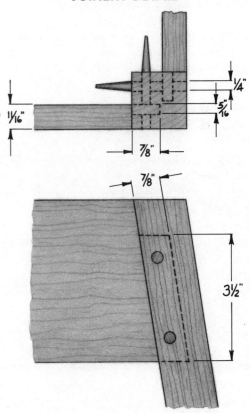

---

used on the original table and it has managed to survive almost 200 years. Remember, though, it is only intended for light duty.

Start the skirts by thickness planing the stock and ripping it to width. If you use a table saw, tilt the blade to rip one edge to 81 degrees. This will be the top edge. Cut the stock to length next, miter-cutting the ends to 81 degrees. Now cut the tenons, as shown in the *Joinery Detail.* Set a sliding T-bevel to 81 degrees and use it to mark the tenon shoulders ⅞ inch from the ends of the skirts. (Keep the T-bevel's setting, as you will need it again.) You can cut the tenons with a router or with a dado blade on a table saw. They are so simple you can also easily do them by hand. Each tenon has one haunch on its upper edge, which can be cut with a backsaw (*Photo 1*).

3. Fit the joints. Fit each tenon to its corresponding mortise. Make any fine adjustments to the tenons with a shoulder plane or rabbet

Photo 1: Cut the haunch on the tenon with a backsaw.

plane. Bevel the edges of each tenon's end so that it will slide easily into the mortise. Before you take the joint apart trace a line on the leg using the skirt's top edge as a guide. This line will help you when you have to trim the leg tops.

TECHNIQUE TIP

As you take apart the mortise-and-tenon joints, number them in sequence from 1 to 8, marking both mortise and tenon with the joint number. This way you can quickly match the parts later.

---

4. Complete the legs. Mold the edges first. This operation is optional, as the outside corners can be left square without seriously affecting the table's appearance. Simply choose from one of the three profiles given in the *Leg Detail.* The ovolo profile can be created with a ³⁄₁₆-inch beading bit, and the double quirk bead can be created with two passes of an edge-beading bit (one pass on each side of the corner). Either operation should be performed with the bit in a table-mounted router.

Trim the tops of the legs, cutting at a compound angle, 81 degrees on each side. This will make the leg tops flush with the skirts and parallel to the tabletop's lower surface. Cut the legs by tilting your table saw blade to 9 degrees off vertical and setting the miter gauge to 81 degrees. Or use the sliding T-bevel to extend onto all four sides the lines you traced along the tops of the skirts. Then use a backsaw to cut on the pencil lines.

Cut the legs to length. Measure 28½ inches from the highest point on the leg's end and make a mark on the opposite end. Use the T-bevel to lay out the same compound angle as at the top. Each line must be parallel to the top edge. Cut on this line using either the table saw or a backsaw.

Finally, taper the legs. Taper only the two inside surfaces — those with the mortises. You can taper the legs on a table saw using a tapering jig, or you can cut the taper on the band saw and clean away the saw marks with a hand plane.

> ### TOOL TIP
>
> **The legs can be tapered quickly with a jointer plane. First, measure and make a mark ¾ inch from each outside edge of the leg's bottom. Next, make a line across the leg that is even with the bottom of the mortises. With a straightedge, draw a taper layout line connecting the two marks. When both tapers have been laid out, set a jointer plane to take a heavy cut and plane to the line.**

5. Join the legs and skirts. Before assembling the legs and skirts, cut four pieces of 2-inch-thick scrap to 9 degrees (the complement of 81 degrees) to act as shims for the bar clamps.

This will enable you to clamp efficiently.

Now assemble the two sides of the table base independently. Apply glue to the mortises and insert the tenons. Span the assembly with a bar clamp, with the two shims protecting the legs. Use the clamp to pull the assembly tightly together — until there is no gap showing between the leg and tenon shoulder. Drill two ¼-inch holes through each joint. Whittle a pin and drive it with a light hammer (*Photo 2*). Saw off the pin, whittle a new one, and repeat for all four holes.

Repeat the entire process for the other side.

The sides are then joined to the end pieces in one operation. Glue all four mortises and insert their tenons. Clamp and pin one end and then the other. Be sure to stagger the pin holes so those on the ends do not intersect those on the sides, as shown in the *Joinery Detail.*

Finally, trim the pins. The same carving gouge used to whittle the pins can be used to shave their ends flush with the legs.

LEG DETAIL

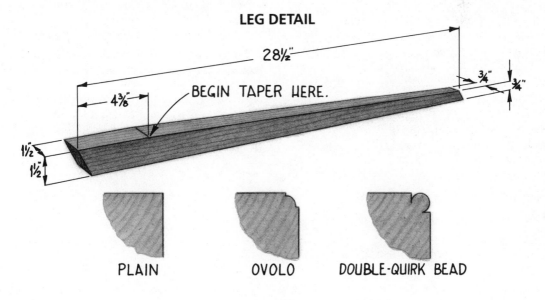

28½"

BEGIN TAPER HERE.

4⅜"

¾"   ¾"

1½"

1½"

PLAIN   OVOLO   DOUBLE-QUIRK BEAD

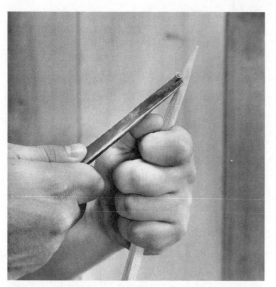

Photo 2: Whittle the ends of the pins to a point and tap them into the holes in the joints to secure the tenons.

6. Attach the top. The top on my table is joined to the base in the same way as the original: nailed to the leg tops with square-head nails. Use a cut nail for this, as the square head runs with the grain and is less obvious than a round head.

Center the top by measuring the overhang. It should be equal on both ends and equal on both sides.

To nail the top, drill a pilot hole for one nail. It must pierce the top and enter the leg. Drive the nail only about halfway. Do the same for the leg diagonally opposite. Now the top (fixed at two points) cannot shift. Do the same for the other two locations. Finally, drive all four nails flush with the top.

STANDING QUILT RACK

Judging by the number of these handy stand-ing quilt racks that have survived, nearly every rural house owned one. Most of them I have seen, however, are not as nice as this one. Quilt racks are often made of a common soft-wood such as pine, but this one is cherry. They are usually low with no more than two rails, but this one stands over 45 inches tall and has three rails. The feet on most racks are short and shapeless, but the feet on this exam-ple are well developed and long enough to make the quilt rack stable—even under the weight of several quilts.

Today, standing quilt racks like this one are usually used in the bedroom for display-ing quilts and other fabrics. They probably served that function in country homes as well. They were, however, also called drying racks, and they were frequently found, draped with laundry, in front of the fireplace or stove. In the fall, racks like this one were probably also used for drying herbs. The herb garden's harvest was tied in small clusters and sus-pended from the rails. Later, the herbs and spices would be used in cooking and in home-made remedies.

I made my copy from cherry—the same as the original—and I finished it with oil. This

CONSTRUCTION OVERVIEW

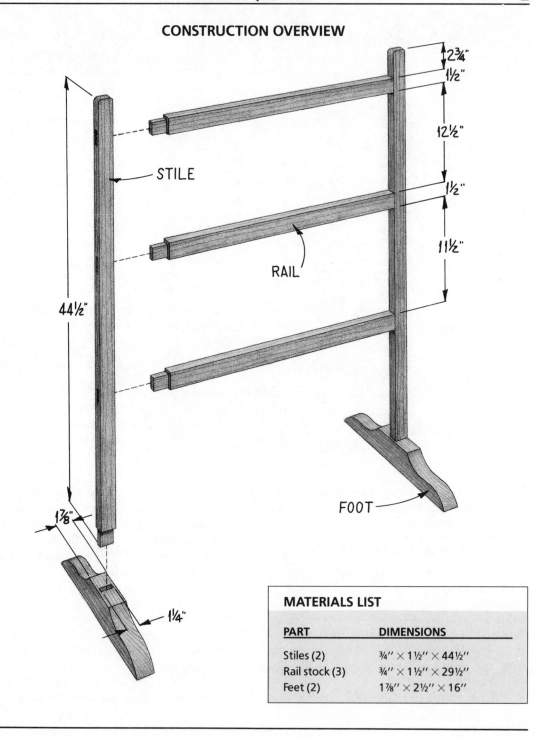

STILE

RAIL

FOOT

44½"

1⅞"

1¼"

2¾"

1½"

12½"

1½"

11½"

MATERIALS LIST

PART	DIMENSIONS
Stiles (2)	¾" × 1½" × 44½"
Rail stock (3)	¾" × 1½" × 29½"
Feet (2)	1⅞" × 2½" × 16"

quilt rack relies heavily on mortise-and-tenon joints, so most of your time will be spent cutting and fitting those joints. The rack has six identical through mortises in the stiles and two blind mortises in the feet. The through mortises are wedged for a tight fit.

MAKE THE PARTS.

1. Prepare the materials. Joint, thickness plane, rip, and cut the stock to the dimensions given in the Materials List. Hand plane all the surfaces to remove planer and saw marks.

2. Round the top ends of the stiles. Round the top corners of each stile with a sanding disk or belt sander, as shown in the *Construction Overview.*

3. Shape the feet. First, make a grid of ½-inch squares on a piece of posterboard, then draw the pattern shown in the *Foot Detail.* Cut out the pattern and transfer the shape to the stock. Cut the feet to shape on the band saw and smooth away the saw marks with sandpaper.

MAKE THE JOINTS.

1. Cut the tenons on the rails and stiles. As shown in the *Joint Detail,* the rails are joined to the stiles with through mortise-and-tenon joints. The stiles are joined to the feet with blind tenons. Cut the tenons on the rails and stiles with a dado blade in the table saw.

First, cut each tenon's wide side, or cheek. Raise the dado blade to ³⁄₁₆ inch above the surface of the table and set the miter gauge to 90 degrees. Clamp a stop block to the rip fence just in front of the dado blade to gauge the tenon length. Lay the first rail flat on the saw table and hold its edge firmly against the miter gauge. Slide the end of the rail against the stop block, then push the miter gauge and rail forward to make the first cut (*Photo 1*). When the first cut has been made, slide the rail away from the fence and cut away the rest of the waste on the cheek (*Photo 2*). Flip the stock over to cut the opposite cheek, then repeat the process to create tenons on the rest of the rails and one end of each stile.

When the cheeks have been cut, adjust the dado blade to a height of ⅛ inch and cut the tenon shoulders using the same stop block and fence setting as for the cheeks.

FOOT DETAIL

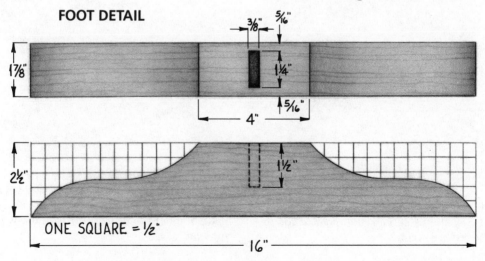

ONE SQUARE = ½"

93

JOINT DETAIL

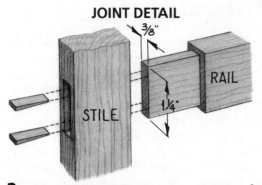

2. Lay out and cut the mortises. Lay out the through mortises on both edges of the stiles, as shown in the *Construction Overview.* Lay out a mortise in the top of each foot, as shown in the *Foot Detail.*

To cut out the mortises, drill a series of holes within the mortise layout lines with a ⁵⁄₁₆-inch-diameter bit in the drill press (*Photo 3*). When drilling the through mortises in the stiles, back up the stock with some scrap to support the wood grain as the bit exits the

> **CONSTRUCTION TIP**
>
> I like to make my through tenon ⅛ inch longer than the stile width (in this case 1⅝ inches long), so I've added ¼ inch to the rail lengths given in the Materials List (⅛ inch for each tenon). I trim this extra length off the tenons with a block plane after the rack is assembled. The trimmed tenons meet the outer edge of the stiles perfectly, and this results in cleaner joints. I recommend this extra step in this piece since the ends of the tenons are very visible.

stock. The mortise in each foot should be 1½ inches deep. When the mortises have been drilled out, clean up the waste to the inside edge of the layout lines with a sharp chisel.

Photo 2: To remove the remaining cheek waste, slide the rail about a dado blade's width away from the stop block and guide it across the blade. Repeat the process until all the waste is removed.

Photo 1: Butt the rail against the stop block, then guide it over the blade with the miter gauge to make the first cheek cut.

Photo 3: Drill a series of ⁵⁄₁₆-inch-diameter holes within the mortise layout lines.

TOOL TIP

With the number of mortises in this project, you may want to consider investing in a mortising chisel attachment for your drill press. The square mortising chisel and bits (available from Woodcraft, 210 Wood County Industrial Park, P.O. Box 1686, Parkersburg, WV 26102) cut clean, square-sided mortises.

ASSEMBLE THE RACK.

1. Adjust and glue the joints. Dry assemble the quilt rack to test the fit of the joints, and make any necessary adjustments. When all of the joints fit correctly, reassemble the rails and stiles with glue and put pressure on the joints with several bar clamps. When the rails and stiles have been joined, glue and clamp the feet to the assembly.

2. Wedge and trim the joints. Two wedges are driven into the ends of each tenon. The wedges strengthen the joint and expand the tenon to fill in any gaps.

First, make several thin ⅜-inch-wide wedges from some scraps of hardwood. Next, make two splits in the end of each tenon with a ⅜-inch chisel. When the splits have been made, spread some glue on the end of a wedge and drive it into one of the splits. Drive the wedge just enough to spread the tenon end and to fill any gaps.

When all of the wedges have been driven, plane the tenons flush with the stiles. Lightly sand the quilt rack.

TECHNIQUE TIP

Rather than cutting 12 separate wedges, make them from a single narrow strip of scrap. Shave a wedge in the end of the scrap with a drawknife or chisel. Drive the first wedge, saw the scrap free, and shave the next wedge.

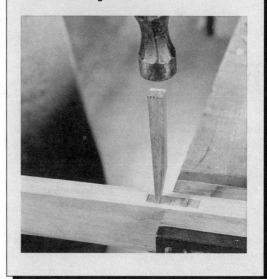

WATCH HUTCH

Before Eli Terry, Seth Thomas, and Silas Hoadley applied the lessons of the Industrial Revolution to clockmaking, clocks were extremely expensive and very few households owned one. The tall clock, mistakenly called a grandfather clock today, was the most valued of all.

Pocket watches were also relatively expensive but were far more common. For example, the ship's captain who built my house did not own a clock when he died in 1805. However, he did have two pocket watches that he probably used in navigation. One of his watches was silver and one was gold. The gold watch was appraised at $45 and the silver one at

$15. Today, that would equal about $7,500 and $2,500 respectively.

Something as valuable as a pocket watch was not carried about every day. It was also too precious to store out of sight in a drawer. If you have inherited a pocket watch, you, too, probably want to display it. In the past, the common solution was to store the watch in a special case called a watch hutch. This way, the expensive watch not only was protected, but also could serve as a small clock.

Watch hutches were usually made of wood. They came in all sorts of sizes and shapes— perhaps the most clever being a miniature tall clock.

CONSTRUCTION OVERVIEW

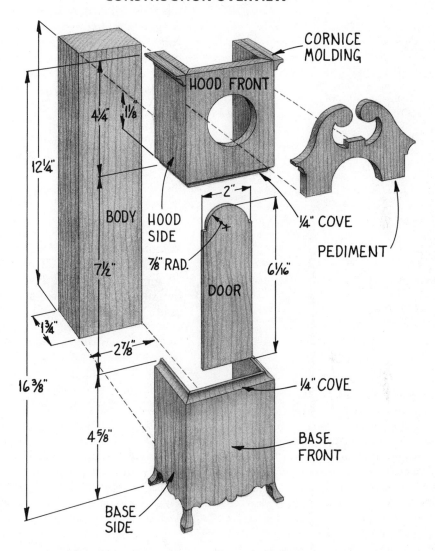

CORNICE MOLDING

HOOD FRONT

¼" COVE

PEDIMENT

4¼"

1⅛"

12¼"

BODY

HOOD SIDE

2"

7⅞" RAD.

7½"

DOOR

6 1⁄16"

1¾"

2⅞"

16⅜"

¼" COVE

BASE FRONT

4⅝"

BASE SIDE

I like this watch hutch because it so closely copies a real tall clock. It is such an accurate copy that, unlike many country pieces, it can be associated with a time and place. It is very similar to tall clocks made in the mid-Atlantic states between about 1790 and 1810.

It is safe to guess that the maker had seen a full-size urban tall clock that he copied from memory. This clock is different from the other projects in this book in that it is an architectural piece of furniture. It has parts that correspond to similar architectural parts found in a room. For example, the clock has a cornice and a pediment. (The cornice is the

MATERIALS LIST

PART	DIMENSIONS
Base front stock	$5/16'' \times 3\frac{3}{4}'' \times 4\frac{5}{8}''$
Base side stock (2)	$5/16'' \times 2\frac{3}{8}'' \times 4\frac{5}{8}''$
Body	$1\frac{3}{4}'' \times 2\frac{7}{8}'' \times 12\frac{1}{4}''$
Hood front stock	$5/16'' \times 3\frac{3}{4}'' \times 4\frac{1}{4}''$
Hood side stock (2)	$5/16'' \times 2\frac{3}{8}'' \times 4\frac{1}{4}''$
Front foot blocks (2)	$3/16'' \times 7/16'' \times 5/8''$
Side foot blocks (2)	$3/16'' \times \frac{1}{4}'' \times 5/8''$
Side back foot blocks (2)	$3/16'' \times 5/16'' \times 5/8''$
Cornice molding stock	$5/16'' \times 2'' \times 5''$
Pediment	$5/16'' \times 4\frac{1}{8}'' \times 2\frac{3}{4}''$
Door stock	$\frac{1}{8}'' \times 2'' \times 6\frac{1}{8}''$

HARDWARE AND SUPPLIES

1" brad (1)

molding on the sides of the hood; the pediment is the arched part that surmounts the clock.) Because it is open at the top, this form is known as a broken pediment.

The watch hutch has other details that are accurately copied from a full-size clock. It has miniature French feet, a favorite detail on Federal-period case furniture made in the Hepplewhite style. The watch hutch's feet are made the same way as on a full-size case piece. They are built up of blocks that are glued on and then carved to shape.

The door is also an accurate copy. Because of its similarity to many gravestones of the same period, the shape is known colloquially as a tombstone door. Both the headstone and door share a common source—a popular molding profile called an astragal. This profile is a half-round set off by two short, square corners called fillets.

On full-size tall clocks, the door was usually covered with a highly figured veneer. To remain close to the model, the original miniature also had a figured wood door. Unlike the doors on full-size tall clocks, this door is glued to the clock body and does not really open.

Only one small brad is used in this watch hutch to suspend the pocket watch. No other nails or hardware are used in the watch hutch. It is made up of several sections that are glued to a solid wood core. Making the hutch requires a lot of drying time, so glue the parts with a fast-drying glue such as Elmer's yellow carpenter's glue. You can further speed up the project if you make the parts for one section and glue them before preparing the next section.

The original hutch was made to fit its owner's pocket watch. I adapted my copy to fit a silver watch I own and of which I am very fond. You will want to fit your copy to your watch. The hole you cut in the hood front should match the diameter of your watch's face. The brad on which the watch hangs should be carefully placed so the watch face fits perfectly in the hole.

The original watch hutch was made of mahogany. I chose to use cherry, as all the projects in this book are made of native wood. I finished my hutch with oil. The door on my copy is cut from a piece of crotch-grain cherry that I had set aside for just such a purpose. I suggest you take the time to find a small piece with a similar grain.

MAKE THE PARTS.

1. Prepare the materials. Joint, thickness plane, rip, and cut the stock to the dimensions given in the Materials List. Cut the foot blocks to size with a dovetail saw. Hand plane or scrape all the surfaces to remove machine marks.

2. Cut and fit the base. First, cut the ¼-inch-radius cove in the base front and base sides, as shown in the *Construction Overview.* Put a ¼-inch-radius cove bit in a table-mounted router and adjust the router table fence and bit height to cut the profile shown. Back up the stock with a piece of scrap as you rout the coves to help prevent tear-out as the bit exits the stock (*Photo 1*).

When the cove has been cut, miter the base front and base sides to fit around the body of the clock, as shown in the *Construction Overview.* Cut the miters on the table saw with the blade set at 45 degrees. Make some test cuts on pieces of scrap first to check the angle.

When the parts have been mitered, make a grid of ¼-inch squares on a piece of posterboard and draw the base skirt shapes on it, as shown in the *Base Front Skirt Pattern* and *Base Side Skirt Pattern.* Cut the shapes from the posterboard and transfer them to the base

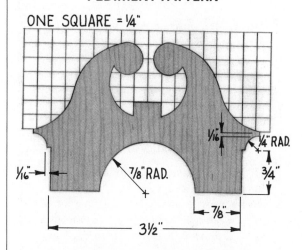

PEDIMENT PATTERN

ONE SQUARE = ¼"

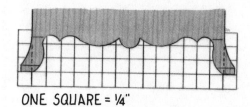

ONE SQUARE = ¼"

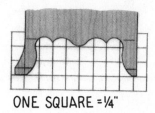

ONE SQUARE = ¼"

Photo 1: Back up the base front stock and base side stock with a piece of scrap as you rout the cove. The scrap will support the grain where the bit exits the stock and prevent tear-out.

front and base side stock. Cut the parts to shape with a scroll saw or coping saw and sand the sawed edges smooth.

3. Glue the base to the body. First, test fit the base front and base sides to the body and make any necessary adjustments. When the parts fit correctly, glue and clamp them to the body, as shown in the *Construction Overview.*

MAKE THE HOOD.

1. Cut and fit the hood. First, cut the ¼-inch-radius cove in the bottom of the hood front and hood sides, as shown in the *Construction Overview*. Cut these coves in the same way you cut those in the base parts.

When the coves have been cut, miter the hood front and hood sides to fit around the body of the clock, as shown in the *Construction Overview*. Cut these miters in the same way you cut those in the base parts.

2. Cut the face hole. Measure the diameter of your watch's dial and cut a hole that size. Make sure you have enough space between the bottom of the hole and the body for the watch case. Depending on the size of the watch's case, you may have to raise the hole's center slightly. Also make sure the hole will not intersect with the pediment.

3. Glue the hood. Test fit the hood front and hood sides and make any necessary adjustments. Glue and clamp the parts to the body, as shown in the *Construction Overview* and the *Hood Back View*.

HOOD BACK VIEW

PEDIMENT

COVE CORNICE MOLDING

1" BRAD

HOOD FRONT

HOOD SIDE

BODY

MAKE THE FEET.

1. Attach the foot blocks. Glue the front foot blocks and side foot blocks to the base front and base sides, as shown in the *Foot Construction Detail*. Each front foot is made up of two foot blocks—make sure the front foot blocks overlap the side foot blocks so the joint is less apparent. Each back foot is made up of only one side back foot block.

2. Shape the feet. The feet are too small to carve easily. I found it easiest to shape them on a sanding drum in my drill press. Sand the feet to the shapes shown in the *Base Front Skirt Pattern* and *Base Side Skirt Pattern*. I blended the blocks into the skirt with a round chain saw file.

FOOT CONSTRUCTION DETAIL

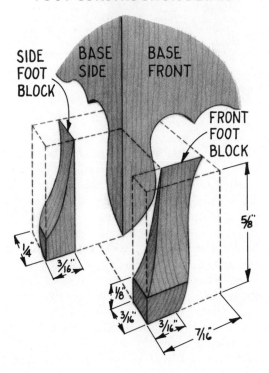

SIDE FOOT BLOCK

BASE SIDE

BASE FRONT

FRONT FOOT BLOCK

1/4"

3/16"

1/8"

3/16"

3/16"

7/16"

5/8"

MAKE THE PEDIMENT AND CORNICE MOLDING.

1. Make and attach the cornice molding. First, rout a cove in the edge of the stock with a 1/4-inch-radius cove bit in a table-mounted router. Next, rip the coved edge of the stock to 5/16 inch wide and cut it into two 2 1/8-inch lengths. Glue and clamp the cornice molding to the top of the hood sides, as shown in the *Construction Overview*.

2. Shape and attach the pediment. Make a grid of 1/4-inch squares on posterboard and draw the pediment shape on it, as shown in the *Pediment Pattern*. Cut the shape from the posterboard and transfer it onto the stock. Cut the pediment to shape with a scroll saw or coping saw; clean up the sawed edges with files and sandpaper. Glue and clamp the pediment to the hood, as shown in the *Construction Overview*. Center the pediment's concave lower edge over the hole for the watch dial.

MAKE THE DOOR.

1. Cut the door to shape. Lay out the shape of the door on the stock, as shown in the *Construction Overview*, with a compass and straightedge. Cut the door to its final shape with a scroll saw or coping saw. Smooth the sawed edges with sandpaper. Clean the square fillets with a sharp chisel. Plane the door's straight edges smooth with a block plane.

2. Attach the door. Glue and clamp the door to the body, as shown in the *Construction Overview*.

3. Hang the watch. Position the watch behind the face opening and mark the location of the 1-inch brad. Remove the watch and carefully tap the brad in place.

RATCHET CANDLE STAND

In the age before electricity, every home owned a variety of lighting devices and accessories. The ability to have light both where and when it was needed was a major concern. Candlesticks and lanterns could be carried from room to room, but they had to be placed on a nearby flat surface. Then the user had to move his or her reading material or work to make the best use of the available light, no matter how inconvenient or uncomfortable this might be.

This ratchet candle stand solves that problem and is a good example of the country ingenuity. Like candlesticks and lanterns, the stand is portable, which allows it to be moved from place to place; however, unlike most candle holders, it is adjustable. The candle can be raised and lowered—this allows the candle to be placed at the most useful height.

Today, we do not usually work or read by candlelight, but this candle stand is still an intriguing decorative accent for a country home. Wooden objects that are mechanical in nature always invite the viewer to look them over and to figure out how they work.

To use the candle stand, lift the ratchet to the desired height. Push the ratchet forward so the nearest tooth rests on the top rail and

CONSTRUCTION OVERVIEW

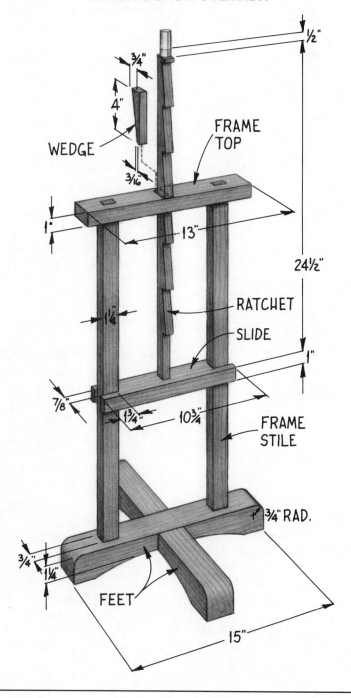

½"

¾"

4"

WEDGE

3/16"

FRAME
TOP

1"

13"

24½"

1¼"

RATCHET

SLIDE

1"

7/8"

1¾"

10¾"

FRAME
STILE

¾" RAD.

¾"

1¼"

FEET

15"

MATERIALS LIST

PART	DIMENSIONS
Feet (2)	$1\frac{7}{8}'' \times 2'' \times 15''$
Frame stiles (2)	$\frac{3}{4}'' \times 1\frac{1}{4}'' \times 25\frac{3}{4}''$
Frame top	$1'' \times 2'' \times 13''$
Slide	$1'' \times 2'' \times 10\frac{3}{4}''$
Ratchet	$\frac{3}{4}'' \times 1\frac{3}{16}'' \times 26''$
Wedge stock	$\frac{3}{4}'' \times \frac{3}{4}'' \times 4''$

HARDWARE AND SUPPLIES

1″ headless brads (2)
$2\frac{7}{8}'' \times 2''$ piece of sheet tin

slide the wedge in behind it to hold it in place.

The original candle stand was made of a hardwood with an even grain, then stained red. I made mine of cherry and wiped it with a thin wash of red milk paint. I then gave the finish more depth by wiping it with a light coating of linseed oil.

MAKE THE PARTS.

1. Prepare the stock. Joint, thickness plane, rip, and cut each part to the dimensions given in the Materials List. Hand plane the parts to remove machine marks.

2. Shape the feet. Lay out the shape of the feet on the stock, as shown in the *Construction Overview*. The curve on the bottom of the feet doesn't need to be an exact radius, but the two feet should be identical to each other. Sand the sawed surfaces to remove the saw marks.

3. Cut the lap joint. The feet are joined with a lap joint, as shown in the *Feet Joinery Detail*. Lay out the position of the notches on the edges of the stock. Cut the lap notches with a dado blade set up in your table saw, and guide the stock with a miter gauge set at 90 degrees.

First, raise the dado blade to $1\frac{3}{8}$ inches above the saw table and cut a $1\frac{7}{8}$-inch-wide notch centered on the bottom of the foot, as shown in the *Feet Joinery Detail*. Next, lower the dado blade to $\frac{5}{8}$ inch above the saw table and cut a $1\frac{7}{8}$-inch-wide notch centered on the top surface of the lower leg, as shown in the *Feet Joinery Detail*.

MAKE THE FRAME.

1. Cut the frame stile tenons. Cut $1\frac{3}{4}$-inch-long tenons on the bottom end of each frame stile and 1-inch-long tenons on the top end of each frame stile, as shown in the *Top Rail Detail* and *Feet Joinery Detail*. Cut the tenons with a dado blade set up in a table saw. Clamp a stop

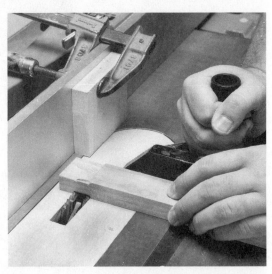

Photo 1: Gauge the length of the tenons with a stop block clamped to the rip fence, and guide the stock into the dado blade with a miter gauge set at 90 degrees.

FEET JOINERY DETAIL

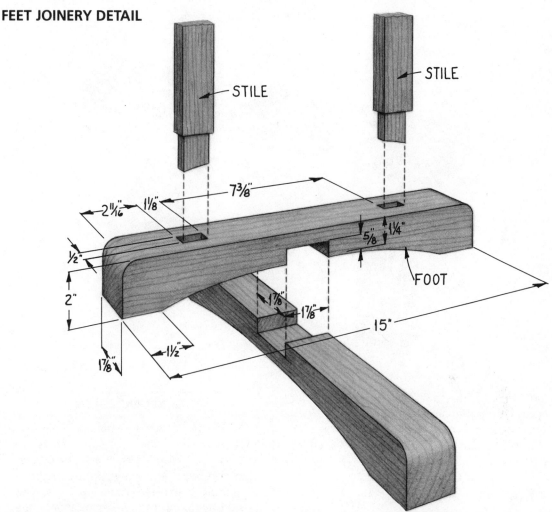

block to the rip fence and adjust it to control the length of the tenons. Guide the stock over the blade with a miter gauge set at 90 degrees (*Photo 1*). Cut the cheeks, or wide edges, of the tenons with the blade raised ⅛ inch above the saw table, and cut the shoulders, or narrow edges, of the tenons with the blade raised ¹⁄₁₆ inch above the saw table. Make as many passes over the blade as necessary to remove all of the waste from the tenon cheeks and shoulders.

2. Cut the mortises in the frame top and feet. The frame top and feet are mortised to accept the frame stile tenons, as shown in the *Top Rail Detail* and *Feet Joinery Detail*. The top rail has an extra mortise that guides the ratchet, as shown in the *Top Rail Detail*. All of the mortises pass all the way through the stock.

First, lay out the position of the mortises on the stock. When the mortises have been laid out, remove most of the waste from the

TOP RAIL DETAIL

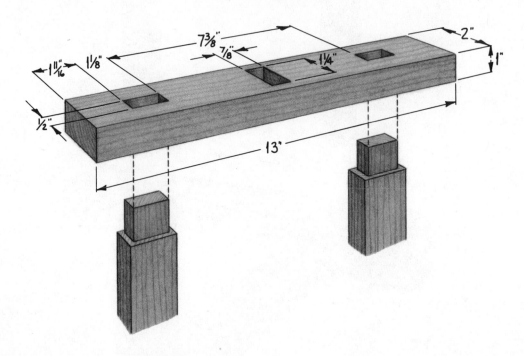

mortises by drilling a series of ⅜-inch-diameter holes within the layout lines (*Photo 2*). Next, square the ends of the mortises with a ⅜-inch chisel, and square the sides with a ¾-inch (or wider) chisel.

MAKE THE RATCHET AND SLIDE.

1. Make the slide. The slide attaches to the bottom of the ratchet and helps guide it as it moves up and down. The slide is notched out on each end to fit over the frame stiles, as shown in the *Construction Overview.* Lay out the notches to the dimensions shown with a marking gauge and try square. Cut the edges of the notches with a band saw, then cut out the waste with a coping saw. Square the ends of the notches with a ¾-inch chisel.

CONSTRUCTION TIP

Make sure that the notches in the slide are slightly wider than the frame stiles are thick. This extra width allows the ratchet to move up and down easily without binding. It also permits the ratchet to lean slightly forward so the teeth catch on the frame top.

2. Make the mortise and tenon. The ratchet is tenoned to fit into a mortise in the slide. Cut the tenon at the bottom of the ratchet with a dado blade set up in a table saw. Cut the tenon using the same technique you applied when cutting the frame stile tenons. Because the ratchet teeth will protrude from the side of the ratchet, the tenon is offset, as shown in

Photo 2: Drill a series of holes within the mortise layout lines to remove most of the waste from the mortises. Drill the holes with a ⅜-inch-diameter drill bit secured in a drill press.

the *Ratchet and Wedge Detail.* To cut the tenon, raise the blade ³⁄₁₆ inch above the saw table to cut one shoulder and both cheeks. To cut the remaining shoulder on the teeth side of the ratchet, raise the blade to ⅝ inch above the table. The result should be a ⅜-inch-square offset tenon.

Center the ratchet mortise on the slide, as shown in the *Ratchet and Wedge Detail.* Cut the mortise in the slide as you cut those in the feet and frame top.

3. Cut the ratchet teeth. Lay out the teeth on the edge of the ratchet, as shown in the *Ratchet and Wedge Detail.* Cut the teeth on a band saw, then remove the saw marks with sandpaper wrapped around a sanding block.

4. Prepare the sheet tin to make the candle socket. Cut a square of sheet tin with tin shears to the dimensions given in the Materi-

als List. In a pinch, even the smooth sides of a tin can will do. Clean the two long edges with either emery cloth or steel wool. Wrap the tin around a short length of ¾-inch-diameter dowel. Tap it lightly with a hammer to round it. With the tin shears, trim the tin so the edges overlap by about ⅛ inch.

5. Solder the candle socket. Remove the dowel and grip the tin in a vise so the two edges overlap by about ⅛ inch. Smear the seam with flux and heat it with a solder iron. When the flux melts, run a narrow bead of solder into the joint (*Photo 3*). Allow the tin to cool.

If you don't feel comfortable doing this metalwork, find a friend who does or have the candle socket soldered at a local machine shop.

Photo 3: Pinch the edges of the tin candle socket together in a machinist's vise. Smear flux along the seam and melt it with a solder iron. Run a narrow bead of solder into the seam and allow the candle socket to cool.

RATCHET AND WEDGE DETAIL

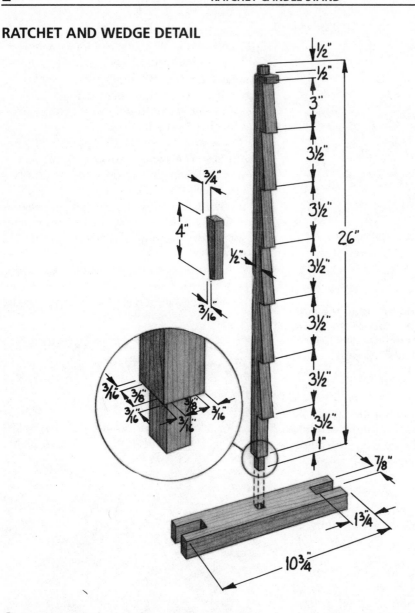

½"

½"

3"

3½"

3½"

26"

3½"

3½"

3½"

3½"

1"

¾"

4"

½"

3/16"

3/16" 3/8" 3/8" 3/16"

3/16" 3/16"

7/8"

1¾"

10¾"

6. Fit the candle socket to the ratchet. The candle socket is held in place by a ¾-inch-diameter tenon at the top of the ratchet. First, cut a ¾-inch-square × ½-inch-long tenon on the top of the ratchet, where shown in the *Ratchet and Wedge Detail*. Next, draw a

¾-inch-diameter circle on the end of the tenon, then chisel and file it to shape.

When the tenon has been cut to shape, slide the candle socket over it. Drill two ¹⁄₁₆-inch-diameter holes on opposing sides of the candle socket. The holes should be parallel, but should not meet in the center of the tenon. Trim two 1-inch brads to ½ inch long with tin snips and drive them into the tenon with a light hammer.

CONSTRUCTION TIP

The original did not include it, but it may be a good idea to add a tin drip ledge to catch wayward candle wax. Simply cut a 4-inch-diameter disk of tin and drill a ¾-inch-diameter hole in its center. Slip the disk over the tenon before you put the candle socket in place. The candle socket will keep the drip ledge from moving.

---

7. Make the wedge. Lay out the shape of the wedge on the stock, as shown in the *Ratchet and Wedge Detail.* Cut the angled edge on a band saw and smooth the sawed surface with sandpaper.

ASSEMBLE THE PIECES.

1. Glue together the feet, ratchet, and frame. First, spread white glue over the lap joints in the feet and clamp them together. Set the feet aside to dry. Next, spread glue in the slide mortise and insert the ratchet tenon. Clamp the ratchet to the slide with a bar clamp.

When the feet and ratchet glue joints are dry, spread glue on the frame stile lower tenons and insert them into their mortises in the feet. Next, slip the slide notches over the frame stiles and put the frame top over the ratchet. Spread glue into the frame top mortises and slip them over the frame stile upper tenons. Pull together the frame top, frame stiles, and feet with bar clamps. Make sure that the assembly is square and allow the glue to dry.

TECHNIQUE TIP

You can fill any gap left in a mortise-and-tenon joint with thin wedges. Rip some thin wedges from leftover scrap wood and carefully tap them between the tenon and mortise edges.

Be very careful not to tap the wedges too hard or the mortised parts may split.

---

2. Clean up the joints. Shave the tenon ends flush with the top of the frame and the bottoms of the feet and slide with a chisel. Clean up any excess glue with a chisel and sandpaper and finish sand the assembled candle stand.

TREENWARE

TURNED BREADBOARD

Most breadboards are no more than flat, square-edged pieces of wood. Some are cut into interesting shapes. This breadboard is far more elaborate—it is both turned and carved.

This type of turned breadboard was very popular in late 19th century rural America. As recently as a decade or two ago, breadboards like this one were easy to find in antique shops. They have since been bought by country collectors. As a result, the originals are now unusual—and expensive—items.

The design is very clever. The outer band is shaped by turning. It is then carved to include the word "Bread" set off in a banner

and two ears of wheat.

The breadboard is a relatively simple turning project, one that offers you a good chance to learn faceplate turning. You'll need access to a lathe that allows you to turn outboard or has at least a 6-inch swing.

The carving looks much more complicated than it really is. All you need is a basic selection of bench gouges and chisels that includes a ¼-inch chisel, a ½-inch chisel, a ¼-inch gouge, a ½-inch gouge, and a 1-inch gouge.

All of the breadboard's carved details are first scored with a chisel, a gouge, or both. As

FRONT VIEW

CROSS SECTION

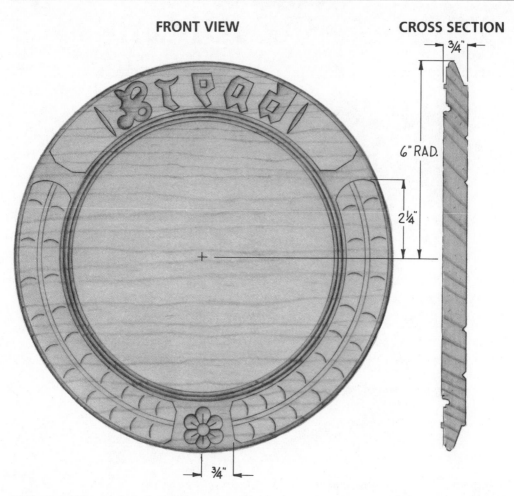

¾"

6" RAD.

2¼"

¾"

MATERIALS LIST

PART	DIMENSIONS
Maple turning blank	¾" × 12" × 12"

HARDWARE AND SUPPLIES

#8 × 1″ drywall screws (as needed)

you score, hold the chisel vertically and push its edge into the wood. A chisel scores a straight line; a gouge scores an arc.

After scoring around a detail, you relieve it by paring away the surrounding wood. On the antique breadboards very little time was spent carving. The word "Bread" and the flower were sketched on the wood. The rest was done freehand. As a result, the paring is very perfunctory and the relieved surfaces are fairly rough. Rather than detracting from the breadboard, this gives it a country appearance. When doing this work, use the tool that feels best for any particular detail.

While most projects in this book can be made out of more than one species of wood, hard (sugar) maple is the appropriate choice for this breadboard. Maple turns cleanly and when carved yields crisp details. It is also hard enough to stand up to repeated slices of the bread knife.

I recommend making the breadboard out of a single piece of wood. A glue joint will be very obvious, especially in light-colored maple. It is difficult to find wide hardwood boards, but if you make the extra effort, you'll end up with a better breadboard.

If you haven't done much turning, you might want to do some extra reading on the subject. In *Woodturning for Cabinetmakers*, I go into much greater detail on this subject.

I left my breadboard unfinished or "in the white." Over time, food oils will penetrate the wood and leave a nice patina.

PREPARE THE BLANK.

1. Prepare the stock. Joint, thickness plane, and cut the stock to the dimensions given in the Materials List. With dividers or a large compass, lay out a 12-inch-diameter circle on

EXPLODED VIEW OF TURNING ASSEMBLY

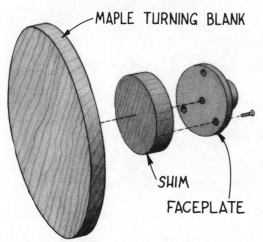

MAPLE TURNING BLANK

SHIM

FACEPLATE

the maple blank's jointed surface. Be sure the stationary leg makes a strong center mark that you can locate easily later. Cut out the circle with a band saw or a bow saw.

TECHNIQUE TIP

When cutting the circular blank's diameter, cut about ¼ inch outside the line. That way you have a little extra in case the blank isn't perfectly centered on the lathe.

---

2. Prepare the shim block. For turning, the breadboard blank is glued to a shim, which in turn is screwed to the lathe's faceplate, as shown in the *Exploded View of Turning Assembly.* Joint, plane, and cut a 1¼-inch-thick piece of hardwood so that it's slightly larger than your lathe's faceplate diameter. Make the shim by tracing the diameter of the lathe's faceplate onto the scrap. Most faceplates have a screw hole in their center that allows them to be used as a screw chuck. Use that hole to make a pencil mark that locates the shim's center.

Use a band saw or a bow saw to cut out the circle. Cut roughly ¼ inch outside the circle so that you end up with a round shim block about ½ inch greater in diameter than the faceplate.

3. Attach the shim block to the breadboard blank. Smear glue evenly over the front of the shim block. Center the shim block on the back of the breadboard blank. Clamp the two securely together.

SAFETY TIP

Let the glue dry for at least 12 hours. Don't risk having a 12-inch-diameter hard maple disk spin out of the lathe because you were impatient.

---

4. Attach the faceplate. When the glue is dry, lay the lathe's faceplate on the shim block. Align the centers of the shim and faceplate and screw the two together with #8 × 1-inch drywall screws (*Photo 1*). Mount the faceplate on the lathe.

TURN THE BREADBOARD.

1. Round the outside edge. Adjust the tool rest so you can work on the outside edge of the breadboard blank. Turn the blank with a ½-inch gouge until the blank is a perfect 12-inch round (*Photo 2*).

2. Joint the surfaces. If the blank's surfaces are not spinning true, you will see a ghost image of the surface as you look at it. Turn the front and back surfaces true with a ½-inch gouge and smooth it with a skew used as a scraper (*Photo 3*).

3. Turn the breadboard. Turn the disk to the shape shown in the *Cross Section* and the

> ### SAFETY TIP
>
> Before turning on the lathe, always turn a blank one revolution by hand to be sure it will clear the tool rest.

Shaping Detail. Note that there are three different levels that serve as references for carving. In the center is the bread cutting surface. It is the same height as the stem ridge. The surfaces on either side of the stem are the next level. They will be the wheat ears. Finally there is the fillet level, established by two narrow fillets—one on the breadboard's extreme outside edge and another on the cove's outside edge.

The center and stem ridge levels were formed when you thickness planed the blank, or when you jointed the surface on the lathe.

Lay out the second level on either side of the stem ridge, as shown in the *Shaping Detail*, by holding a pencil against the spinning stock.

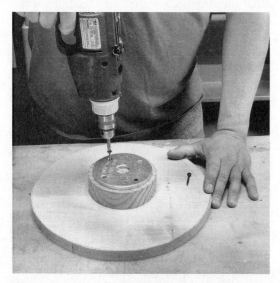

Photo 1: Screw the faceplate to the back of the shim.

Photo 2: Turn the blank round with a ½-inch gouge.

Photo 3: Smooth the surface of the blank with a skew.

Photo 4: Turn the second level with a square scraper or a skew.

Cut down to the second level with a square scraper or a skew laid on its wide surface (*Photo 4*).

Cut the fillets with a ¼-inch skew laid on its wide side and used like a scraper (*Photo 5*). Cut the cove with a ¼-inch turning gouge, known as a lady finger gouge (*Photo 6*). Cut the bead with the point of a skew.

4. Remove the breadboard. Hold the head-stock spindle with a wrench and unscrew the faceplate. Remove the screws.

Holding the breadboard in a vise, use a handsaw to cut off most of the shim block. Leave about ¼ inch so the saw teeth do not scratch the breadboard's lower surface.

5. Remove the waste. Lay the breadboard face down on the workbench and grip it between bench dogs. Remove the remainder of the waste with a gouge. Flatten the surface with a hand plane and use a cabinet scraper to smooth away any plane marks.

CARVE THE DETAILS.

1. Lay out the ears. With a pencil and straightedge, divide the breadboard into quar-

Photo 5: Scrape the fillets with a skew.

ters. To lay out the top of the wheat ears, measure 2¼ inches along one of the lines, as shown in the *Front View.* To mark the top of the wheat ears, draw in the dotted line shown. Score the round wheat ear tops with the 1-inch gouge.

Lay out the bottom of the ears by measuring ¾ inch from either side of the diameter line, as shown in the *Front View.* Score the bottom of the stems with a chisel.

2. Pare away the excess stem. The stem ridge is removed where it protrudes beyond both ends of the wheat ears, as shown in the *Front View.* Remove this with a chisel.

3. Set off the banner. Measure ⅝ inch from the tops of the wheat ears, and with a ½-inch

Photo 6: Cut the cove with a ¼-inch gouge.

chisel score a line that is centered across where the stem used to be. Make two angled cuts with the ½-inch chisel, as shown in the *Front View.* Pare the wood away until the wood is nearly at the same level as the fillet (*Photo 7*). Enough of the fillet should remain to give definition.

4. Carve the flower. In pencil, draw the flower shape shown in the *Front View.* To score the center of the flower, hold a ¼-inch gouge vertically and push its edge into the wood. About four cuts are required to cut a circle. Cut the round ends of the flower's petals with two slightly overlapped cuts of a ½-inch gouge. Hollow the petals with the same gouge. Make the veins by pushing the ½-inch chisel into the center of each petal (*Photo 8*). The chisel thrust is biased so the line is heavier closer to the center of the flower.

5. Relieve the flower. Pare away the wood around the flower to the fillet level. Use a

SHAPING DETAIL

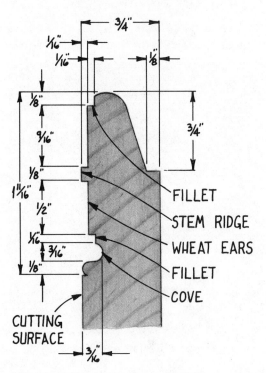

FILLET
STEM RIDGE
WHEAT EARS
FILLET
COVE

CUTTING SURFACE

Photo 7: Pare the wood between the wheat ears and the banner to the fillet level.

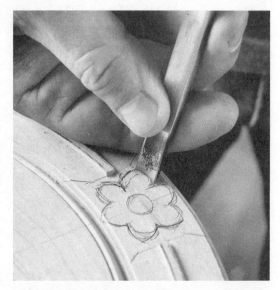

Photo 8: Score the flower with a chisel and gouge.

chisel to bevel the ends of the wheat ears toward the flower.

6. Carve the word "Bread." Sketch the word so it is centered on the diameter layout line. Score around the letters with the ¼- and ½-inch chisels and gouges. Pare away the wood that surrounds the letters to just above the fillet level (*Photo 9*). Use a carver's V parting tool to cut the lines in the banner that frame the word "Bread."

7. Score the ears. Make the curved lines that represent the grains of wheat with a ½-inch gouge. Place the gouge so the back of the blade faces away from the flower. Tap the gouge with a mallet. Make the lines in pairs. Notice the pairs are closer together near the bottom.

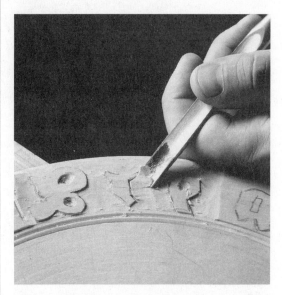

Photo 9: Pare away the wood from around the letters.

PASTA ROLLER

Like many kitchen tools, the pasta roller has almost vanished from the scene. But in the days when cooks made their own noodles, rollers like these were essential. The cook first rolled dough flat with a rolling pin and then rolled the pasta roller across it. The ridges of the roller cut the dough into uniform noodles.

In this country, boxed pasta has made the roller obsolete. Europeans still make much of their own fresh pasta, but generally use a more expensive pasta machine to cut the noodles. Yet, if the number of pasta rollers found in antique stores is any indication, the roller was once found in nearly every kitchen.

It also may have been used to create decorative effects on pastries.

In order to create pasta without ragged edges and to make sure the strands do not cling to the utensil, the roller's ridges have to be crisp and clean. For both reasons, it is important to use a piece of even-grained hardwood, such as maple or birch. Do not use an open-pored wood, like walnut, as the pores will fill with dough and the roller will be very difficult to clean.

The pasta roller is a turning project. Its basic shape is very simple and can be made very quickly. Your time will be spent in mak-

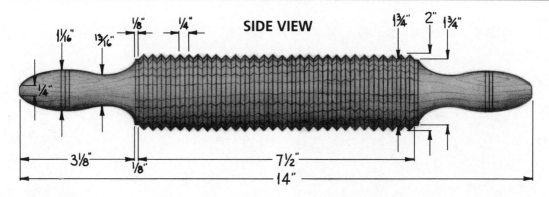

SIDE VIEW

1¹⁄₁₆" 1³⁄₁₆" ⅛" ¼" 1¾" 2" 1¾"

¼"

3⅛" ⅛" 7½"

14"

MATERIALS LIST

PART	DIMENSIONS
Pasta roller blank	2¼″ × 2¼″ × 15″

ing the individual ridges. For the sake of appearance, they should be very uniform, so careful layout is important.

Each ridge is made with slicing cuts done with a skew. The skew has a well-deserved reputation as the most cantankerous of turning tools. In certain operations, the spinning wood grabs it and sends the tool spiraling up the turning. This operation, however, is so simple that a beginner can master it quickly.

Like many other kitchen utensils, country pasta rollers were usually left unfinished. If you choose, wipe on a nontoxic salad bowl oil finish. Never immerse the roller in water or put it in a dishwasher. Clean it with a damp sponge.

PREPARE THE MATERIALS.

1. Make the blank. Cut a turning blank 15 inches long from stock that is a full 2¼ inches thick. This is both longer and thicker than the finished piece. The extra length leaves you ½ inch for waste on the end of each handle. The extra thickness allows you to turn the

blank to a 2-inch cylinder even if you accidentally mount it off-center.

2. Lay out the centers. Locate the centers on both ends by connecting the corners of the stock with an X.

TURN THE ROLLER.

1. Shape the body and handles. Put the turning blank in the lathe and adjust the tool

Photo 1: Turn the body with a ¾-inch spindle gouge.

Photo 2: Set off the handles with a parting tool. Use a pair of calipers to determine the diameter.

Photo 3: Smooth the body with a skew.

TECHNIQUE TIP

Your turning blank can also be riven, or split, directly from a log. If you have access to a cordwood pile, you may be able to find a suitable piece of maple or birch. Be careful to avoid a piece that is spalted or has any other staining that would detract from the completed turning.

---

rest. Rotate the stock by hand to make sure the corners clear the tool rest.

Turn the blank round with a ¾-inch spindle gouge. First, turn the roller's body (*Photo 1*). Then use a parting tool to create the fillets that set off the handles from the body (*Photo 2*). Plane the body smooth with a skew (*Photo 3*). Sand the entire roller if necessary. Use the heel (lower corner of the cutting edge) of the skew to make a series of three light scribe lines on the thickest area of each handle, as shown in the *Side View.* Such

lines were common decorations on country turnings.

2. Lay out the ridges. Turn off the lathe and hold a ruler against the pasta roller body. Make a mark ⅛ inch from the inside edge of the left fillet. Next, make a series of marks ¼ inch apart to indicate each ridge. If the last mark is more than ⅛ inch from the edge of the right fillet, turn on the lathe and shorten the body as needed by slightly increasing the width of the fillet. When you've laid out all the marks, turn on the lathe and lightly touch a pencil against the spinning wood at each ¼-inch mark (*Photo 4*). This will result in a series of fine lines ¼ inch apart, each marking the point of a ridge.

3. Cut the ridges. The ridges are created by cutting a series of V-shaped valleys. Each valley is made by adjacent cuts with the skew. Make the first cut by holding the skew with the long point down (*Photo 5*). Raise the handle to bring the chisel into the wood, and angle it so that you're cutting a slope into the wood at about 45 degrees (*Photo 6*). Move to the adjacent line and make the same slicing cut back toward the cut you just completed (*Photo 7*). The chip between the two cuts should be completely severed and fall away.

It doesn't matter which ridge you start with, as long as it isn't either of the end ridges. Also, it does not matter whether the first cut angles to the right or left. The cut should be at about a 45 degree angle and should extend to a point midway between the lines.

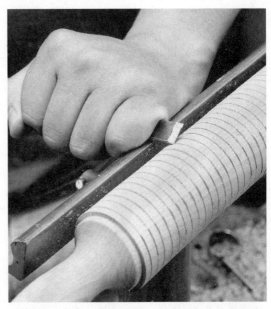

Photo 5: Hold the skew with the heel down.

> ### TOOL TIP
>
> You will find your skew is easier to handle if you round-over the edge that rides on the tool rest. A square edge rocks on its corners and can be hard to control. Round-over the edge with a file and smooth it with an emery cloth.

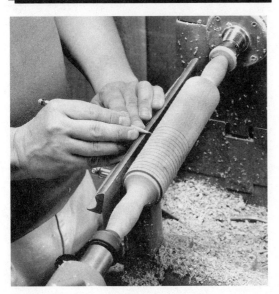

Photo 4: Touch a pencil to the spinning stock to define the ridge tops.

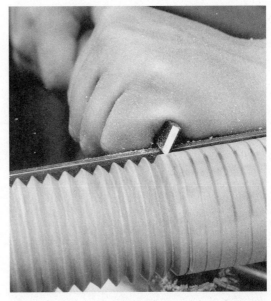

Photo 6: Cut a slope into the wood at about 45 degrees.

Photo 7: Cut back toward the original cut to remove the waste between the ridge tops.

TECHNIQUE TIP

Now that you have turned nice, sharp pasta-cutting ridges on the pasta roller, you don't want to dull them with sanding. Instead, hold a handful of wood shavings against the spinning stock. The shavings will burnish the ridges to a glassy smoothness.

4. Cut off the waste. Remove the pasta roller from the lathe. Cut the waste from each handle with a dovetail saw.

JULIA'S MORTAR AND PESTLE

There was a time when a mortar and pestle was used in every kitchen. In cooking, it was used to grind and press herbs and spices. It was also used to make home remedies. Today, gourmet cooks still use the mortar and pestle in dishes such as pesto to crush fresh basil and pignolia (pine nuts) in olive oil.

The mortar is a substantial, standing vessel in which the herbs or spices are worked. The actual crushing is done with the pestle — a round-bottom masher, akin to a potato masher (page 133). If you cook with fresh ingredients, you will still find a mortar and pestle to be very handy for your herbs. It is also a very attractive ornament when displayed on a mantle or a shelf.

Unlike much country woodworking, the history of this mortar and pestle is well known. It was a gift to my wife and me from our dear friend Dr. Dorothy Vaughan. Dorothy is credited with reviving Portsmouth, New Hampshire, the colonial seaport city where we live. Dorothy was also the founding force behind Strawbery Banke, a well-respected house museum in Portsmouth that preserves the city's Puddle Dock area.

The mortar and pestle belonged to Dorothy's grandmother, Julia Gage Smith, who

MORTAR TURNING LAYOUT   PESTLE TURNING LAYOUT

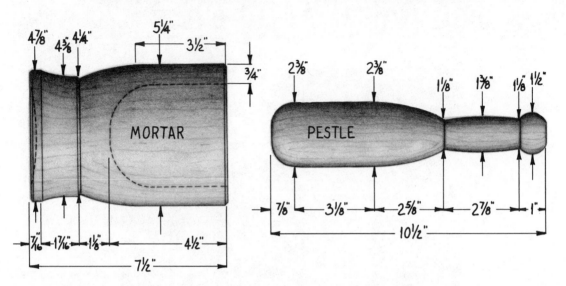

used it in her kitchen. Julia was born in Penacook, New Hampshire, in 1853 and married Oscar Smith in 1878. We keep a note Dorothy wrote about the piece tucked inside the mortar in the hope that its history will be preserved.

This is a turning project that requires both spindle and faceplate turning. The pestle is a spindle turning. The outside of the mortar is also spindle-turned; the mortar is then mounted on a faceplate and the inside is hollowed. In my directions, I explain how to turn the piece with the gouge and skew, tools that I use often as a Windsor chairmaker. If you're more comfortable using scrapers, you can turn this project with a roundnose chisel and a skew held flat on the tool rest. Simply scrape the wood away to create the desired profile. I outline my technique more thoroughly in *Woodturning for Cabinetmakers*. *Creative Woodturning*, by Dale Nish, explains both scraping and gouge work.

Julia's mortar and pestle appears to be made of maple, but the pieces have darkened

MATERIALS LIST	
PART	**DIMENSIONS**
Pestle blank	2⅜″ × 2⅜″ × 11½″
Mortar blank	5½″ × 5½″ × 10″

so much it is hard to be sure. You can substitute another species, but the one you choose should be heavy, strong, stable, and even-textured, like maple. You can make each turning blank from 10/4 (ten-quarter) stock or glue it up from thinner stock. You can also split the blank directly from a log. If you choose to split, or rive, the stock, you can probably find a suitable piece in the firewood pile. Choose an extra-long piece that doesn't include the unstable center of the tree. If the ends of the blank are split or checked, cut away the imperfections.

Finish both the mortar and pestle with a nontoxic salad bowl oil. Apply several coats of finish to the inside of the mortar to better seal it from food liquids and oils.

MAKE AND TURN THE BLANKS.

1. **Make the mortar and pestle blanks.** Note that the blanks are longer than the completed parts. The extra length allows you to mount the pieces on the lathe.

If you're making the blanks by gluing up thinner stock, joint the mating surfaces. Spread the glue evenly and clamp the stock using even pressure. Locate the centers on each end of the blank by connecting the four corners with an X. When you mount the pieces on the lathe, put the lathe centers in the center of the X. If you use riven blanks, round the long edges with a drawknife and mount the piece as best you can by eye.

2. **Turn the pestle blank.** Put the pestle blank between centers on the lathe. First, turn the pestle blank to a 2⅜-inch-diameter cylinder with a ½-inch gouge. Next, turn a groove at each diameter indicated in the *Pestle Turning Layout* (*Photo 1*). Once you've laid out the diameters, turn the pestle to its rough shape with a gouge (*Photo 2*). Use the grooves as layout lines and turn the proper profiles between them.

You can either sand the pestle smooth or plane it with a skew (*Photo 3*). Remove the pestle from the lathe and cut off the waste.

SAFETY TIP
Before turning on the lathe, always turn a blank one revolution by hand to be sure it will clear the tool rest.

3. **Turn the mortar blank.** Mount the mortar blank between centers. Place the bottom end on the spur center, which is nearest the headstock. With a ½-inch gouge, turn the out-

Photo 1: Lay out the rough shape of the pestle by turning a series of grooves with a parting tool. Push the tool into the wood to start the groove. Check the diameter with a pair of calipers.

Photo 2: To cut with a gouge, rest the bevel on the turning cylinder. Raise the rear of the handle slowly until the tool begins to cut.

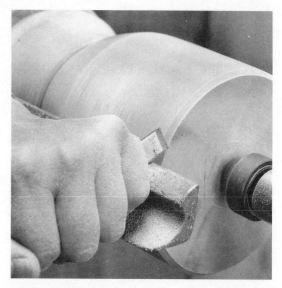

Photo 3: You can either sand the wood or plane it with a skew. Rest the bevel on the turning cylinder. Raise the rear of the handle slowly until the tool begins to cut.

Photo 4: Chamfer the edge of the rim and foot with a skew.

side to the shape and dimensions given in the *Mortar Turning Layout*. Make a cut about ½ inch deep with a parting tool to lay out the bottom of the mortar and then chamfer the foot and rim with the skew (*Photo 4*). Finish shaping and smoothing the outside of the mortar with sandpaper or a skew.

4. Turn the inside of the mortar. Remove the mortar from the lathe. With the lathe center mark as a guide, center and mount the faceplate on the bottom end of the mortar. Secure the faceplate with 2-inch-long screws. Mount the faceplate on the lathe and position the tool rest at the top end of the mortar. Turn on the lathe, and hollow out the mortar with a roundnose scraper (*Photo 5*). Start the cut with the scraper about ¾ inch from the left edge of the mortar and work the tool toward the center. Make successive cuts from the edge to the center until the depth and

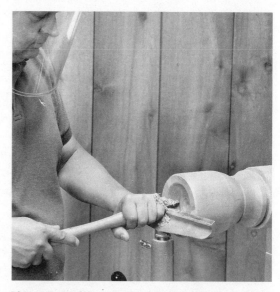

Photo 5: Position the tool rest at the top of the mortar. Hollow out the interior with a round-nose scraper. Make successive cuts, working from the left edge to the center.

TECHNIQUE TIP

When cutting my mortar out of the lathe, I made the second cut with the parting tool immediately next to the first cut. This double cut was wide enough to allow me to reach inside the cut with a diamond point, which I used for facing off the bottom surface. Facing off (slicing a thin shaving) creates a glassy-smooth bottom. I also made a slightly concave cut. Thus, like a wine glass, the mortar rested not on a flat bottom but on one that had a slight rim.

shape approximate that shown in the *Mortar Turning Layout.* Periodically check the depth of the cut with a ruler, and the thickness of the edge with calipers. Pay attention to your finish work to be sure you produce a smooth, even bottom. When you've hollowed out the mortar, remove the tool rest and carefully sand the inside of the mortar smooth.

5. Separate the mortar. Use a parting tool to deepen the cut that defines the bottom of the mortar. If you are confident in your turning skills, you can part the mortar out of the lathe. If you are not, shut off the lathe, unscrew the faceplate, and cut off the waste with a handsaw.

CLOTHESPIN

Chances are that your household has a clothes drier and you do not need clothespins. If you still hang your laundry on a line, you surely buy spring-loaded clothespins at the hardware store where they are sold by the bag. Even with these readily available, mass-produced clothespins, I decided to make my wife a supply of handmade clothespins for some special jobs. She occasionally likes to display quilts and other fabrics, and in the fall she brings the garden's copious harvest of herbs into the house to dry on the herb racks that hang from the kitchen ceiling. Clothes-

pins are handy for both jobs. Throughout the year she uses dried herbs and flowers to create seasonal decorations, and some of these are hung with the help of my clothespins. We also display our Christmas stockings with these handmade clothespins.

Why handmade clothespins? The modern mass-produced equivalent would detract from the country look. Such attention to detail may seem somewhat obsessive, but as mentioned in the first three chapters, details are what create depth, and without them a decor is superficial.

TURNING LAYOUT

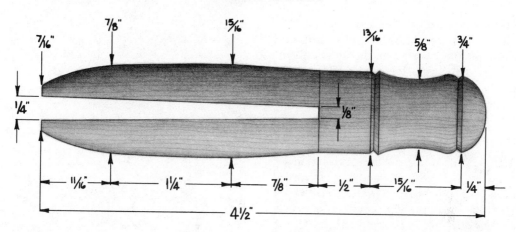

These clothespins were copied from a group of five handmade examples I found in an antique shop. As with many country accessories, it is impossible to say when they were made, but it is a safe bet that they predate the mass-produced product.

Clothespins like these were everyday treen items and it was not intended that they be looked at and admired. A household needed many of them, but it was expected only that they do their job of securing wet laundry to the clothesline.

Such mundane items used to be "mass-produced" by a woodworker who repeated a single process over and over. At the time, this fast method of hand production was the only way small, utilitarian objects could be made in large quantities. Today's machine-mass-produced, identical items make us appreciate the rough charm and individuality of handmade crafts.

These considerations (speed and wide tolerances) make these clothespins an excellent practice project to teach yourself turning, or to refresh skills you already have. Because you do not have to focus your attention on making exact duplicates, you can concentrate

MATERIALS LIST	
PART	**DIMENSIONS**
Clothespin blanks (as needed)	1⅛″ × 1⅛″ × 6″

on developing technique and tool skill, still knowing that you will manage to create a useful object every time.

Make your clothespins from a straight-grained hardwood that will turn crisply. I used birch. Avoid any woods that might stain fabrics. I suggest that you not sand at all. Instead, try to create a smooth surface with just the lathe tools. Any tool marks you do leave add to the clothespin's rough charm. Over time, regular use will polish the wood to a natural sheen.

Clothespins are usually left raw—a state that was once called "in the white." It would not be wise to oil your pins if they are going to come in contact with fabric. If you choose, you can paint them decorative colors, but use an oil paint and give it time to dry thoroughly. Milk paint can run if it gets wet and can also rub off if the fabric is rough and abrasive.

MAKE THE BLANKS.

1. Prepare the stock. Rip the stock to the width given in the Materials List. Cut the blanks to length. Notice that the length given in the Materials List is longer than the length shown in the *Turning Layout*. There is extra stock included for waste at each end.

> ### TECHNIQUE TIP
>
> Clothespin blanks are also easy to rive from a log. Just cut the log or billet to the length given in the Materials List and split the rough blanks with a hatchet or froe. Round the blanks with a drawknife and center them in the lathe by eye.

Photo 1: Define the ends of the blank with a parting tool.

ing gouge. Round the blank to the body's maximum diameter, as shown in the *Turning Layout*. Establish the pin's overall length with two parting tool cuts, one on each end (*Photo 1*).

2. Locate the centers for turning. Locate the center on each end of the stock by making an X across the corners.

TURN THE BLANKS.

1. Round and shape the blank. The blank is small and can be rounded with either a ½-inch spindle gouge or the same size rough-

Photo 2: Cut the head and the slope of the body with a ½-inch spindle gouge.

With a gouge, reduce the head to the diameter given in the *Turning Layout,* and smooth the transition between it and the body's diameter (*Photo 2*). Taper the ends of the legs and round the head with rolling cuts made with a skew (*Photo 3*).

2. Make the decorative cuts. Use a skew to make a V-groove just below the head's rounded top, as shown in the *Turning Layout.* Use the point of a skew to make one of the groove's beveled sides. Roll the skew over and make the other beveled edge (*Photo 4*). Move down the pin about ⅞ inch and make a second V-groove. While you have the skew in your hands, make a light scribe line 1⅝ to 1¾ inches from the top of the head.

3. Make the cove. Cut the cove between the grooves in the head with a ¼-inch spindle gouge (also called a lady finger). Cut down from each side of the cove. Both cuts should merge at the bottom of the cove.

4. Remove the pin from the lathe. Shut off the lathe and remove the clothespin. Cut off the waste on each end with a dovetail saw or backsaw. Pare away any of the stem that remains with a carving gouge or bench chisel.

MAKE THE LEGS.

1. Cut the legs. Lay out the taper of the legs, as shown in the *Turning Layout.* If you choose, you can cut the tapered legs on a band saw. However, I am very wary of put-

Photo 3: Taper the ends of the legs and round the crown of the head with a skew.

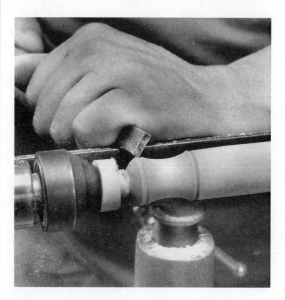

Photo 4: Cut the V-grooves with a skew.

ting my fingers that close to any blade that is being driven by a motor. Instead, I recommend gripping the pin in a vise with the bottom end up. Start two short saw kerfs with a dovetail saw. They should be parallel and about ¼ inch apart. Continue the cuts all the way to the turned scribe line, as shown in the *Turning Layout,* with a 10-point handsaw. If the cuts do not meet, remove the wedge by undercutting it with a coping saw.

2. Sand the inside of the legs. If you will be using your clothespins to display quilts or other fabrics, smooth the saw marks on the inside of the legs with sandpaper. The rough wood could snag and damage fabric.

POTATO MASHER

In country kitchens, food was still being prepared by hand long after city folk were buying
the processed stuff. As a result, such implements as this masher remained in common
use until recent times. In fact, during the two
world wars the German army used a type of
hand grenade that had an explosive cylinder
on the end of a wooden handle. Its shape was
so similar to this implement that the grenade
was known as a "potato masher," indicating
that this wooden tool was a standard in country kitchens well into the 20th century.

Though it may be old-fashioned, this
wooden masher is guaranteed to work as well
as any modern variety. It will work equally
well on other vegetables that are commonly
mashed, such as turnips and squash. Like other
treen (common wooden) implements in this
book, this potato masher also makes an attractive decoration in a country kitchen.

The potato masher is a simple turning
project. If you have little experience on the
lathe, it is a good place to practice. It is largely
gouge work, but if you have the skill to use a
skew or want to learn, it is an easy shape to
plane.

TURNING LAYOUT

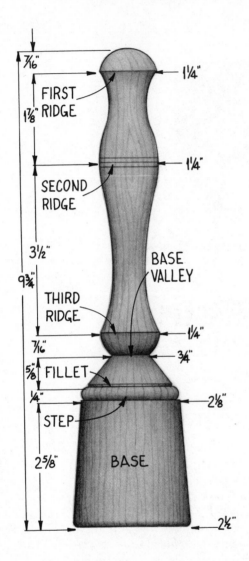

FIRST RIDGE

SECOND RIDGE

BASE VALLEY

THIRD RIDGE

FILLET

STEP

BASE

$\frac{7}{16}$"

$1\frac{1}{4}$"

$1\frac{7}{8}$"

$1\frac{1}{4}$"

$3\frac{1}{2}$"

$9\frac{3}{4}$"

$\frac{7}{16}$"

$1\frac{1}{4}$"

$\frac{3}{4}$"

$\frac{5}{8}$"

$\frac{1}{4}$"

$2\frac{1}{8}$"

$2\frac{5}{8}$"

$2\frac{1}{2}$"

MATERIALS LIST

PART	DIMENSIONS
Turning blank	$2\frac{3}{4}'' \times 2\frac{3}{4}'' \times 10\frac{7}{8}''$

When turning the potato masher, do make an effort to duplicate the pattern as closely as possible. However, even major deviations from the form shown in the *Turning Layout* will not affect the potato masher's function. No matter what your skill level, you are all but assured a successful turning.

This masher is also a good place to use up a small piece of 10/4 (ten-quarter) stock left over from another project. As with many other pieces of treen, it, too, can be made out of a riven blank pulled from a pile of firewood. The masher should be made of a very hard wood with an even texture. I used American beech, but maple, birch, cherry, apple, or pear would be fine. Do not use wood with open pores, such as oak. I would worry that small particles of food could press into the pores and create a health problem. You can leave the masher unfinished or you can seal it with nontoxic salad bowl finish.

PREPARE THE BLANK AND TURN THE POTATO MASHER.

1. Dimension the blank. Rip and cut the blank to the width and length given in the Materials List. The length given is 1 inch longer than the length shown in the *Turning Layout* in order to leave ½ inch of waste at each end.

2. Turn the potato masher. Before you start turning, make a storyboard template from a piece of ¼-inch stock to help lay out critical dimensions of the turning. Indicate the ends, base, ridges, and any other crucial dimensions shown in the *Turning Layout*.

If you start with a square turning blank, locate the centers with a center locator or by drawing an X from corner to corner on each end. The point where the lines intersect is the

TECHNIQUE TIP

If you use a riven blank, you can cut down on the amount of rough-rounding you have to do with lathe tools by first rounding the blank with a drawknife.

Photo 1: Hold the storyboard template against the stock and transfer the layout lines to the spinning stock with a pencil.

center. If you use a riven blank, center it as best you can by eye.

First, turn the blank round with a gouge to about a 2½-inch-diameter. Check the diameter with a pair of calipers. Next, lay out the different sections of the turning with the storyboard template (*Photo 1*). With the sections of the turning determined, make sizing cuts with a parting tool to indicate the position and diameter of the handle ridges and step, as shown in the *Turning Layout* (*Photo 2*). Determine the diameter of the cuts with a pair of calipers. Also, make cuts to about a ¾-inch-diameter that indicate the ends of the potato masher.

With the sizing cuts made, it is easy to turn the blank to shape with a gouge. First, turn the handle to its 1¼-inch diameter and, if you wish, draw new layout lines to indicate the ridges. When you are shaping the handle,

Photo 2: Make sizing cuts with the parting tool that determine the position and diameter of the ridges and step.

Photo 3: When turning with a gouge, always cut from the top of the ridges to the bottom of the valleys.

Photo 4: Smooth the body of the potato masher by planing with a skew.

always work the gouge from the top of the ridges to the bottom of the valleys (*Photo 3*). Next, shape the sloping base, step, fillet, and base valley, as shown in the *Turning Layout*. When the basic shape of the potato masher has been turned, plane the entire length smooth with a skew (*Photo 4*) and, if necessary, sand lightly to remove the tool marks. Finally, cut the decorative lines at the second ridge with the heel of the skew, remove the completed turning from the lathe, and cut off the waste.

SPICE ROLLER

Before the development of modern food processing, many of the exotic spices used in cooking were purchased whole at the country store or from a peddler. These spices were ground by the cook as they were needed. This spice roller was one of the tools used in a country kitchen to prepare spices.

Although today's spices usually come preground, many cooks still prefer to prepare them fresh. If you cook, or if there is someone in your household who likes to cook, this spice roller may be a welcome addition to your kitchen.

The spice roller is a cylinder that crushes spices in a narrow trough. The roller has two handles that allow a lot of weight to be applied on a narrow bearing surface. The trough is an enclosed track that keeps the spice under the roller. Once the spice is prepared, it can easily be poured from the trough into a measuring container.

The roller is a simple turning project. It has a 3½-inch finished diameter. If you do not have any 4-inch hardwood stock, you may have to glue up a blank. Since the roller and trough should be harder than the spices that will be crushed between them, make them from a dense, nonporous hardwood like sugar maple. With use, sugar maple takes on a very pleasing, glasslike smoothness. The trough is

ROLLER TURNING LAYOUT

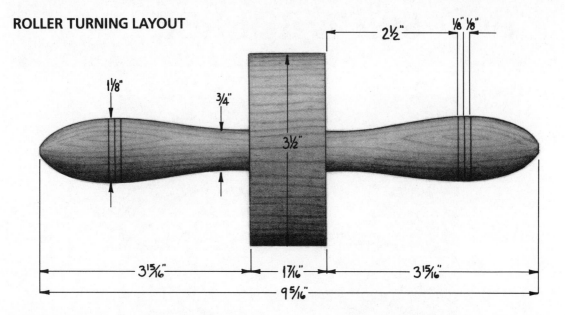

glued up from three pieces—a core block and two thin sides. The sides are a nice place to use some small pieces of special figured wood. I made the sides of my trough out of curly maple.

The spice roller comes in contact with food, so finish it with a nontoxic finish such as salad bowl oil. Or simply leave the piece unfinished and allow it to develop a natural patina. Never immerse the spice roller in water. Instead, clean it with a moist sponge.

CONSTRUCTION TIP

Cut the trough walls ½ inch wider and longer than the trough core. With the extra length and width, you don't have to worry about the sides shifting as you glue them to the trough core. When the glue is dry, the edges can be hand planed flush. The dimensions for the trough sides in the Materials List already have the extra width and length added.

MATERIALS LIST

PART	DIMENSIONS
Trough core	1½″ × 3½″ × 10″
Trough sides (2)	¼″ × 4″ × 10½″
Roller	4″ × 4″ × 10⁵⁄₁₆″

MAKE THE TROUGH.

1. Prepare the materials. Joint, thickness plane, cut, and rip the stock to the dimensions given in the Materials List. Since the trough walls are only ¼ inch thick, I made them by resawing a ¾-inch-thick piece of curly maple on my band saw.

2. Lay out the curved trough. Lay out the 7¼-inch-radius curve on the trough core, as shown in the *Trough Construction Overview.* As shown, the center point of the curve is 6¹⁄₁₆

TROUGH CONSTRUCTION OVERVIEW

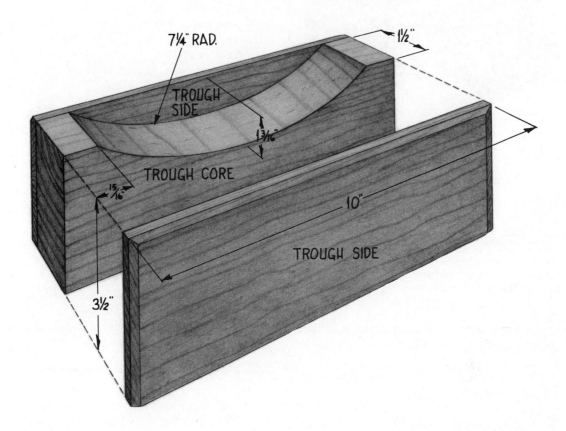

7¼" RAD.

1½"

TROUGH SIDE

1³⁄₁₆"

TROUGH CORE

15⁄₁₆"

10"

TROUGH SIDE

3½"

inches above the center of the top edge of the trough core. Lay a wide piece of 1½-inch-thick stock next to the trough core on your workbench. Lay out the centerline across the trough core and the scrap and draw the curve with a pair of dividers set at 7¼ inches (*Photo 1*).

Cut out the curve with a band saw or bow saw, and sand away the saw marks.

3. Glue up the trough. Smear glue on both sides of the trough core. Put the trough sides

in place and clamp the assembly in several places to create even pressure.

Allow the glue to dry overnight.

4. Surface the trough. Joint the sides of the trough flush with the core, using a hand plane. Sand the outer surface smooth.

5. Chamfer the edges. Both ends and the top edge of the trough sides are chamfered, as shown in the *Trough Construction Overview*. Set a marking gauge to ⁵⁄₁₆ inch and

Photo 1: Draw the centerline across the trough core and the scrap and swing the curve with a pair of dividers.

scribe a line on the ends and top edge of the sides. Chamfer to the scribe lines with a block plane.

MAKE THE ROLLER.

1. Prepare the stock. Cut the roller blank to the length given in the Materials List. Note the blank's length is 1 inch longer than that shown in the *Roller Turning Layout*. This length includes ½ inch of waste on each end.

If you do not have any 16/4 (sixteen-quarter) hardwood stock, glue up stock for the necessary thickness.

2. Turn the blank. Locate the centers of the blank with a center locator or by drawing an X from corner to corner on each end. The point where the lines intersect is the center. Put the blank between centers on the lathe and turn it to a 3½-inch diameter with a gouge.

TOOL TIP

Sanding is the usual way to smooth highly figured woods without tearing the grain. However, sanding by hand is very slow, and a belt sander can grind away wood too fast. For the best control with no tear-out, use a cabinet scraper.

Plane the edge smooth with a skew (*Photo 2*).

When the blank is round and smooth, measure and lay out the position of the roller with a pencil. Make two plunge cuts on either side of the roller with a parting tool. Plunge all the way down to the ¾-inch diameter of the handles (*Photo 3*). Check the diameter with calipers. Shape the handles to approximate the outline shown in the *Roller Turning Layout*. Make the three decorative lines on each handle with the edge of the skew and sand the handles smooth. Smooth the roller's edges with facing cuts made with a skew or a diamond point, or simply sand them smooth. Remove the roller from the lathe, cut off the waste, and smooth the handle ends.

Photo 2: Plane the surface of the spinning blank by guiding the skew along its length.

Photo 3: Using the parting tool, make two plunge cuts down to the ¾-inch handle diameter. This defines the edges of the roller.

MITTEN AND SOCK STRETCHERS

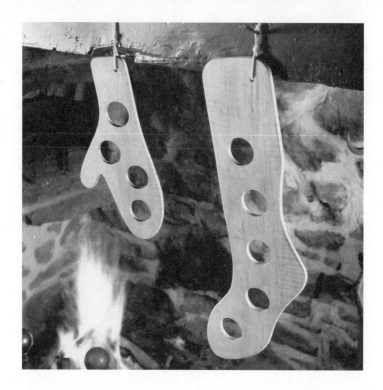

Before the second half of the 20th century, most fabrics were made of natural fibers. Wool was so warm it was the fiber of choice for mittens and winter socks, but wool has the disadvantage of shrinking if heated while drying. This is well known to anyone who has ever dried a wool sweater in a clothes drier. It ends up big enough only for a doll.

Before central heat, a country house was heated by fireplaces and wood stoves. Clothes had to be dried near these heat sources because the rest of the house was too cold and damp. To prevent expensive mittens and socks from shrinking, they were dried on wooden stretchers like those shown here. To help a wet mitten or sock fit more easily over the stretcher, the edges were rounded, and several large holes were drilled through the stretchers to allow air to circulate and speed drying.

To care for the many different sizes of soiled and snow-soaked socks and mittens, country folk owned numerous mitten and sock stretchers. They kept the stretchers handy by hanging them on a nail near the stove or fireplace. Today, most mittens and socks are made of synthetic fibers that can be dried in a clothes drier. But even with our modern fabrics, mit-

STRETCHER PATTERNS

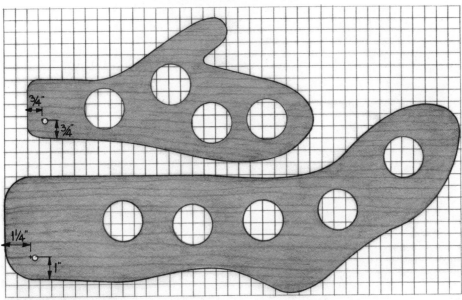

ONE SQUARE = ½"

MATERIALS LIST

PART	DIMENSIONS
Sock stretcher stock	¼" × 7" × 20½"
Mitten stretcher stock	¼" × 6" × 12½"

HARDWARE AND SUPPLIES

12" length of cotton twine

ten and sock stretchers can add interest to your home when hung near a fireplace or stove.

The original stretchers were made of ¼-inch-thick, even-grained birch or maple and were left unfinished. If your stretchers will be purely decorative, you might want to make them out of a figured wood. You can give your mitten and sock stretchers a clear finish like oil or varnish, or you can paint

them to add a dash of color to your stove area or fireplace.

I made my stretchers to match my feet and hands. I am of average size and take a size 9 shoe. To make larger or smaller stretchers, scale your patterns up or down and adjust the stock width and length given in the Materials List as needed.

MAKE THE STRETCHERS.

1. Prepare the stock. Thickness plane the mitten and sock stretcher stock to ¼ inch. Hand plane the stock to remove any machine marks.

2. Cut out the patterns. Make a grid of ½-inch squares on a piece of posterboard and draw the mitten stretcher and sock stretcher on it, as shown in the *Stretcher Patterns.*

Cut the shapes from the posterboard and trace the patterns onto the stock. Cut the mitten stretcher and sock stretcher to shape with a band saw, scroll saw, or coping saw. Clean up the sawed edges with a spokeshave and sandpaper. As you clean up the saw marks, round the edges of the stretchers so that they will not snag and damage wool socks or mittens.

3. Drill the air holes. The air hole diameter is not critical, so I suggest using any large bit you own rather than buying a new one. I bought a 1⅝-inch-diameter Forstner bit for another project and used that bit to make the air holes in my stretchers. Lay out the air holes roughly where shown in the *Stretcher Patterns* and drill them on the drill press. Put a piece of scrap under the stretchers as you drill the air holes. The scrap will support the wood fibers

and minimize tear-out as the bit penetrates the stock.

When the air holes have been drilled, drill a ¼-inch-diameter string hole in each stretcher, as shown in the *Stretcher Patterns*.

CONSTRUCTION TIP

It is not critical for the air holes to be located exactly where shown in the *Stretcher Patterns*, but the holes should not be too close together. If the holes are spaced too closely, the stretchers will be weakened.

---

4. Attach the string. For each stretcher, cut a piece of cotton twine 6 inches long. Pass one end through the ¼-inch hole and tie it into a loop. Trim the string's ends.

EGG HOLDER

Country homes had to be self-sufficient. Some goods were obtained during the occasional trip to town, but most of what a family ate was produced on the family plot. Every house had an herb and vegetable garden outside the kitchen door.

Every family also had at least one cow, and a number of chickens always scratched around the barnyard. These birds were kept for their meat and, more important, for their eggs. Since there was no refrigeration, the eggs were eaten promptly—a country family ate fresh eggs nearly every day. Some country woodworker made this egg holder to store his family's daily supply of eggs.

The egg holder sat on a counter or table. Each morning the children gathered the eggs, washed them, and placed them in the egg holder. Not only were the eggs handy when they were needed in cooking but, sitting in the holder, they were protected and less likely to be broken.

Today, most of us buy eggs at the store and they come in their own protective carton. When we get the eggs home, we keep them in the refrigerator. But this piece is still an attractive decoration for a country kitchen. You might consider turning some wooden eggs to keep in it, and at Easter the egg holder is perfect for displaying decorated eggs.

CONSTRUCTION OVERVIEW

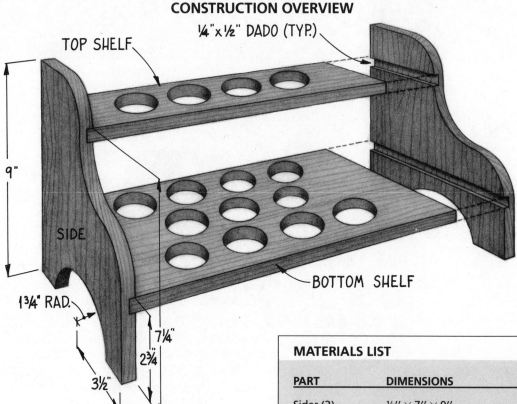

TOP SHELF

¼" x ½" DADO (TYP.)

SIDE

9"

1¾" RAD.

7¼"

2¾"

3½"

BOTTOM SHELF

MATERIALS LIST

PART	DIMENSIONS
Sides (2)	½" × 7" × 9"
Bottom shelf	½" × 7" × 14"
Top shelf	½" × 3¾" × 14"

HARDWARE AND SUPPLIES

1¼" finishing nails (as needed)

The original egg holder was painted white, but since most eggs are white, they do not show up well. I painted my pine egg holder blue because I wanted more contrast.

MAKE THE PARTS.

1. Prepare the stock. Joint, thickness plane, cut, and rip the stock to the dimensions given in the Materials List. Hand plane the stock to remove any machine marks.

2. Cut the dadoes. The shelves fit into dadoes in the sides, as shown in the *Construction Overview.* Cut the dadoes on the table saw with a ½-inch-wide dado blade. Adjust

the dado blade to make a ¼-inch-deep cut. Set the table saw fence 2¼ inches away from the blade and cut the bottom dado in each side. Readjust the fence to 1¾ inches from the blade and cut the top dado in each side.

3. Cut the sides to shape. First, make a grid of ½-inch squares on a piece of posterboard and plot the side shape on it, as shown in the *Side Pattern.* Cut out the pattern and trace it

SIDE PATTERN

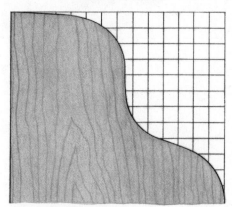

ONE SQUARE = ½"

onto the outside surface of the sides. Cut the sides to shape with a band saw or coping saw.

Next, lay out the radius on the bottom of each side with a compass and cut the waste away to create the feet. Clean up the edges with a spokeshave and sandpaper.

DRILL THE EGG HOLES AND ASSEMBLE THE PARTS.

1. Lay out the egg holes. Lay out the grid shown in the *Egg Hole Layout* with a try square. Mark the center of each hole with an X and drill the holes.

TOOL TIP

I recommend drilling the holes with a 1⅝-inch-diameter Forstner bit. A Forstner bit is great for drilling large-diameter, smooth-sided holes.

2. Nail the joints. Nail the sides to the shelves with 1¼-inch finishing nails.

Fill the nail holes and sand the egg holder smooth.

TECHNIQUE TIP

Save some time by cutting both sides in one operation. Clamp or tape the sides together with the dadoes facing inward. Draw the shape and radius on one of the sides and cut the assembly to shape on the band saw. Sand the sawed edges smooth while the sides are still together.

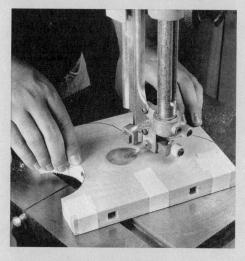

EGG HOLE LAYOUT

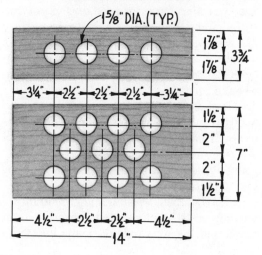

BOOTJACK

In New England, where I was raised and still live, we call early spring mud season. As winter fades and the ground begins to thaw, every dirt walkway and road turns into brown soup. It's always necessary to walk on paved surfaces, for only they allow an easy and clean passage.

In past centuries, when most Americans lived in rural communities and paved surfaces were virtually unknown, mud was a fact of life. As a result, everyone wore boots when going outside. Upon entering the house, they had to pull off their mud-covered footwear.

The bootjack was a helping hand for removing boots. It eliminated the need to sit down and tug at a pair of heavy boots. In-

stead, you placed one foot on the jack and fit your booted ankle in the yoke end. To remove the boot, you pointed your toe and raised your leg. Because you had to place all your weight on one foot, it was best to have a chair nearby to steady yourself.

Because nearly everyone wore boots much of the year, every country house had a bootjack near the door. As a result, antique bootjacks are a common item on the antique market. Although many are made of wood, cast iron was also a popular material. A very popular iron bootjack was cast in the form of a cricket, whose oversize and curled antennae created the yoke. We own an iron bootjack in the form of a devil whose horns form the yoke. Perhaps the best-known cast-iron bootjack is called Naughty Nellie, a scantily clad Victorian woman whose raised legs helped gentlemen remove their footwear.

The floor is the place to use the bootjack, of course, but it's more convenient to hang it when it's not in use. The most practical solution is to keep the bootjack at a handy height near the door. For that reason, the narrow end has a hole in it.

The yoke on this bootjack is wide enough for an adult's foot, but may be too big for a child's. You can adapt this plan to little feet by scaling it down.

The bootjack can be made of just about any wood you choose. It is a very simple form, but it is hung at a handy height, making it quite visible. Thus, the bootjack is a good

place to use a short piece of highly figured wood, like curly or bird's-eye maple. The original bootjack was left unfinished and has darkened to a rich brown.

Some finishes are inappropriate for the

CONSTRUCTION OVERVIEW

MATERIALS LIST

PART	DIMENSIONS
Top	¾″ × 6″ × 20″
Shim	1¼″ × 1¾″ × 5″

149

bootjack. Since you stand on it, any finish you apply will become scuffed by your boot soles. This means that a hard finish, such as paint or varnish, will soon be scratched. I recommend a soft finish, such as linseed oil, as this can be renewed from time to time.

On the other hand, the bottom of a bootjack receives no wear, and it is the surface that faces outward when you hang it on the wall. Therefore, the bottom of the bootjack offers a protected, flat surface that can be painted and decorated.

MAKE AND ASSEMBLE THE PARTS.

1. Prepare the stock for the top. Thickness plane the stock, and hand plane the top and bottom surfaces to remove the machine marks. Cut the piece to length.

2. Cut out the top. Transfer the shape shown in the *Construction Overview* to the top. Use a tapering jig on the table saw to taper the sides, or cut them freehand on the band saw. Cut the narrow end and the yoke to shape on a band saw or with a bow saw. Remove the saw marks from the tapered edge with a jointer plane or block plane. Sand the yoke smooth.

3. Drill the hole. Drill a ⅜-inch-diameter hole located 1⅜ inches from the narrow end and centered on the top, as shown in the *Construction Overview.*

4. Make the shim. Rip the wood to the width given in the Materials List. Tilt your table saw's arbor to 85 degrees and bevel the shim, as shown in the *Construction Overview.* Straighten the saw blade and set your table saw's miter gauge at 85 degrees (*Photo 1*). Taper both ends of the shim block to match the angle of the top. Remove any saw marks on the four

---

> ### CONSTRUCTION TIP
>
> When making the bootjack, round-over the yoke's edges with a spokeshave or sandpaper. If they are left sharp they will cause undue wear to your boots. Also round-over the lower edge of the narrow end with a block plane. When you rest your weight on the bootjack, you do not want to drive a sharp corner into the floor.

straight surfaces with a hand plane. Sand the end grain to remove saw marks.

5. Glue the shim. Spread glue on the shim's angled upper surface. Position the shim on the top so the two ends of the shim are flush with the edges of the top. Clamp the shim with a wooden hand screw to achieve even pressure along the entire joint. Wipe away any glue that squeezes out with a moist cloth. Set the assembly aside to let the glue set before applying a finish.

Photo 1: Cut the ends of the shim by guiding the stock past the blade with a miter gauge set at 85 degrees.

DUSTPAN

Country woodworking traditions predate most of the labor-saving inventions that have transformed housekeeping. Although we are more inclined to use carpet sweepers and vacuum cleaners, we still need dustpans because we still sweep floors between cleanings or to take care of an accidental spill. Thus, no house, shop, or business can be without at least one dustpan.

Country woodworking also predates the Industrial Revolution—a time when many everyday utensils began to be mass-produced.

Before that time, many items that we know of only in plastic or stamped sheet metal were made of wood. This wooden dustpan is a good example. Most of us have never seen a dustpan that was not mass-produced. However, I think you will agree that this dustpan is more interesting and pleasant to look at than a plastic one. You will also find that this one will work every bit as well as one its modern cousins, and it's a lot more classy.

This dustpan's handle is shaped to make the piece more decorative. The maker relied

CONSTRUCTION OVERVIEW

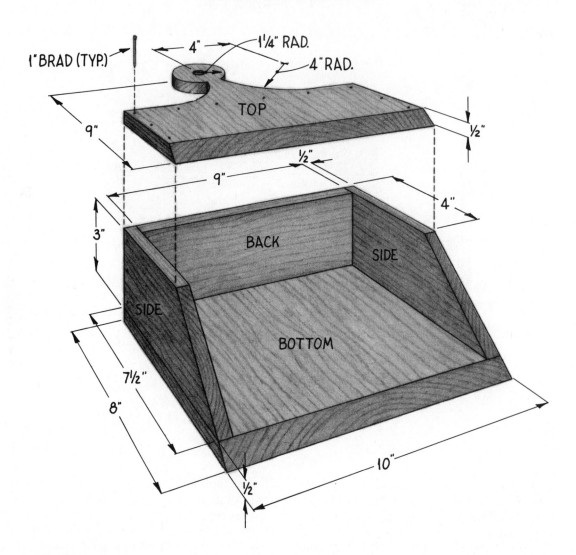

1"BRAD (TYP.)
4"
1¼" RAD.
4" RAD.
TOP
9"
½"
½"
9"
4"
3"
BACK
SIDE
SIDE
BOTTOM
7½"
8"
½"
10"

on a geometric shape, as did most other country woodworkers. The handle fits nicely into the palm of your hand.

When not in use, this dustpan can be suspended by a loop of string or leather tied through the hole in the handle. It could also be hung directly from a nail, although over time this will wear and disfigure the hole. When a string wears out and breaks it can easily be replaced.

When hanging on the wall, the dustpan is readily visible, so some thought should be given to how you will integrate it into your country decor. There are two obvious choices:

MATERIALS LIST

PART	DIMENSIONS
Back	½″ × 3″ × 9″
Sides (2)	½″ × 3″ × 7½″
Bottom	½″ × 10″ × 8″
Top	½″ × 10″ × 9″

HARDWARE AND SUPPLIES

1″ brads (as needed)

decorate it with paint, or select a species of wood with either an interesting color or grain pattern. If you decide to paint and decorate your dustpan, use some easy-to-work wood with an even grain, such as pine. If you want to see an interesting grain or a particular color, consider woods like curly maple or walnut, and give the dustpan an oil finish.

MAKE THE PARTS.

1. Prepare the stock. Joint and thickness plane all the materials to ½ inch, then hand plane the parts to remove any machine marks. Rip the stock to the widths given in the Materials List. Joint the edges and square the ends.

TECHNIQUE TIP

As shown in the Materials List, the dustpan contains five separate parts, but they have only two different widths. When planning the project, try to cut the top and bottom from the same piece of wood. The sides and back are also the same width and can be cut from a single board.

2. Cut the parts to size. Cut the back to the length specified in the Materials List. Set your table saw's miter gauge to 45 degrees and cut the angle in the sides' front edges, as shown in the *Construction Overview.*

Tilt your saw's arbor to 45 degrees and cut the bevel in the bottom's front edge and the top's front edge, as shown in the *Construction Overview.* Clean up the sawed edges with a block plane.

TECHNIQUE TIP

Instead of making separate cuts to form the 45 degree edges on each side and the mitered front edges on the top and bottom, plan your work so you only have to make one of each cut. A single 45 degree cut made in the middle of the 3-inch-wide board will result in the sloping ends for both sides. The same applies when cutting the beveled front edges of the bottom and top. Cut the miter in the center of one 18-inch-long board. One half will serve as the top, and the other as the bottom.

3. Cut the top to shape. Use a band saw, bow saw, or coping saw to cut the top's handle. Smooth the curved edges with either a sander or a spokeshave. Clean up the corner formed by the circular handle with a chisel. Drill a ⅜-inch-diameter hole centered on the circular end.

ASSEMBLE THE PARTS.

1. Nail together the bottom, sides, and back. Nail the bottom to the sides with 1-inch brads. Make sure the 45 degree mitered edges on the sides line up with the beveled edge of the bottom. Fit the back between the sides. If necessary, trim it to fit. Nail the bottom and sides to the back.

Photo 1: Before attaching the top, even up the top edges of the sides and back with a block plane.

2. Attach the top. If the top edges of the sides and back are not perfectly flush, run a block plane over them to make them all the same height (*Photo 1*). This will ensure that the top fits tightly. Nail the top in place with 1-inch brads.

CONSTRUCTION TIP

When nailing the top and bottom, try to space your nails evenly. The dustpan's bottom is seen when the dustpan is hung and the top is visible when it is used. Uniform spacing looks better.

PLATE HOLDER

All of us have a few cherished objects around that we display in a manner that reflects how much they mean to us. Our love for collecting and displaying things is apparent in the several projects found in this book that were made specifically for that purpose by country woodworkers.

This plate holder is dedicated to displaying a fine plate—perhaps a gift from a close friend or one passed down from a great-grandmother. The plate holder keeps the plate upright so that it can be admired. I've also found that this plate holder supports a book quite nicely.

The rack is a small piece, providing a good opportunity to use up those special scraps you've been saving because they were too

good to run through the stove. However, the holder's purpose does raise a dilemma—since the holder's function is to support a precious treasured object, should it be made of the most handsome, precious wood you have, or should you make the holder from a bland, less obvious wood? The original plate holder was made of maple or birch, but it was painted black so it would not compete with the object it was displaying. I compromised by making my copy from cherry, which has a pleasant color but not a strong figure. I gave it an oil finish. I bought a ¼-inch cherry dowel (available from The Woodworkers Store, 21801 Industrial Boulevard, Rogers, MN 55374; part #21055) to match the cherry sides.

CONSTRUCTION OVERVIEW

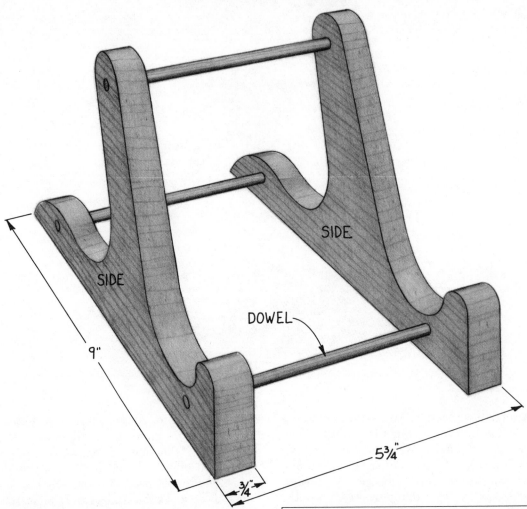

SIDE

SIDE

DOWEL

9"

5¾"

¾"

MAKE AND ASSEMBLE THE PARTS.

1. Make the sides. Joint and thickness plane the side stock to ¾ inch, then hand plane the stock to remove any machine marks.

Make a grid of ½-inch squares on a piece of posterboard and draw the side shape on it, as shown in the *Side Pattern*. Cut out the

MATERIALS LIST

PART	DIMENSIONS
Sides (2)	¾″ × 5¾″ × 9″
Dowels (3)	¼″ dia. × 5¾″

pattern and transfer it to the stock. Cut the sides to shape on the band saw, then sand and file the sawed edges smooth.

SIDE PATTERN

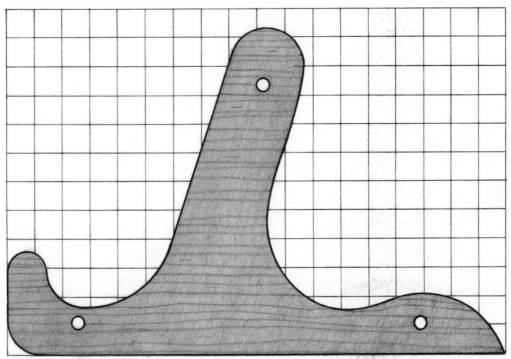

ONE SQUARE = ½"

2. Drill the holes. Drill the ¼-inch-diameter dowel holes through the sides, as shown in the *Side Pattern.* Put a piece of scrap underneath the sides as you drill the holes. As the bit penetrates the side, the scrap will support the wood fibers and minimize tear-out.

3. Cut the dowels. Cut the dowels to the length given in the Materials List.

TECHNIQUE TIP

To ensure that the holes align perfectly, clamp the two sides together and drill the holes in both sides at the same time.

4. Assemble the parts. Glue the dowels into one of the sides. If they are tight, tap them into place with a light hammer. Align the second side with the dowels and glue it in place.

BOXES

PIPE BOX

The original of this distinctive box dates from before the Revolutionary War and was designed to hold long-stemmed clay pipes. The pipes were placed in the open upper section, while the narrow drawer held tobacco.

I have my copy of this box hanging by the back door, and each day, as I bring in the mail, I put any new bills in it. This way, they are all in one spot. I keep stamps in the drawer.

This pipe box may seem unremarkable to some people, but I really see it as a sophisticated design. In part, the sophistication stems from the box's curvilinear upper edges that flow both forward and down in a three-dimensional cascade, moving from the top of the fishtail back to the deepest point of the cutout front. The length of this unbroken movement is almost equal to the height of the box itself. Furthermore, the curves actually appear to wrap around the corners. This illusion is accomplished by a distinctive rabbet joint produced by a narrow, low shoulder with a curved corner.

On the original, the profiles of the sides and front duplicated common molding profiles. The box's curves were shapes its owners and users certainly recognized, for they were surrounded everywhere by them. No matter where this pipe box hung, one or more of the moldings used on the house's interior woodwork was the same shape as the pipe box's cutout edges. It was not merely an object in the room; it became part of the room.

I painted my pipe box a deep matte red. The red adds a splash of color to the wall and also shows off those curves. The original box

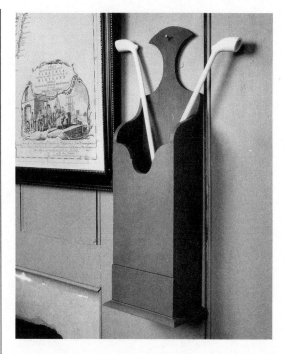

is made of pine, but almost any even-textured wood (hard or soft) will do. I made the one shown here out of basswood.

MAKE THE PARTS.

1. Cut the parts to size. Much of the stock is quite thin. You may want to resaw 4/4 (four-quarter) or 5/4 (five-quarter) stock on a band saw, then thickness plane the stock to dimension. In any case, hand plane all surfaces to remove any machine marks. Joint, rip, and square the individual pieces to the dimensions given in the Materials List.

159

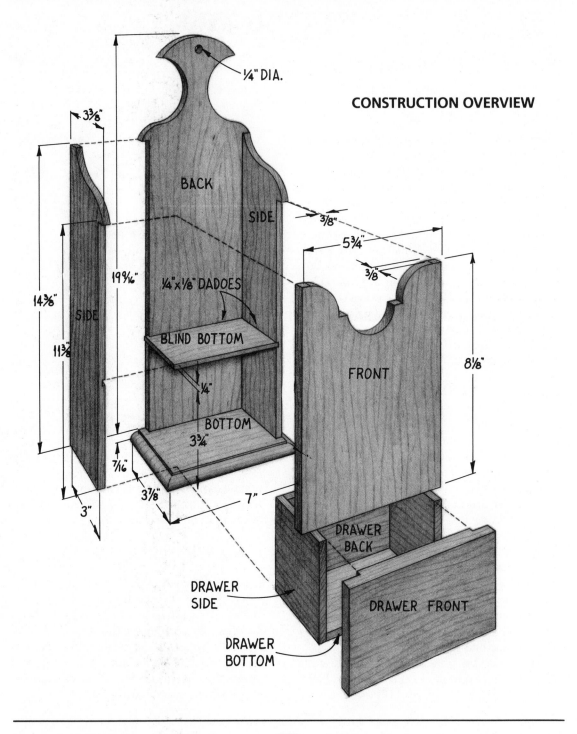

CONSTRUCTION OVERVIEW

¼" DIA.

3⅜"

BACK

SIDE

3/8"

5¾"

3/8"

19⁹⁄₁₆"

¼" x ⅛" DADOES

14⅜"

SIDE

11⅜"

BLIND BOTTOM

FRONT

8⅛"

¼"

BOTTOM

3¾"

7⁄16"

3⅞"

7"

3"

DRAWER
BACK

DRAWER
SIDE

DRAWER FRONT

DRAWER
BOTTOM

MATERIALS LIST

PART	DIMENSIONS
Front	3/8" × 5¾" × 8⅛"
Sides (2)	3/8" × 3⅜" × 14⅜"
Back	3/8" × 5¾" × 19⁹⁄₁₆"
Blind bottom	¼" × 2¾" × 5¼"
Bottom	7/16" × 3⅞" × 7"
Drawer front	11/16" × 3¼" × 5¾"
Drawer sides (2)	¼" × 2⁷⁄₁₆" × 3¼"
Drawer back	¼" × 3" × 4⅜"
Drawer bottom	¼" × 2⁷⁄₁₆" × 4⅜"

HARDWARE AND SUPPLIES

1" brads (as needed)

Brass mushroom knob (optional)

2. Lay out and cut the front, sides, and back.
Lay out the curved profiles on the front, sides, and back, as shown in the *Back Pattern*, *Side Pattern*, and *Front Pattern*. If you cut them on a band saw, use a narrow, fine-tooth blade. (You can cut the curves just as quickly with a coping saw.) Clean up the edges with a drum sander or a combination of hand tools, including a spokeshave, files, and sandpaper.

The blind bottom fits into dadoes cut in the sides and back. Cut them ¼ inch wide and ⅛ inch deep, as shown in the *Construction Overview*.

Locate and drill a ¼-inch hole in the back. The hole is centered on a line between the points of the fishtail.

BACK PATTERN

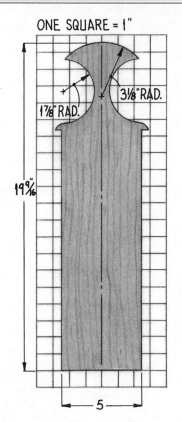

SIDE PATTERN

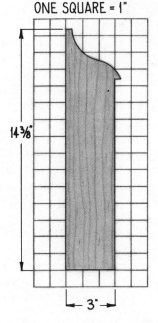

FRONT PATTERN

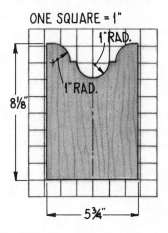

The dadoes for the blind bottom are short, narrow, and shallow. They can be cut very quickly by hand. Lay out the dadoes with a try square and scratch awl. (The awl creates a very fine line and is therefore more accurate than a pencil.) Score the edges of the dadoes with a utility knife and pare out the waste with a ¼-inch chisel.

Photo 1: Bury most of the ¾-inch roundover bit in the router table fence. Guide the stock against the fence to cut the thumbnail.

3. Make the bottom. The bottom's edge has a shape called a thumbnail (the name's inspiration is clear if you look at your thumb's profile), as shown in the *Construction Overview.* I formed the edge profile with a specialized plane. To approximate the profile with a router, use a ¾-inch roundover bit, engaging only the outer segment of the cutter. (A smaller roundover bit will produce too blunt a profile.) Because the workpiece is small, do this on a table-mounted router (*Photo 1*). An alternative approach—slightly less refined but quite acceptable—is to bevel the edges with a block plane.

ASSEMBLE THE BOX AND DRAWER.

1. Assemble the box. The box is simply nailed together. Attach the sides to the back first. Use 1-inch brads. Insert the blind bottom into its dadoes. Make sure the front edge is flush with the sides. Nail the front in place, then the bottom.

2. Make the drawer. Like the box itself, the drawer is simply nailed together with brads. The sides and bottom fit into rabbets cut into the front, as shown in the *Drawer Top View* and the *Drawer Side View.* The rabbets on the ends of the drawer front (these are for the sides) are $^{11}/_{16}$ inch wide and ¼ inch deep. The rabbet on the bottom of the drawer front is ¼ inch wide and ¼ inch deep. Cut these rabbets with a dado blade in the table saw.

DRAWER TOP VIEW

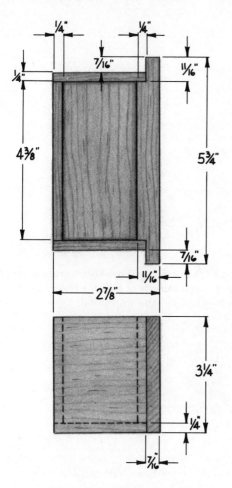

DRAWER SIDE VIEW

Assemble the drawer by nailing the two sides to the front with 1-inch brads. Fit the back between the two sides and nail it in place. Insert the bottom. If any adjustment needs to be done to make the bottom fit, use a block plane to trim it to the proper size. Nail the bottom in place.

The original pipe box has no drawer pull. Rather, it is opened by gripping the edges; over the years, repeated use has worn away the paint and even rounded the edges — a very charming effect. If, however, it's an effect that doesn't appeal to you, add a pull. A small brass mushroom knob would be appropriate. To install such a knob, locate the drawer front's center and make a pilot hole with a brad awl. Screw the knob into this hole.

TOOL TIP

The drawer front is quite small, so the rabbets in it can easily and quickly be cut with a dovetail saw. Use a marking gauge and try square to lay out the rabbets, then cut them with the saw. Clean up the saw cuts with a shoulder plane.

HEXAGONAL CANDLE BOX

In other chapters I have underscored the importance candles and lamps had in a country home. Using these early forms of lighting required a household to have all sorts of accessories, including a place to store candles. Usually the candles were kept in a special candle box.

Although we no longer have to light our homes with candles, it is a rare house that does not have a few on hand. We need them for emergency lighting in a power failure or for creating a more intimate atmosphere at meals, parties, and other gatherings. All candle boxes are long and narrow, reflecting the

shape of their contents. However, this candle box is indeed different because it is hexagonal rather than rectangular. Country woodworkers generally created their own designs, and they often chose to use geometric shapes. The hexagon, however, was not a frequent selection, and its unusual shape is just what makes this box so delightful.

The original candle box from which this was copied had a type of hinge that, in the past, was quite common on country woodwork, although today we would find it unusual. The hinge was a long, narrow strip of leather tacked to the edge of the lid and the top. Leather is

CONSTRUCTION OVERVIEW

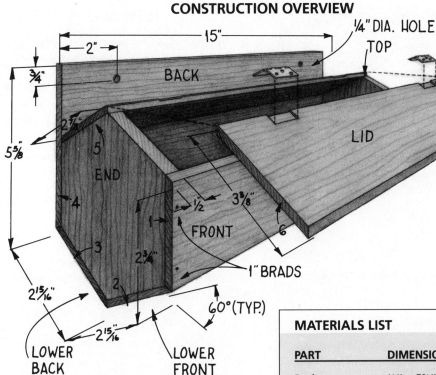

MATERIALS LIST

PART	DIMENSIONS
Back	$1/4'' \times 5\frac{5}{8}'' \times 15''$
Lid	$1/4'' \times 3\frac{3}{8}'' \times 15''$
Top	$1/4'' \times 2\frac{7}{8}'' \times 15''$
Lower front	$1/4'' \times 2\frac{15}{16}'' \times 15''$
Lower back	$1/4'' \times 2\frac{15}{16}'' \times 15''$
Front	$1/4'' \times 2\frac{3}{4}'' \times 15''$
Ends (2)	$1/2'' \times 4\frac{5}{8}'' \times 5\frac{3}{8}''$

HARDWARE AND SUPPLIES

1'' brads (as needed)
$1'' \times \frac{13}{16}''$ brass butt hinges (2)

tough and flexible and it endures hard use almost as well as metal does. In fact, the leather hinge on the original still works well today after almost two centuries of use. On my copy I chose to use lightweight brass hinges. I flush-mounted the hinges by cutting shallow mortises for the hinge leaves. I also inverted the hinges so the knuckles were hidden by the lid's rear edge.

I painted my pine candle box with green milk paint. The candle box could also be decorated with country designs.

MAKE THE PARTS.

1. Prepare the stock. Joint and thickness plane all the stock to the dimensions given in the Materials List, then hand plane it to remove any machine marks. Joint the edges and hand plane them to remove the jointer marks. Cut the stock to length.

2. Cut the bevels. Set your table saw's arbor to 30 degrees. Rip parts 1 through 6 to width, referring to the *Construction Overview* for proper bevel directions (*Photo 1*).

Photo 1: Cut the bevels in the side pieces as you cut them to width.

TECHNIQUE TIP

Even though there are critical differences between them, many of the sides look very much alike. To avoid confusion, follow these tips and refer frequently to the drawing. Use a pencil to mark the ends Right and Left. Next, number each of the six sides on each end, as shown in the *Construction Overview.* It is important to begin the numbering on an edge grain side so the front and back will be parts #1 and #4. Use the pencil to number the sides to match the edges. The front is #1, the lower front is #2, the lower back is #3, the back is #4, the top is #5, and the lid is #6.

3. **Drill the holes in the back.** Drill two holes in the back with a ¼-inch-diameter bit, as shown in the *Construction Overview.*

4. **Make the ends.** Locate the center of each end and trace a centerline that runs in the

TECHNIQUE TIP

Plan your cuts so you obtain as many pieces as possible from each width of lumber. I used standard 10-inch-wide lumber (actually measuring 9½ inches) and needed three 15-inch-long lengths. There was some left over, which is handy if you make a mistake.

same direction as the grain. Place a 60 degree triangle (or a sliding T-bevel set to that angle) on the centerline and use it to lay out the six angled sides. Screw an extension fence to the table saw miter gauge and set the miter gauge to 60 degrees (*Photo 2*). Guide the end stock with the miter gauge as you cut the angled sides.

Check your work by measuring the six sides. They should all be equal. Make any final adjustments to the six sides on a disk sander.

Photo 2: Screw an extension fence to the miter gauge and guide the end stock with it as you cut the 60 degree sides.

ASSEMBLE THE PARTS.

1. Attach the back. To avoid splitting the ends when nailing, use a $5/64$-inch-diameter drill bit to make three pilot holes in the edges of the back. Center the pilot holes on the ends' thickness. Apply a light coating of glue to edge #4 on each end. Align the back's beveled edge with the ends' corners, as shown in the *Construction Overview*, and secure the back with three 1-inch brads on each end.

2. Attach the remaining sides. First, attach the lower back (#3). Drill two pilot holes at each end and secure the joints with brads. To allow for the ends' seasonal expansion and contraction, do not apply glue to their remaining edges.

Next, add the remaining sides. Secure each to the ends with two brads. Glue only the beveled edge joints between the sides.

CONSTRUCTION TIP

To obtain a perfectly straight joint where the beveled edges meet, eliminate any saw marks by carefully smoothing each joint with a block plane. Adjust the block plane to remove a small amount of wood so that you have little risk of altering the angle.

FIT THE HINGES.

1. Cut the hinge mortises. First, lay out the hinge positions by measuring in 2 inches from each end of the lid. Make a pencil mark at each spot. Lay the lid against the top and transfer the marks to the top.

Next, lay the outside edge of each hinge on its mark on the lid and trace around the leaf. Carefully score the outline with a utility knife and pare away the waste with a sharp chisel, matching the thickness of the leaf. Repeat the process on the top.

2. Fit the hinge knuckles. Since the hinge knuckles face in, a small recess must be cut for them in the lid and the top. Cut a half-round channel in the lower front edge of each hinge mortise with a small carving gouge. Hold the hinges in place and test the fit of the lid against the top. Cutting the channel will cause the hinge leaf to project back further than the rear edge of the mortise. When you are satisfied with the fit of the knuckle in the channel, trace a new rear edge and extend each mortise.

The in-turned hinge knuckles can cause the lid to bind. To prevent this, use a block plane to relieve the corners of the top and lid, as shown in the *Construction Overview*.

3. Attach the hinges. Hinges are generally countersunk for screws on the knuckle side. Since the hinges on this candle box are reversed, you must rebore the hinge countersinks. I used a $1/4$-inch-diameter drill bit held in my hand. The brass is so soft that the bit's sharp edge easily peeled it away.

When the screw holes have been countersunk, hold the hinges in the lid mortises and bore pilot holes with a brad awl. When everything seems to be fitting properly, drive in the brass screws.

Because the screws are longer than $1/4$ inch, they will pierce the lid's underside — simply file away their points.

OPEN WALL BOX

Most boxes found in a country home were intended for general use and held many of the small things that were needed to keep a household running smoothly. Storing these items in a hanging wall box kept them in one easy-to-reach place. Things kept in a small wall box could include anything from sewing implements to notions to materials for starting a fire. Hanging wall boxes were so handy that no country home was without one or more.

Although this box is a very simple project held together with only nailed joints, its design merits some mention. As is true of many small country wooden objects, its maker relied on basic geometric shapes to create visual interest.

Above the box sides, the back is essentially a right triangle topped by a circle. Simple half-circles are cut out of the sides of the triangle. When first seen, this design appears more intricate and complicated than it really is.

The box's front and sides slope at 96 degrees. The bottom's front and side edges are also angled at 96 degrees to accommodate the sloped front and sides.

I made the box shown here as an exact copy of the original. Later, my wife thought

CONSTRUCTION OVERVIEW

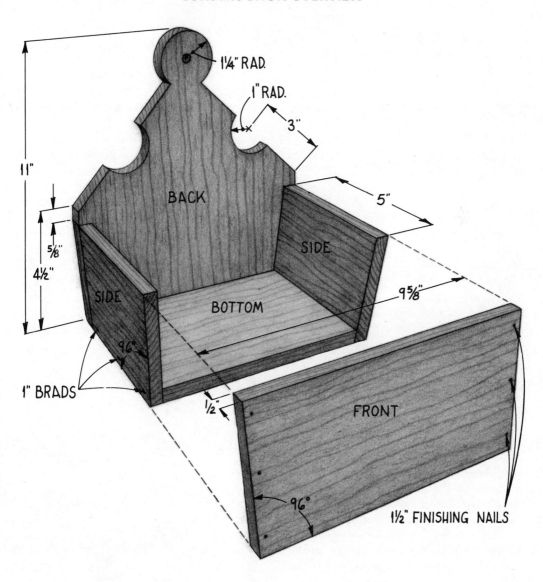

1¼" RAD.

1" RAD.

3"

11"

BACK

5"

SIDE

5/8"

4½"

SIDE

BOTTOM

9⅝"

96°

1" BRADS

½"

FRONT

96°

1½" FINISHING NAILS

she might like to use my copy to hold a box of tissues; however, it was just a little too short. If you would like to make your box to hold tissues, make the bottom 5 inches wide × 10 inches long, and expand the back, front, and sides to match.

To help brighten up the out-of-the-way corners in which they were hung, small coun-

MATERIALS LIST

PART	DIMENSIONS
Back	½″ × 9⅝″ × 11″
Front	½″ × 3⅞″ × 9⅝″
Sides (2)	½″ × 3⅞″ × 5″
Bottom stock	½″ × 5″ × 8″

HARDWARE AND SUPPLIES

1½″ finishing nails (as needed)
1″ brads (as needed)

try objects like this wall box were often given a very colorful finish. For that reason, I applied a false grain finish using a yellow ground and red glaze, drawing out the glaze with a very coarse graining comb. See "False Graining" on page 8 for instructions on applying a false grain finish.

MAKE THE PARTS.

1. Prepare the stock. Thickness plane the stock to ½ inch. Hand plane the stock to remove any tool marks.

2. Make the back. First, rip and cut the back to the dimensions given in the Materials List. Lay out the shape of the back on the stock, as shown in the *Construction Overview.*

Next, set your table saw's miter gauge to 84 degrees and cut an angle on the lower corners of the back, as shown in the *Construction Overview.* Cut out the remainder of the back on a band saw or scroll saw or with a coping saw. Use a disk sander and small drum sander to smooth away the saw marks. Drill a ¼-inch-diameter hole centered in the top circle.

3. Make the front, sides, and bottom. Set your table saw's arbor to 6 degrees and rip the bottom to width as you bevel its front edge. The bottom is not beveled along its back edge, but it is beveled on its ends, as shown in the *Construction Overview.* Guide the bottom with the table saw miter gauge set at 90 degrees as you bevel its ends while cutting it to length.

Although the sides and front are treated as three separate pieces in the Materials List, it is most efficient to cut them from a single piece. Start with a piece of wood about 22 inches long to allow for waste. Again, bevel the edges with the table saw blade tilted at 6 degrees. Flip the piece over and rip a bevel in the other edge that is parallel to the first, as shown in the *Construction Overview (Photo 1)*. When you cut the front's angled ends, measure carefully so that each cut also produces a side *(Photo 2)*. Then, set the miter gauge to 90 degrees and cut the sides to length.

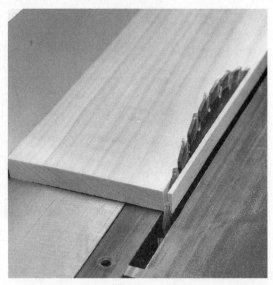

Photo 1: Bevel both edges of the side and front stock as you rip it to width. The beveled edges should be parallel.

Photo 2: Lay out the cuts on the stock so that, as you cut the front's angled ends, you also produce the sides' angled ends.

Hand plane the edges to remove the saw marks.

ASSEMBLE THE PARTS.

1. Nail the front and back to the sides. Hold one of the sides in a vise and nail the front to it with 1½-inch finishing nails, as shown in the *Construction Overview.* Repeat the process for the remaining side, then nail the back to the sides with three 1½-inch finishing nails per side.

2. Fit the bottom. Adjust the bottom's width and length until it fits all the way into the opening created by the back, front, and sides. Make the adjustments with a hand plane or on a disk sander. As you adjust the size of the bottom, make sure the corners remain square. When the bottom fits correctly, nail the bottom in place with 1-inch brads.

CLOSED SHELF

This hanging wall shelf is different from the other shelves in this book because both its shelves have closed fronts that, in essence, create a box. These two fronts will cover at least part of the objects placed on the shelf, so the piece is intended more for storing objects like knitting or sewing supplies than for displaying knickknacks.

In recent years the heart cutout has become the motif most associated with country woodwork, and it is used far more today than it was in the past. However, the original shelf *really does* have a heart cutout. If you're tired of looking at this sometimes overused motif,

omit the cutout or substitute another shape. Both of the shelf fronts would also be a good place for a chip-carved decoration or a carved date. You could also decorate the shelf fronts with painted designs.

The original shelf was made of pine and that is what I used. Most hardwoods would also be appropriate. If you use a wood with an attractive figured grain, such as cherry, apply a clear oil finish to bring out the grain. You could also paint the shelf to match your home's decor. I left my shelf raw because raw pine turns a very warm pumpkin color and its grain becomes more pronounced. Since the shelf

CONSTRUCTION OVERVIEW

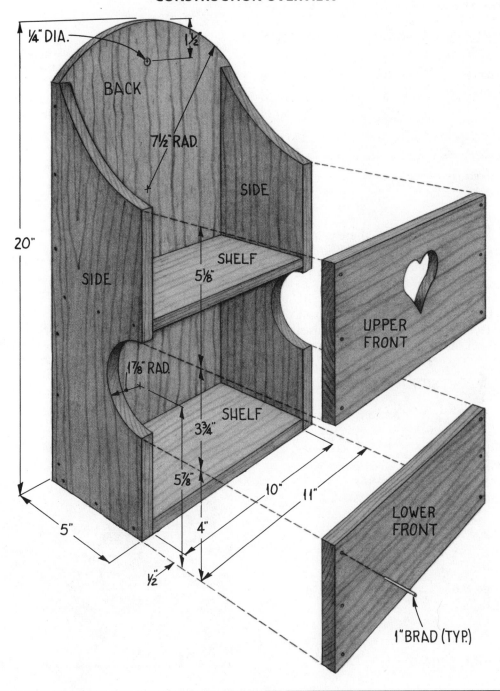

¼" DIA.

1½"

BACK

7½" RAD.

SIDE

20"

SHELF

5⅛"

SIDE

UPPER
FRONT

1⅞" RAD.

SHELF

3¾"

5⅞"

10"

11"

4"

5"

½"

LOWER
FRONT

1" BRAD (TYP.)

MATERIALS LIST

PART	DIMENSIONS
Back	½″ × 11″ × 20″
Sides (2)	½″ × 5″ × 17⅜″
Shelves (2)	½″ × 4½″ × 10″
Upper front	½″ × 5⅛″ × 11″
Lower front	½″ × 4″ × 11″

HARDWARE AND SUPPLIES

1″ brads (as needed)

will not be handled often, there is no need to worry about dirt and grime building up on the raw wood from contact with fingers.

There isn't any tricky joinery in this shelf. All you'll find here is the lowly butt joint, which is completely satisfactory for a piece this size. You can probably build this shelf in an afternoon.

SIDE PATTERN

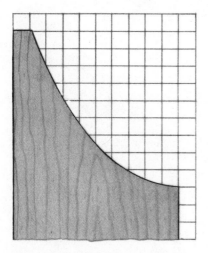

ONE SQUARE = ½″

MAKE AND ASSEMBLE THE PARTS.

1. Prepare the stock. Joint and thickness plane the stock to ½ inch thick. Rip and cut the stock to the dimensions given in the Materials List. Joint the edges of the stock and square the ends. Hand plane all the parts to remove any machine marks.

2. Lay out and cut the curves. Lay out the curves on the back and sides, as shown in the *Construction Overview*. As shown in the *Side Pattern*, plot the sides' upper curves on a grid of ½-inch squares. Cut the curves with a band saw, jigsaw, or coping saw, and clean up the saw marks with a spokeshave and sandpaper.

TECHNIQUE TIP

You can clean away saw marks and produce a clean, tight joint with a combination of two hand planes. First, smooth most of the long edge with a block plane. Next, smooth all of the way into the corner with a chisel plane.

Drill a ¼-inch hole centered on the back, 1½ inches from the top, as shown in the *Construction Overview.*

3. Cut out the back to accept the sides. Rip a ½ × 17⅜-inch cutout in each side of the back, as shown in the *Construction Overview.* Make the long rip and short crosscut on the band saw. Sand the sawed edge smooth.

4. Lay out and cut the heart. Draw a vertical centerline on the upper front. Lay out a 1⅛-inch-radius circle on the centerline. Draw the heart freehand within the circle. Drill a hole through the heart for a coping saw or scroll saw blade and cut out the heart shape. Smooth away the saw marks with a half-round mill file and sandpaper.

5. Join the parts. First, attach the sides to the back with 1-inch brads. Next, put the shelves in place and secure them by driving brads through the sides. Finally, nail the upper and lower fronts to the sides and shelves and give the shelf a quick sanding.

KEEPING BIN

A country household had to store grain and other bulk food for both itself and its livestock. While animal feed was generally kept in a barn grain bin, food for humans, such as flour, meal, beans, and grain, was usually stored in wooden barrels kept in the pantry. Ironically, while country collectors actively seek grain bins for use in their homes, most would be aghast at the idea of owning barrels.

This project strikes a middle ground. It is more attractive than barrels and much nicer than rustic grain bins. The keeping bin was obviously meant to be used in a kitchen; its size indicates that this piece was definitely in-

tended for use in the house rather than the barn. And the shaped front, back, and sides, as well as the bootjack feet, make this piece too handsome to store away in a pantry.

Notice the maker's choice of shiplap joints. The bin is essentially a deep wooden box. If the front and back were made from a single board (or several boards glued together), they would expand and contract as much as ⅜ inch between winter and summer. Given this kind of movement, it's unlikely the piece would survive for long. Shiplapping solves this problem. This joint, made by rabbeting the edges of adjoining boards, allows the pieces to over-

CONSTRUCTION OVERVIEW

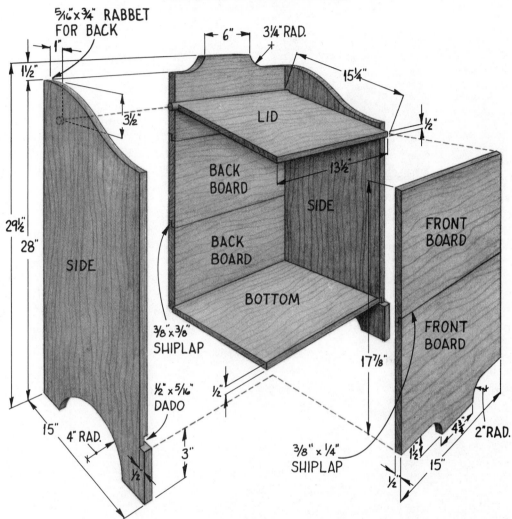

lap and slide against each other without creating an opening into the box.

Instead of using metal hinges to attach the lid, the maker made the lid an integral part of the bin. A hole in each side receives lugs on the edge of the lid. Make note of the lid's length in the Materials List. It is given as 15 inches, although the lid proper is only 13½ inches. The lugs account for the extra length.

The lid is glued up from two pieces of wood. The wood that faces the center of the tree is the bottom surface of the lid. As a result, the board will be slightly concave when it warps. Interestingly, the curve in the upper edges of the sides camouflages the warp. The primary purpose of shaping the edges may, in fact, have been to remove the straight lines that would make the warping obvious.

MATERIALS LIST

PART	DIMENSIONS
Front boards (as needed)	½″ × (variable) × 15″
Back boards (as needed)	¾″ × (variable) × 14⅛″
Sides (2)	¾″ × 15″ × 28″
Lid	½″ × 15″ × 15¼″
Bottom	½″ × 13¾″ × 14⅛″

HARDWARE AND SUPPLIES

6d cut nails (as needed). Available from
Tremont Nail Company, 8 Elm Street, P.O.
Box 111, Wareham, MA 02571.
Part #N-21 Std.

I oiled my pine bin with a mixture of boiled linseed oil (buy boiled linseed oil at the store—don't attempt to boil it yourself) thinned with turpentine, as described on page 7. I applied oil to the inside surfaces of the sides above and sightly below the lid. I didn't oil the inside since it will come into contact with food.

MAKE THE PARTS.

1. Prepare the stock. Joint and thickness plane the materials to the dimensions given in the Materials List. Glue up stock for the wider parts as necessary. Rip all parts to width and cut them to length. Hand plane all the surfaces to even the glue joints and to remove thickness planer chatter marks.

2. Cut the parts to shape. Cut to shape the appropriate parts of the front, back, and sides with a band saw or bow saw, as shown in the *Construction Overview* and the *Side Pattern.* Clean up all curved sawed edges with a spokeshave or a drum sander. Set your saw blade to cut a 75 degree angle and trim the lid's front

SIDE PATTERN

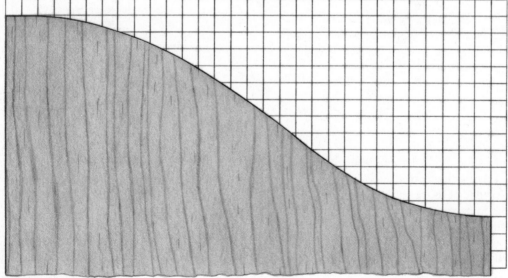

ONE SQUARE = ½″

edge and the upper front board's upper edge. Smooth both with a hand plane.

3. Make the hinge lugs. The lid is hinged to the sides by two ½-inch-diameter lugs on the lid's back corners. First, define the front edge of each lug by making a ¾-inch-deep cut with a dovetail saw. Next, set your band saw's fence to ¾ inch and trim away the waste in front of the lugs. Clean up the sawed edges with a block plane and chisel.

Lay out the lugs in pencil. Cut away the corners with a dovetail saw and pare the lugs round by making plunge cuts with a sharp bench chisel. Test the shape of each lug by test fitting it in a ½-inch hole drilled in a piece of scrap. If you are using pine, twist the lug in the test hole several times to round the facets created by the chisel. If you are using a harder wood, smooth the lug with a file.

Round-over the lid's back edge with a hand plane to prevent it from binding when the lid is opened.

Lay out the hinge holes in the sides, as shown in the *Construction Overview*. Drill the holes through the sides with a ½-inch bit.

CUT THE JOINTS.

1. Make the dadoes. Dado the sides for the bottom with a dado head on your table saw, as shown in the *Construction Overview*.

Photo 1: Guide the router with a fence attachment as you rout the stopped rabbets in the sides.

2. Rabbet for the back. Rabbet the sides for the back with a router and a ¾-inch-diameter straight bit (*Photo 1*). Guide the router with

Photo 2: The rabbets can be cut in the front boards and back boards with a fillister plane.

its fence attachment. Stop the rabbets when they meet the dadoes.

3. Cut the sides to hold the front boards. The sides are cut away to house the front, as shown in the *Construction Overview*. First, make a ½-inch-deep cut with a dovetail saw to define the bottom of the cutaway. Set the band saw's rip fence to ½ inch and rip the edge of the cutaway. Smooth the cut with a block plane and chisel.

4. Shiplap the front boards and back boards. The front boards and back boards have interlocking rabbets, or shiplaps, that allow the boards to expand and contract. Cut the rabbets, as shown in the *Construction Overview*, with either a dado blade in a table saw or a fillister plane (*Photo 2*).

ASSEMBLE THE PARTS.

1. Attach the lid and back boards. Nail one end of the upper back board to one of the sides with 6d cut nails. Before nailing the other side in place, insert the hinge lugs in their holes. Nail the other end of the upper back board in place to trap the lid. Nail the remaining back boards in place.

TECHNIQUE TIP

Drill pilot holes for the cut nails to prevent the wood from splitting. The pilot holes should be at a very slight angle so the nail points don't break through the inside edges of the bin.

---

2. Insert the bottom. Slide the bottom into its dadoes and tap it lightly with a mallet if it binds. Make sure its back edge butts tightly against the back board.

3. Attach the front boards. Use a bar clamp to pull the sides tightly against the bottom and check to make sure the case is square. Put the top front board in place first, then attach the remaining front boards with 6d cut nails.

KNIFE BOX

In a country house during the 19th century, everyday tableware was usually stored in an open, double-sided box. Between meals the box was kept in the pantry. It was carried to the kitchen or dining room when the table was being set for meals. After being washed, knives and forks were laid in the knife box and returned to the pantry until the next meal. Spoons were kept in a separate container called a spooner.

Because every house had a knife box, antique examples are common. However, because these boxes were so utilitarian, most amount to no more than a rectangular painted box that is nailed together. This example is certainly a cut above the norm. It has a turned handle rather than a simple cutout finger hole. It also has sloping sides that are joined with dovetails. The sloped sides make the box interesting to look at, but present you with some extra considerations: Make sure when ripping the sides that you make their beveled edges parallel, and lay out the direction of the bevels and miters before you do any cutting.

The original knife box was a wedding present, given to my wife and me by the mother of one of my college roommates. My wife displays antique tableware in it, and some-

CONSTRUCTION OVERVIEW

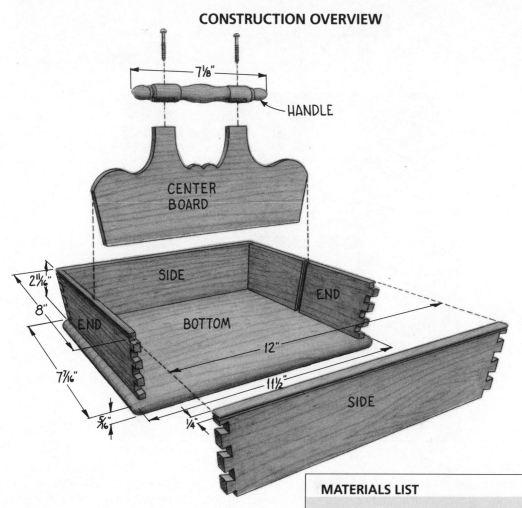

sometimes she uses it to hold flower arrangements. In either case, it helps decorate her country kitchen.

The original box is finished with orange shellac that, over time, has darkened to a rich brown. This makes it very hard to identify the wood from which it was made. I can only say that it has a very even grain. I made my copy from basswood that I sawed from a tree that used to grow in front of my house. Birch, a good wood for turning, was my choice for the

MATERIALS LIST

PART	DIMENSIONS
Sides (2)	¼″ × 2¾″ × 12″
Ends (2)	¼″ × 2¾″ × 8″
Center board stock	¼″ × 5¼″ × 11¾″
Handle stock	¾″ × ¾″ × 9″
Bottom	⁵⁄₁₆″ × 7⁷⁄₁₆″ × 11½″

HARDWARE AND SUPPLIES

#4 × ¾″ flathead wood screws (13)
#8 × 1¼″ brass roundhead wood screws (2)

handle. Birch's color is close to that of basswood; if you want more contrast in your knife box, make the handle out of a darker wood such as walnut. I finished my knife box with nontoxic salad bowl oil.

MAKE THE PARTS.

1. Prepare the stock. Thickness plane all the stock, then hand plane it to remove any machine marks.

2. Cut and shape the bottom, sides, and ends. First, rip and cut the bottom to the dimensions given in the Materials List.

Next, bevel the edges of the sides and ends as you cut them to width. Tilt your saw's arbor to 9 degrees and bevel one edge of each side and end. Set the fence to 2¾ inches and rip the second bevel. Make sure the second

bevel is parallel to the first, as shown in the *Construction Overview.*

When the sides and ends have been beveled, reset the table saw arbor to square (0 degrees) and set your miter gauge to 9 degrees. Cut the sides and ends to length as you angle their ends, as shown in the *Construction Overview.* Note that the sides and ends all angle toward the bottom.

3. Cut the center board to shape. First, rip the center board to width.

Next, make a grid of ½-inch squares on a piece of posterboard and draw one half of the center board pattern on it, as shown in the *Center Board Pattern.* Cut out the pattern and transfer the shape to the stock. Flip the pattern to draw the second half of the center board; as you do so, make sure the base of the center board is $10^{13}/_{16}$ inches long (*Photo 1*).

CENTER BOARD PATTERN

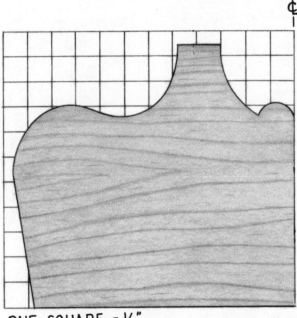

ONE SQUARE = ½"

Photo 1: Lay out the first half of the center board with the pattern, then flip the pattern over to fill in the second half.

When the pattern has been laid out on the stock, set the table saw miter gauge to 9 degrees and cut the angled ends of the center board. Cut the upper part of the center board to shape with a scroll saw, band saw, or coping saw. Remove the saw marks with a chisel, file, and sandpaper.

4. Round the edges of the bottom. Mount your router in a router table and round the edges of the bottom with a ⅜-inch-diameter bull-nose bit. Recess most of the bit in the router table fence and guide the stock against the fence as you rout.

5. Turn the handle. Turn the handle to the shape shown in the *Handle Turning Layout*. The handle length given in the Materials List includes ½ inch of waste at each end.

First, chuck the handle stock in the lathe and turn it to a ¾-inch diameter with a gouge. Next, measure and lay out the sections of

---

TOOL TIP

The edges of the bottom can also be rounded with a block plane. Round the end grain first, holding the block plane at a slight angle so that the blade slices across the wood. Finish up on the sides, then sand all four edges to round any flat spots.

---

the turning, including the grip, the attachment points, and the acorn-shaped ends, by touching a pencil to the spinning stock at those points. When you have made your layout marks, turn the handle grip with a ½-inch gouge. Finally, turn the acorn-shaped ends with a skew (*Photo 2*).

If you haven't done much turning, you might want to do some extra reading on the subject. In *Woodturning for Cabinetmakers*, I go into much greater detail on the subject than is possible here.

Photo 2: Turn the acorn-shaped ends with a skew.

HANDLE TURNING LAYOUT

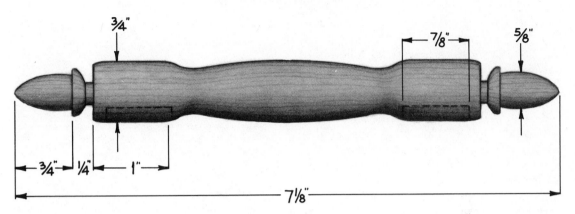

¾" ⅞" ⅝"

←¾"→ ¼" ← 1" →

7⅛"

6. Lay out the handle mortises. The handle has two shallow mortises that fit over the center board tenons, as shown in the *Construction Overview.* The handle is then secured with two #8 × 1¼-inch roundhead wood screws. Lay out the mortises while the handle is still chucked in the lathe with a shop-made center locator, as described in "Lathe Center Scribe" on page 27.

With the handle still in the lathe, trace three parallel lines ⅛ inch apart on both handle cylinders (*Photo 3*). The two outside lines lay out the mortises' width, while the third line marks their centers. Place the center board's tenons on the layout lines to determine the length of the mortises.

CUT THE JOINTS.

1. Make the dovetails. Dovetailing is precise work that demands concentration when the sides of a box are merely square. Here, the sloping box creates additional complications.

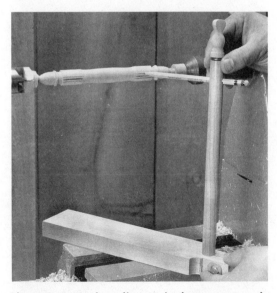

Photo 3: Trace three lines ⅛ inch apart on each handle cylinder to lay out the mortises.

The difference here is that the tails must angle across the width of the sides, and the angle of the pins must compensate, as shown in the *Construction Overview.*

For the most part, you can follow the dovetail cutting process outlined in "Cutting Dovetails" on page 20. First, set a marking gauge to ¼ inch (the width of the sides and ends) and scribe a line around the ends of the sides and ends. Next, lay out the tails on the outside surface of the sides, as shown in the *Dovetail Layout.* Then, set a sliding T-bevel to 99 degrees and extend the tails across the end grain of the sides (*Photo 4*). After the lines have been extended, lay out the tails on the inside surface of the sides. Following the layout lines, cut out the tails with a dovetail saw, then cut and chisel away the waste (*Photo 5*).

Trace around the tails to lay out the pins on the ends (*Photo 6*). After tracing the pins, extend the layout lines to the scribe line with the T-bevel set at 99 degrees (*Photo 7*). Be sure that the blade of the T-bevel is always

Photo 4: Extend the dovetail layout lines across the ends of the sides with a sliding T-bevel set at 99 degrees.

parallel to the end's upper edge. Cut out the pins by guiding a dovetail saw along the layout lines, and saw and chisel away the waste.

DOVETAIL LAYOUT

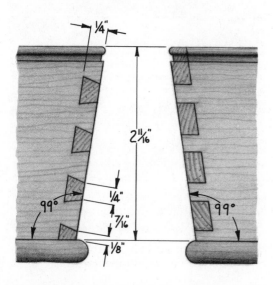

Photo 5: Cut out the tails by guiding a dovetail saw along the angled layout lines.

Photo 6: Lay out the pins on the ends by tracing around the tails.

2. Dado the ends for the center board. Locate the centerline on the inside surface of each end. Make a mark ⅛ inch to each side

Photo 7: Extend the pins' layout lines across the end grain with a sliding T-bevel set at 99 degrees.

of the centerline and extend the dado layout lines across the width of the ends with a square.

The dadoes are very shallow and are easily cut by hand. Score the edges of the dadoes by running a utility knife blade along the layout lines. Guide the knife along a straightedge as you make the cut. Pare out the waste between the layout lines with a ¼-inch chisel to create a ¹⁄₁₆-inch-deep dado.

3. Cut the handle mortises. Rest the handle in a V-block for support and drill a series of ¼-inch-deep holes within the mortises' layout lines with a ³⁄₁₆-inch-diameter brad-point bit in a drill press. The centerline acts as your guide for locating the bit's point. Clean up the mortises' edges and square their ends with bench chisels. Test fit the center board tenons in the mortises.

> **TECHNIQUE TIP**
>
> You might wonder why I choose to use a ³⁄₁₆-inch-diameter bit to drill the ¼-inch-wide handle mortises rather than a ¼-inch-diameter bit. With the ³⁄₁₆-inch-diameter bit, you have some leeway. If the holes fail to line up perfectly, you can trim away any unevenness with a chisel as you trim the mortises to ¼ inch.

ASSEMBLE THE BOX.

1. Assemble the dovetails. Spread a thin layer of glue on the dovetails and assemble the four sides. Test the corners with a try square to make sure the box is square. Set the box aside to allow the glue to dry. When dry, sand the dovetails to level them and to remove any glue that may have squeezed out of the joints.

2. Level the edges. Run a sharp block plane around the box's top and bottom edges to even the corners. The block plane will also remove any saw marks left from beveling the edges.

TOOL TIP

The bead can be easily made with a scratch stock. I use a #8 × 1¼-inch flathead wood screw driven into a small piece of scrap. The corner formed by the slot in the head makes an excellent cutting tooth. The screw can be backed out or screwed in to adjust the scratch stock's setting.

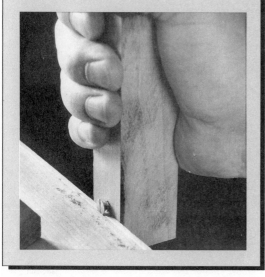

---

3. Bead the top edges. Mount your router in a router table and rout a bead on all four top edges with a ⅛-inch-diameter edge-beading bit. The goal is to produce the bead shown in the *Construction Overview.* Recess the bit in the router table fence and guide the side and end assembly against it as you rout.

4. Join the bottom to the sides. Screw the bottom to the sides using #4 × ¾-inch flathead wood screws. Drill pilot holes to prevent the risk of their splitting. Use three screws per side and two per end. Do not glue the bottom to the sides—this would inhibit seasonal movement.

5. Join the center board to the box. Slide the center board into its dadoes. Tap it with a light hammer to make sure it fits tightly on the bottom. If necessary, trim the ends of the center board to fit. Screw the center board to the bottom with three #4 × ¾-inch flathead wood screws.

6. Join the handle to the center board. Place the handle mortises on the center board's tenons. Tap the handle with a light hammer to seat the joints. Use a 9⁄32-inch-diameter bit to drill two pilot holes, one centered above each mortise. Secure the handle with two #8 × 1¼-inch brass roundhead wood screws.

SERVING TRAY

Every household has an occasional use for a serving tray, but we don't use trays nearly as much as they were used in the past. Back then, serving tea and coffee was a daily social ritual; also, meals were not usually eaten in the kitchen. In the morning it was common for adults to eat at a breakfast table in their bedroom. Every house had a dining room where the day's other meals were taken. All of these customs required transporting food from the kitchen where it had been prepared. Carrying that food safely and efficiently required serving trays.

Most households owned several serving trays, but in those days they were known as waiters. Many waiters were made of tin and were painted and decorated, but there were also plenty of wooden waiters. In the city, the preferred type of wood was mahogany. In the country, where native woods were more commonly used in woodworking, waiters were made of locally harvested hardwoods.

The use of cherry in the original of this tray indicates it is a country piece. So does the decoration. The tray's serpentine edges, made up of mirror-image S-curves, are the sorts of details country woodworkers enjoyed using. The same applies to the flattened, heart-shaped handles. The heart is the quintessential country design element. Since the tray may come in contact with food, I finished mine with nontoxic salad bowl oil.

CONSTRUCTION OVERVIEW

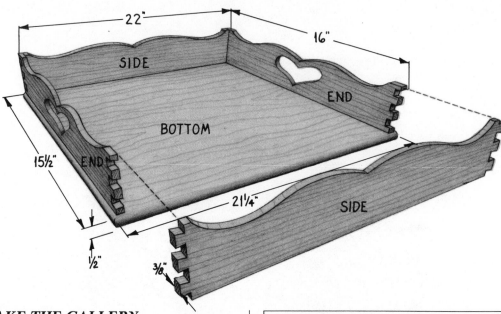

MAKE THE GALLERY.

1. Prepare the materials. Start by preparing the sides and ends of the raised rim, or gallery, of the serving tray. Thickness plane the side stock and end stock. Hand plane the stock to remove any machine marks.

2. Rip and cut the sides and ends. First, rip the bevel in the edges of the stock. Tilt your saw's arbor to 9 degrees and bevel an edge on the side stock and end stock. Flip the stock over and rip the stock to width as you cut the second bevel. The bevels should be parallel, as shown in the *Construction Overview.* Hand plane the edges to remove any saw marks.

Next, angle the ends of the side stock and end stock. Square up the table saw blade and set the miter gauge to 81 degrees. Guide the stock with the miter gauge and angle the ends as you cut the parts to length.

MATERIALS LIST

PART	DIMENSIONS
Ends (2)	3⁄8″ × 3½″ × 16″
Sides (2)	3⁄8″ × 3½″ × 22″
Bottom	½″ × 15½″ × 21¼″

HARDWARE AND SUPPLIES

#6 × 1″ brass flathead wood screws (12)

3. Make the dovetails. Dovetailing is precise work that demands concentration when the adjoining sides are merely square. Here, the sloping sides of the serving tray create additional complications. The difference here is that the tails must angle across the thickness of the sides, and the angle of the pins must compensate, as shown in the *Construction Overview.*

SIDE PATTERN

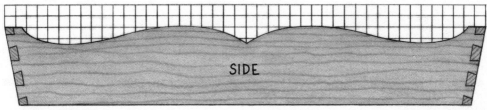

ONE SQUARE = ½"

ONE SQUARE = ½"

END PATTERN

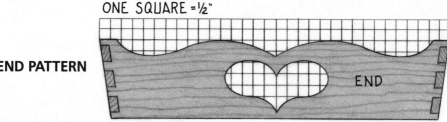

For the most part, you can follow the dovetail cutting process outlined in "Cutting Dovetails" on page 20. First, set a marking gauge to ⅜ inch (the width of the sides and ends) and scribe a line around the ends of the sides and ends. Next, lay out the tails on the outside surface of the sides, as shown in the

Dovetail Layout. Then, set a sliding T-bevel to 99 degrees and extend the tails across the end grain of the sides (*Photo 1*). After the lines

Photo 1: Extend the dovetail layout lines across the ends of the sides with a sliding T-bevel set at 99 degrees.

DOVETAIL LAYOUT   PIN LAYOUT

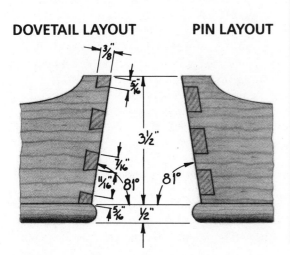

Photo 2: Cut out the tails by guiding a dovetail saw along the angled layout lines.

have been extended, lay out the tails on the inside surface of the sides. Cut out the tails by following the layout lines with a dovetail saw (*Photo 2*), and cut and chisel away the waste.

Photo 3: Extend the pins' layout lines down to the scribe line with a sliding T-bevel set at 99 degrees.

Trace around the tails to lay out the pins on the ends. After tracing the pins, extend the layout lines to the scribe line with the sliding T-bevel set at 99 degrees (*Photo 3*), as shown in the *Pin Layout*. Be sure that the blade of the sliding T-bevel is always parallel to the end's bottom edge. Cut out the pins by guiding a dovetail saw along the layout lines, and saw and chisel away the waste.

Test fit the pins and tails without glue and, if necessary, pare the pins to fit the tails with a sharp chisel.

CONSTRUCTION TIP

The half-pins in the corners of the gallery ends are very fragile. I know from experience that forcing an overtight joint will cause the pins to crack off. So, carefully pare the joint to fit precisely without causing undo strain on the pins. If a pin does split off, you can glue it back together, but hopefully you can avoid that extra step.

SAFETY TIP

As woodworkers, we tend to have a lot of respect for the noisy, spinning, motorized cutting tools in our shops, and that's good. But don't forget to respect the razor-sharp edges of your hand tools. *Always* keep your free hand behind your chisel's blade, and *watch out* for the jagged, sharp teeth of your dovetail saw. Hand tools are responsible for many shop injuries, and it doesn't hurt to be reminded.

4. **Lay out and cut the sides and ends to shape.** Make a grid of ½-inch squares on a piece of posterboard and plot the shapes of the sides and ends on it, as shown in the *Side Pattern* and *End Pattern*. Make templates of the side and end shapes (including the heart-shaped handles) and trace them on the stock.

Drill a ¼-inch hole near the center of each handle and pass a scroll saw or a coping saw blade through it. Cut the handles to shape. Use a half-round mill file and sandpaper to smooth the handles.

The top edge of each of the sides and ends is beveled at 9 degrees. Tilt your band saw table to 9 degrees and cut the edges to shape as you cut the bevel (*Photo 4*). Clean up the edges with either a spokeshave or sandpaper.

> **TOOL TIP**
>
> The curved and beveled edges of the sides and ends can be cut with a jigsaw. Simply tilt the base of the jigsaw to 9 degrees and carefully follow the layout lines.

5. Assemble the gallery. Spread glue on the dovetail joints and assemble the four sides. Use bar clamps to keep the joints under pressure as the glue dries. While the glue is still

Photo 4: Shape and bevel the top edges of the sides and ends at the same time by tilting your band saw table to 9 degrees.

wet, square the assembly by measuring diagonally across the corners. The distances between the opposite corners should be equal.

When the glue is dry, level the dovetail joints with a belt sander. Finish sand the entire gallery.

MAKE THE BOTTOM AND ASSEMBLE THE TRAY.

1. Prepare the material. Thickness plane the bottom stock to ½ inch. Glue together enough stock for the proper width. When the glue is dry, hand plane the stock to smooth the joint and to remove any machine marks.

Rip and cut the bottom to the dimensions given in the Materials List.

> **CONSTRUCTION TIP**
>
> Before cutting the bottom to size, check your gallery's dimensions to see how closely they conform to the drawing. Adjust the bottom's dimensions if necessary.

2. Round-over the edges. Round-over the edges of the bottom on a belt sander. Or use a block plane or spokeshave and smooth the facets with sandpaper.

3. Assemble the tray. Attach the bottom to the gallery with #6 × 1-inch brass flathead wood screws. Drill pilot holes for 12 evenly spaced screws with a ⅛-inch-diameter bit. Countersink the holes and screw the bottom in place.

> **CONSTRUCTION TIP**
>
> To prevent your tray from scratching your tabletops, apply self-adhesive round felt tabs to the four corners and midway along each side.

OCTAGONAL CANISTER

Country folk used numerous ground, powdered, flaked, and shredded products that they kept handy in covered containers. Most of these products were foods, such as coffee, tea, spices, flour, and sugar, but they also kept dried tobacco and various dried medicines on hand. All these products were valuable, so they were stored in containers that were nicer than just an ordinary jar. Tea, for example, was often stored in caddies made of silver. Foodstuffs were kept in decorated tin canisters.

I am fond of this canister not only because it is very handsome but also because some anonymous country craftsperson made it from

my favorite material—wood. The canister has a strong Chinese influence, which may seem to be an unusual design source for a country object. However, shortly after the Revolutionary War, American merchant ships began trading with China, and Americans became absolutely fascinated with things Chinese.

Anything imported over such a great distance was very expensive and could be afforded only by the wealthy. I suspect an anonymous country woodworker made this canister from memory, copying a form he had seen in the city. The original object was probably made from silver or tin, as those metals achieve

CONSTRUCTION OVERVIEW

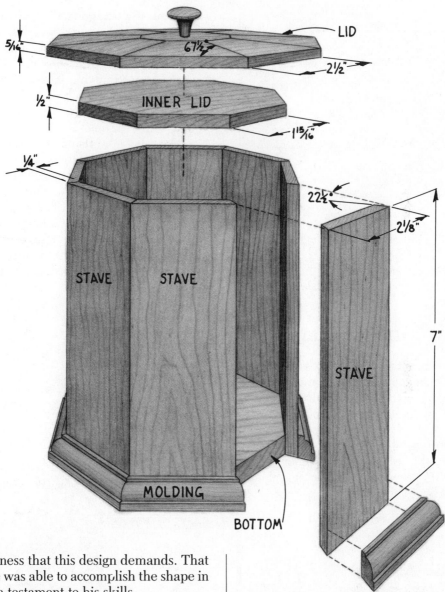

the crispness that this design demands. That someone was able to accomplish the shape in wood is a testament to his skills.

This canister is a small but challenging project. It is assembled with a technique called coopering—the eight sides are fitted like a barrel's staves. Coopering requires cutting small pieces very accurately, so you must keep your wits about you at all times.

I made my copy of the original in pine. To further the Chinese association, I painted it a

MATERIALS LIST

PART	DIMENSIONS
Lid	¾" × 7" × 7"
Inner lid	½" × 5½" × 5½"
Bottom	½" × 5½" × 5½"
Staves (8)	¼" × 2⅛" × 7"
Moldings (8)	¼" × ½" × 2½"

HARDWARE AND SUPPLIES

1" brads (as needed)
Small brass cabinet pull

bright red, but left the inside, which will come in contact with food, in the raw. You may want to make a set of canisters rather than just one. If so, make sure you have enough wood for the whole set.

PREPARE THE MATERIALS.

1. Plane the materials. Thickness plane the stock to the dimensions given in the Materials List. Hand plane the stock to remove machine marks left by the thickness planer.

2. Cut the materials to size. Cut out the squares from which the bottom, lid, and inner lid will be made. Crosscut the stave material into strips 7 inches long, but do not rip the strips to width yet.

CONSTRUCTION TIP

The tolerances in this project are very close and the chances are good that you will make at least one part a bit too small. I recommend cutting several extra staves and lengths of molding.

MAKE THE BOTTOM AND LID.

1. Lay out the octagons. First, use a compass to draw 5-inch-diameter circles centered on the bottom and the inner lid, and a 6½-inch circle centered on the outer lid. With a try square, draw a line that intersects the center (a diameter line) on each circle. Make a mark to identify the side of the stock against which you laid the try square.

Next, lay a draftsman's 45 degree triangle against the try square and draw a second diameter line at a right angle to the first. Then, draw two additional diameter lines at 45 degrees to the first. The four diameter lines divide the circle into eight equal segments, as shown in the *Top View* and *Bottom View.* Connect the points where the lines intersect the circle with a straightedge (*Photo 1*).

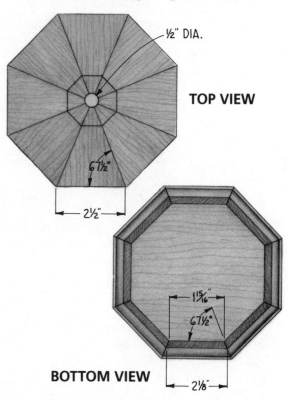

½" DIA.

TOP VIEW

6½°

2½"

1⁵⁄₁₆"

6½°

BOTTOM VIEW

2⅛"

Photo 1: Connect the adjacent points where the diameter lines intersect the circle to form an equilateral octagon.

2. Cut out the octagons. Set your table saw's miter gauge to 67½ degrees and place the side of the square with the mark you made in step 1 against the fence. Trim one side of the octagon. Reset the miter gauge to 45 degrees in the opposite direction and cut the remaining seven sides.

The point of each of the eight angles of the sawed octagons must merge exactly on the diameter lines. If the point of the angle is slightly off the line, adjust one side by carefully trimming it. I did this final trimming with a hand plane and shooting board. The shooting board affords very precise control. The final trimming can also be done against a sanding disk in your table saw, but be careful: The sanding disk removes stock very quickly.

MAKE THE STAVES.

1. Rip the staves. First, set your saw's arbor to 22½ degrees. Set your rip fence to produce a stave that is slightly wider than the stave's final width. I set mine to 2½ inches. Rip one side of each stave.

Next, set your saw's fence so that a rip cut will result in a width of 1 15/16 inches on the stave's inside surface. To make sure you rip the second edge in the proper relationship to the first, lay each stave on its outer surface with the first beveled edge against the fence.

2. Fit the staves. Place a strong elastic band around the edge of the bottom and, one at a time, slip the end of a stave between the bottom and the elastic. The structure, while flimsy at first, will strengthen and stabilize with each additional stave. When the octagon is complete, check the results. If any of the staves is wider than its corresponding edge on the bottom, carefully trim that stave with a block plane.

ASSEMBLE THE BOX.

1. Glue the staves. When all of the staves fit properly, spread a light layer of glue on the left edge of each stave. Reclamp the staves around the bottom with elastic bands. Rest the box on your saw table and lightly tap each stave with a hammer to make sure the staves' bottom ends align. When all of the parts are aligned, tighten a band clamp over the entire assembly.

2. Attach the bottom. When the glue is dry, secure the bottom to the staves with one 1-inch brad per stave.

MAKE THE BASE MOLDINGS.

1. Make or purchase the base molding. If you are making your canister from pine, you should be able to purchase the ovolo molding or a similar molding at most building supply stores. If you are working in another species of wood, you will probably need to make your own molding.

To make your own molding, chuck a ¼-inch-radius roundover bit in a table-mounted

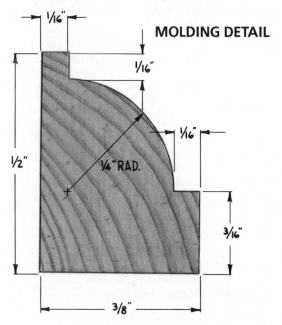

MOLDING DETAIL

1/16"

1/16"

1/16"

½"

¼" RAD.

3/16"

3/8"

router. Recess the bit in the fence and adjust the fence and bit height to produce the profile shown in the *Molding Detail.*

2. Miter the moldings. The moldings are mitered to fit around the canister. Cut the miters on the table saw with the miter gauge as your guide. Attach a wooden extension fence to the miter gauge to support the moldings and to prevent chipping. Set the miter gauge to 67½ degrees away from the blade and trim the end off the extension. This ensures that the extension reaches all the way to the blade and gives the delicate molding excellent back support while being cut. Hold the molding stock with its back edge against the miter gauge fence and cut eight 3-inch-long sections.

To make the second cut, move the miter gauge to the slot on the other side of the blade and reverse the miter gauge angle to 67½ degrees in the opposite direction. Again, cut off the extension fence where it meets the blade. Place each length of molding against a side of the canister and make a mark on its back edge where the cut should be made. Hold the molding against the extension and, with your eye at tabletop level, advance the molding until the mark is just visible beyond the end of the extension. Cut the second set of miters (*Photo 2*).

3. Fit and apply the moldings. Glue the moldings to the box one at a time. Apply a light layer of glue to the back of one of the molding pieces. With the canister on its side, put the molding in place and hold it there with a weight rather than a clamp. Attach each molding piece in this manner. If you have to make any adjustments to the ends of the moldings, simply hold a piece of sandpaper on a flat surface (like the saw table) and draw the molding's mitered end over it until the molding fits in place. Be careful not to round the mitered end.

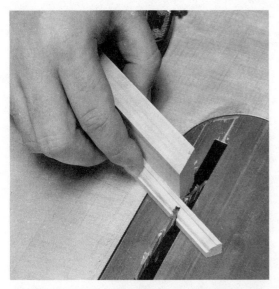

Photo 2: Mark the position of the second miter on the molding stock, line up the mark with the edge of the miter gauge extension fence, and cut the miters.

ASSEMBLE THE LID.

1. Make the lid. Use a tenoning jig to cut the eight facets on the lid. Tilt the saw's arbor to 12 degrees and raise it high enough that it will completely cut off a wedge. Clamp the lid in the jig with one edge flat on the saw table. Set the jig so its cut leaves a 5⁄16-inch-thick edge, as shown in the *Construction Overview.* Make the first cut and then return the jig to the front of the table by lifting it out of its groove. Rotate the octagonal lid by one edge and make the next cut. Repeat this process on all eight edges.

2. Clean up the facets. Remove the saw marks and make any adjustments to the lid facets with sandpaper wrapped around a sanding block. The center of the lid (what remains of the original surface) should also be an octagon, and the original eight layout lines should intersect the points of its angles.

3. Fit the inner lid. The inner lid should fit snugly, but not tightly, inside the canister's body. Adjust the fit of the inner lid by removing stock from its edges with a sanding disk.

4. Join the lids. Glue the inner lid to the lid's lower surface. Orient their grains at right angles to prevent warping.

5. Attach the pull. Screw the pull into the center of the original circle that laid out the octagonal lid. Sand the canister and apply the finish.

COFFEEPOT

As I write this chapter, I recall when my wife found the original of this wooden coffeepot. My reaction was, "Why? What is the purpose?" You can't put this coffeepot over a flame. It isn't watertight, and even if it were, the liquid would dissolve the glue and the pot would fall apart.

All I can say with certainty is that someone took a lot of time to make a wooden coffeepot whose purpose I can only surmise. Perhaps it was made on a whim by a country woodworker who just wanted to show off. Since country woodworking was eminently practical, however, I tend to doubt it.

My guess is that it was given by some anonymous woodworker to his wife on their fifth anniversary, for which the appropriate gift is made of wood. Tea or coffee sets were common gifts on other anniversaries such as 10 years (tin), 20 years (china), and 25 years (silver).

I suspect that the woodworker's wife of long ago used her wooden coffeepot the way mine does. She places a glass of water inside and uses it to hold fresh-cut flowers from her garden. In the winter, the glass is not necessary, as she makes floral arrangements with silk flowers. Other times it sits on a shelf as a curiosity.

CONSTRUCTION OVERVIEW

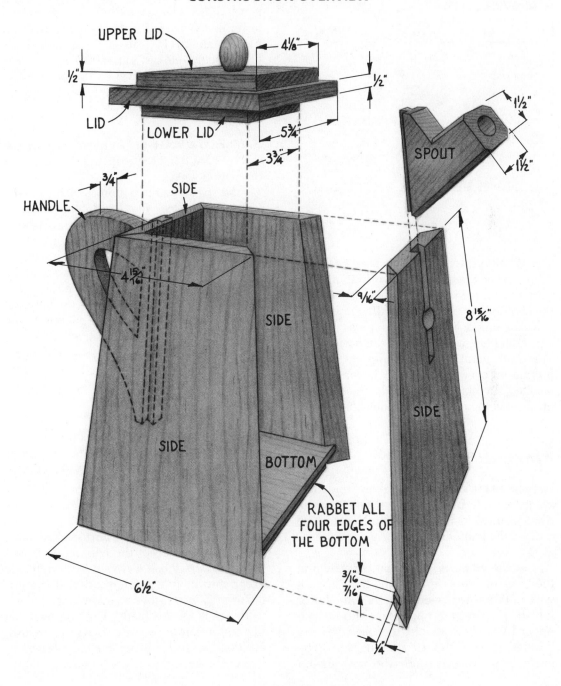

UPPER LID

4⅛"

½"

½"

LID

LOWER LID

5¾"

SPOUT

1½"

1½"

3¾"

3⅓"

HANDLE

SIDE

¾"

4¹⁵⁄₁₆"

9⁄₁₆"

8¹⁵⁄₁₆"

SIDE

SIDE

SIDE

SIDE

BOTTOM

RABBET ALL
FOUR EDGES OF
THE BOTTOM

6½"

3⁄16"

7⁄16"

¼"

MATERIALS LIST

PART	DIMENSIONS
Lid	½″ × 5¾″ × 5¾″
Upper lid	½″ × 4⅛″ × 4⅛″
Lower lid	½″ × 3¾″ × 3¾″
Bottom	9⁄16″ × 5¾″ × 5¾″
Sides (4)	9⁄16″ × 6½″ × 8¹⁵⁄16″
Handle	¾″ × 3⁵⁄16″ × 7⅜″
Spout	1½″ × 2⁷⁄16″ × 3⁹⁄16″

HARDWARE AND SUPPLIES

Finial (1)

Whatever its intended purpose, the pot is a fun and challenging woodworking project. It requires some joints you do not use often — the standing miter and the sliding dovetail.

The original pine coffeepot was painted a powder blue. I did mine the same way using blue milk paint. I did not apply a coat of linseed oil over the paint, as leaving it dry resulted in a color and texture that most closely duplicated the original's powder blue paint.

MAKE THE PARTS.

1. Prepare the materials. Joint and thickness plane the materials to the dimensions given in the Materials List. Hand plane the stock to remove the planer marks.

2. Cut the lid parts. Note that, as shown in the *Construction Overview,* the lid is a sandwich of three layers glued together: the lower lid, the lid, and the upper lid. The lid and upper lid are both visible, so their edges are beveled to mimic the pot's sloping sides. The lower lid's edges fit inside the pot's mouth and are cut at 90 degrees. Set your miter gauge at 90 degrees and use it to guide the lower lid as you cut it to the dimensions given in the Materials List. To cut the lid and upper lid, set your table saw's arbor to 5 degrees. For each piece, rip the bevel on the sides of the stock, then crosscut it to length with the miter gauge.

3. Make the bottom. With your saw's arbor still tilted at 5 degrees, rip and then crosscut the bottom to size.

Next, rabbet the bottom, as shown in the *Construction Overview.* Lay out the rabbet on all four edges of the bottom with a pencil. With the blade still set at 5 degrees, adjust the blade height to ⅜ inch. Place the miter gauge in the right-hand slot of the table to guide the stock as you cut the rabbet. Cut the shoulder of the rabbet on all four sides of the bottom's lower surface. Shift each side slightly to the right and remove the remaining waste by making a second pass over the saw blade. As shown in the *Construction Overview,* the rabbet produces a lip that has both an edge and a shoulder at 5 degrees.

4. Cut the sides to length. Keep your table saw's arbor tilted at 5 degrees and your miter gauge at 90 degrees. Cut the bottom edge of each side. Turn each side end for end and cut the top edges.

5. Cut the grooves for the bottom. The sides are grooved to accept the bottom, as shown in the *Construction Overview.* With your saw arbor still tilted at 5 degrees, set the depth of cut to ¼ inch. Move your rip fence ½ inch to the right of the blade. Cut a groove for the bottom on the inside of each piece. Reposition the fence to widen the grooves to 3⁄16 inch.

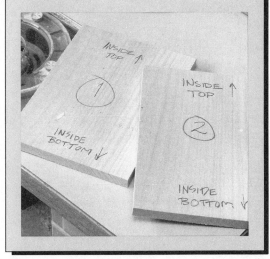

Photo 1: Guide the stock against the router table fence as you cut the dovetail grooves.

(*Photo 2*). Cut a test dovetail in a ¾-inch piece of scrap and test its fit in a groove. If it is too loose, bury more of the bit. If the fit is too

MAKE THE JOINTS.

1. Make the sliding dovetails. The stopped dovetail grooves in the sides for the spout and handle are routed with a ⅝-inch-diameter dovetail bit in a table-mounted router. The positions of the grooves are shown in the *Construction Overview.*

To rout the grooves, adjust the bit to a height of $\frac{5}{16}$ inch and guide the stock against a fence as you rout (*Photo 1*). Square the ends of the dovetail grooves with a chisel.

Rout the sliding dovetails in the spout and handle stock with the bit at the same height. Adjust the fence on the router table so that the dovetail bit is partially buried in it

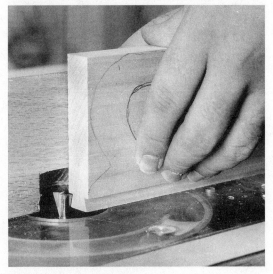

Photo 2: Partially bury the bit in the fence to cut the edges of the sliding dovetails.

tight, adjust the setup to expose more of the bit. When satisfied with the fit, cut the dovetail in the handle stock.

Repeat the process for the spout, but this time cut the test dovetail in a 1½-inch piece of scrap.

2. Cut the left-hand standing miters. First, cut the left-hand miter (as seen from the outside) on each side. Set your saw's arbor to 44¾ degrees and place the miter gauge in the left-hand slot. Set the miter gauge to 85 degrees tilting away from the blade. Place a side on the table with the outside surface facing up and with the top end against the miter gauge (*Photo 3*). Align the side's corner with the blade and make the cut. Repeat on each of the four sides.

3. Cut the right-hand standing miters. Lay out the right-hand cut on each side with a sliding T-bevel set at 85 degrees. Reset the sliding T-bevel to 44¾ degrees to continue the line across the top edge.

To cut the right-hand standing miter, put the miter gauge in the slot to the right of the blade. Lay a side on the table with the inside surface facing up and with the bottom edge against the miter gauge (*Photo 4*). Align the layout line with the saw blade as you begin the cut. As you feed the wood into the blade, watch closely to make sure the cut stays outside the layout line. Cut the miter on all four sides.

MAKE THE HANDLE AND SPOUT.

1. Cut the handle and spout to shape. Make patterns for the handle and spout, as shown in the *Handle Pattern* and the *Spout Pattern*. Plot the patterns on a full-size grid and transfer the shapes to the stock. Cut the parts to shape with a band saw, coping saw, or scroll

Photo 3: Cut the left-hand standing miter with the side's outside surface facing up and its top end against the miter gauge.

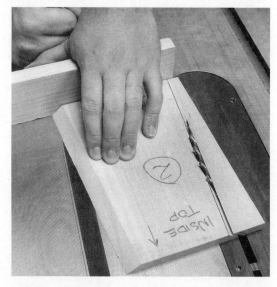

Photo 4: Cut the right-hand standing miter with the side's inside surface facing up and its bottom end against the miter gauge.

HANDLE PATTERN

SPOUT PATTERN

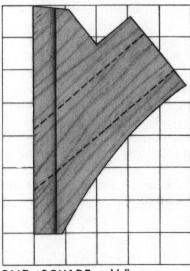

ONE SQUARE = ½"

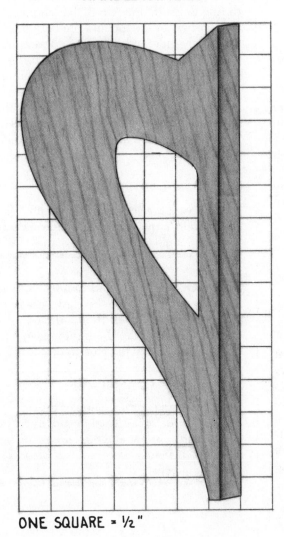

ONE SQUARE = ½"

saw. To cut the inside of the handle, drill a hole through the waste and then pass a scroll saw or coping saw blade through it and cut the inside pattern.

While the spout end is still square, lay out its center by connecting the corners with an X. Relieve the spout's upper corners with a chisel and smooth the sides of the V-notch with a file.

Smooth away the saw marks from the handle's outside edges and the spout's lower edge with sandpaper or a spokeshave. Slightly round all of the corners. File the inside edges of the handle smooth. Round the edges at the same time and smooth them with sandpaper.

2. Drill the spout hole. Slide the spout's dovetail into its dovetail slot. To prevent splintering when you drill the spout hole, clamp a piece of scrap to the interior surface of the side. Put another clamp on the spout to help prevent splitting.

Because the spout hole is so short, you can align the hole by eye. Using a ¾-inch-diameter bit, drill the spout hole completely through the side. Remove the spout and flare the hole's inside edge with a file.

ASSEMBLE THE PARTS.

1. Glue the sides. Spread a layer of glue on the mitered edges of the front and rear sides. Place the tongue of the bottom in its grooves. This loose assembly will stand on its own. Put the other two sides in place. Slip several heavy rubber bands over the pot's body to act as clamps. Space them evenly along its height. Check the miter joints from both above and below to make sure they have no gaps. This should ensure that the body is square, but you can also test it with a small try square. Set the assembly aside to let the glue set.

2. Glue the lid. To help position the pieces during glue-up, draw an X that connects the four corners of the top and the bottom of the lid. Apply glue and align the corners of the lower lid with the lines of the X on the bottom of the lid. Clamp the lids together and allow the assembly to dry. Repeat the process to glue the upper lid in place on the top of the lid. When the second joint is dry, make a light X on the upper lid and screw on the finial at the intersection.

CONSTRUCTION TIP

To prevent the lid from warping, position the grain in the upper lid and lower lid at a right angle to the lid's grain direction.

---

3. Attach the spout and handle. Spread a light layer of glue on the surfaces of both dovetail grooves. Insert the spout and handle and, if necessary, tap them into place with a light mallet. Allow the glue to dry.

TECHNIQUE TIP

If the top and bottom edges of the coffeepot are misaligned, level the pot by holding it first upright and then upside down on a belt sander. Stop sanding when the edges are even.

WALL-HUNG SHELVES

SHELVES

AND

RACKS

TWO-DRAWER HANGING SHELF

Every country home possessed numerous small objects and utensils that had to be stored in a handy location. As a result, country woodworkers produced countless simple boxes. This pine hanging shelf evolved from those simple boxes. Because of the drawers, the box is wider and deeper than usual. The greater size necessitates some additional design considerations. The piece has a double-hanger back because a larger, heavier box needs to be hung from two locations. Double hangers not only are stronger but they also provide stability. The box will hang level even if most of the weight is to one side.

The dovetails provide strength to the case. With some minor adjustments, however, you can make this shelf even if you are not experienced at cutting dovetails. Instead of dovetailing, rabbet the top and bottom of the sides. Nail the top and bottom into the rabbets with 1½-inch headless brads. Because the nails are horizontal, they'll resist the pull of gravity.

You can also rabbet the edges of the drawer fronts and assemble the drawers with 1-inch headless brads. If you do this, adjust the length of the sides and back accordingly.

I painted the case of my hanging shelf blue and gave the drawers a clear oil finish.

CONSTRUCTION OVERVIEW

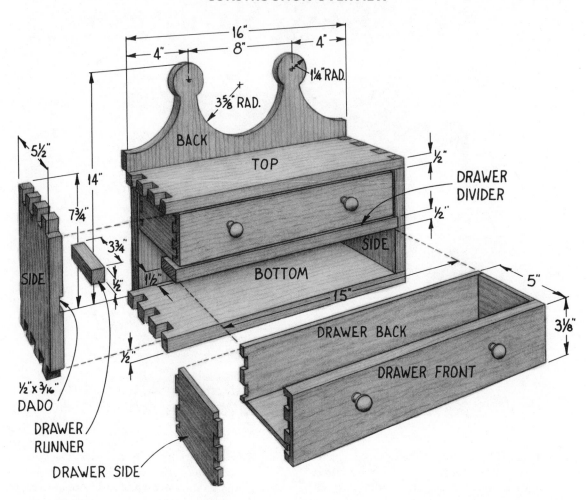

MAKE THE CARCASE PARTS.

1. Prepare the back. Thickness plane the stock to ½ inch and glue up boards to produce the necessary width. When the glue is dry, hand plane both surfaces to smooth the glue joints and to remove machine marks.

2. Make the back. Joint one edge of the back and rip it to width. Square the bottom edge to

the sides. Remove the saw marks from the edges with a hand plane. Lay out the shape of the back on the stock, as shown in the *Back Detail.* Cut the back to shape with a band saw or coping saw. Smooth the sawed edges with sandpaper or a spokeshave and file. Drill a ¼-inch hole centered on each of the two circles.

3. Prepare the remaining case parts. Hand plane the top, bottom, sides, drawer divid-

MATERIALS LIST

PART	DIMENSIONS
Back	$\frac{1}{2}'' \times 16'' \times 14''$
Sides (2)	$\frac{1}{2}'' \times 5\frac{1}{2}'' \times 7\frac{3}{4}''$
Top	$\frac{1}{2}'' \times 5'' \times 16''$
Bottom	$\frac{1}{2}'' \times 5'' \times 16''$
Drawer divider	$\frac{1}{2}'' \times 1\frac{1}{2}'' \times 15\frac{3}{8}''$
Drawer runners (2)	$\frac{1}{2}'' \times \frac{1}{2}'' \times 3\frac{3}{4}''$
Drawer fronts (2)	$\frac{1}{2}'' \times 3\frac{1}{8}'' \times 15''$
Drawer sides (4)	$\frac{1}{4}'' \times 3\frac{1}{8}'' \times 4\frac{13}{16}''$
Drawer backs (2)	$\frac{1}{4}'' \times 2\frac{3}{4}'' \times 15''$
Drawer bottoms (2)	$\frac{1}{4}'' \times 4\frac{5}{8}'' \times 14\frac{3}{4}''$

HARDWARE AND SUPPLIES

1'' headless brads (as needed)

$\frac{1}{2}''$ diameter wooden mushroom
    drawer pulls (4)

BACK DETAIL

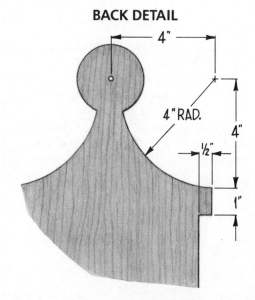

er, and drawer runners to remove any machine marks. Rip and cut the parts to width and length. Hand plane the edges to remove saw marks.

MAKE THE JOINTS.

1. Cut the back to fit around the sides. The edges of the back are cut out to fit around the sides, as shown in the *Back Detail* and *Construction Overview.* Cut the shoulder of each joint with a dovetail saw. Set the rip fence of your band saw or table saw to $\frac{1}{2}$ inch and rip the joints. If you use a table saw, stop well short of the corners, as the lower edge of the circular blade's cut is longer than the top. Complete the cut with a handsaw. Since the joints are so short, you can also rip them completely with a fine-tooth handsaw. Clean up the sawed edges with a block plane.

2. Cut the dadoes. The sides are dadoed to accept the drawer divider and runners, as shown in the *Construction Overview.* Cut the dadoes with a dado blade in your table saw, with a router and a straight bit, or by hand.

DOVETAIL THE CARCASE.

1. Lay out the dovetails. The sides are dovetailed into the top and bottom, as shown in the *Construction Overview.* Set a marking gauge to $\frac{1}{2}$ inch and scribe a layout line on all four surfaces of each end of the sides, top, and bottom. Lay out the dovetails with a sliding T-bevel set at 76 degrees (14 degrees off square). The exact spacing of the dovetails is not important. However, because the joints are visible to the viewer and are part of the piece's character, the dovetail spacing should appear approximately the same on all four corners.

2. Cut the dovetails. Cut the dovetails and use each set as a template to lay out its matching set of pins. Test fit each corner after you cut it. For more on this technique, see "Cutting Dovetails" on page 20.

A block plane will reach only part of the surface you need to plane. Plane the surface with a Stanley #71 router plane instead. To guide the plane, clamp two boards with jointed edges to the back, as shown. Guide the sole of the plane along the boards. Smooth into the corner with a ½-inch cutter set to the rabbet's depth.

ASSEMBLE THE CASE.

1. Fit the dovetail joints. Spread a thin layer of glue on the inside edges of either the tails or the pins. Assemble the sides, top, and bottom. Push the dovetails and pins together with bar clamps. Make sure the case is square by measuring across the diagonals—equal diagonals indicate the case is square. Make any necessary adjustments and let the glue dry.

2. Fit the drawer divider and drawer runners. Insert the drawer divider into its dadoes and secure it on each end with two 1-inch headless brads driven through the sides.

Put a spot of glue only in the center of each drawer runner and press each runner into its dado. Clamp the drawer runners in place while the glue dries. Leave about ⅛ inch of space on each end of the drawer runners. This way, seasonal movement will not cause the drawer runners to press against the drawer divider and back and push them out of place.

3. Install the back. Set the back in place and secure it with 1-inch headless brads.

MAKE THE DRAWERS.

1. Make the parts. Joint, thickness plane, rip, and cut the drawer stock to the dimensions given in the Materials List. Hand plane all the parts to remove marks left by the saw and the thickness planer.

2. Cut the bottom grooves. The drawer sides and drawer fronts have ⅛ × ⅛-inch grooves cut along their length to hold the drawer bottoms, as shown in the *Drawer Side View.* Position your table saw fence ¼ inch from the blade and set the blade to cut a groove ⅛ inch deep. Push the parts over the blade with a push stick.

3. Lay out, cut, and assemble the dovetails. Lay out the dovetails, as shown in the *Drawer Side View.* The exact width of the tails is not crucial.

I like to lay out the dovetails first and use them as templates to lay out the matching pins. This works well on the front corners of the drawer. On the back corners, however, the bottom pin must line up with the groove. Cut the pins first, aligning the lower pin with the top of the groove, as shown in the *Drawer Side View.* For more on this technique, see "Cutting Dovetails" on page 20.

Photo 1: Bevel the lower edges of the drawer bottoms with a hand plane.

Spread a light layer of glue on the joints' recessed surfaces and assemble them. Clamp the assembly and make sure it is square by measuring across the diagonals.

4. Make and fit the drawer bottoms. Bevel the lower edges of the drawer bottoms with a hand plane (*Photo 1*). Slide the bottoms under their backs and into their grooves. If they bind, tap them lightly with a hammer. Secure the bottoms by driving two 1-inch headless brads into the backs.

5. Mount the drawer pulls. Measure in $3\frac{1}{2}$ inches from the ends of each drawer front and screw the pulls in place.

DRAWER SIDE VIEW

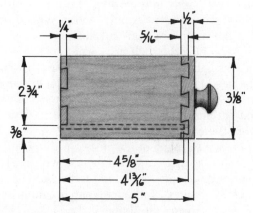

DRAWER TOP VIEW

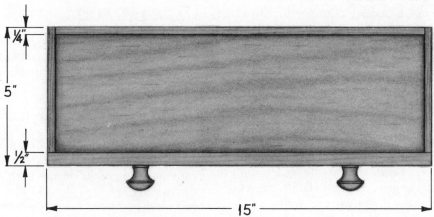

CORNER CANDLE SHELF

Today we live in houses lit by electric bulbs, so we have a hard time imagining what it was like to live before electricity. Then, when the sun went down, the house became as dark as a tomb; the orange glow of a candle or a lamp lit only the immediate area. As a result, a lot of concern and attention was directed to lighting needs.

This shelf provides a surface on which to rest a candlestick. Unlike a sconce, this candle shelf hangs in a corner, where it is protected from drafts. Its tall wooden sides protect the wall from heat and soot.

Hanging the shelf in a corner causes it to cast its light across the room. A pair of these shelves hung in opposite corners could light much of a room's living space. Because of its flat bottom, the shelf can also be taken down from the corner and set on any flat surface.

Like so many other pieces in this book, this shelf is made more elaborate with basic geometric shapes. The top of the back is a circle. The sides' cyma curves end in a quarter-circle, mirroring the shape of the bottom.

Your house is undoubtedly electrified and you do not have to light it with candles. However, candle flame still has a magical quality for us. It elicits such emotions as intimacy, romance, and hospitality.

The high sides of this shelf help reflect light. The more pale their color, the more effectively they do this job. If you paint the shelf, choose a light color. If you use a natural finish (or no finish at all), make the shelf from a light-colored wood. Basswood, poplar, and pine would be good choices. Dark woods, such as walnut, will not work as well.

MAKE THE PARTS.

1. Prepare the stock. Joint, thickness plane, and cut the stock to width. Hand plane to remove the machine marks and cut the ends square.

CONSTRUCTION TIP

When cutting the sides to final width, tilt your saw's arbor to 45 degrees to create the mitered corner on the back edge of each side.

CONSTRUCTION OVERVIEW

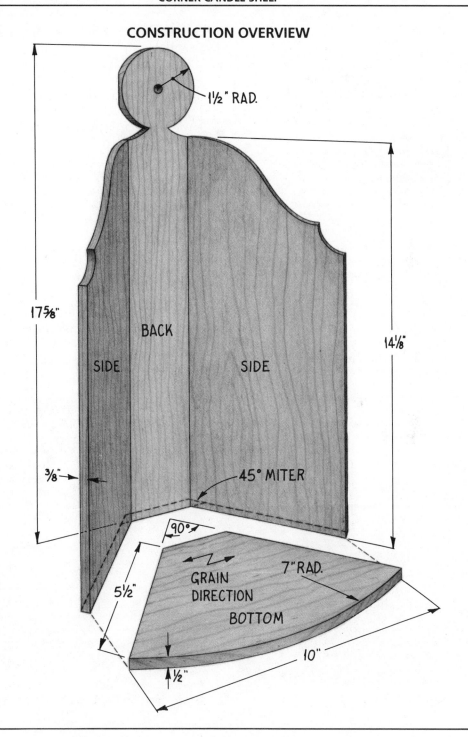

1½" RAD.

17⅝"

14⅛"

BACK

SIDE

SIDE

⅜"

45° MITER

90°

GRAIN
DIRECTION

BOTTOM

7" RAD.

5½"

10"

½"

MATERIALS LIST

PART	DIMENSIONS
Back	3/8" × 3" × 175/8"
Sides (2)	3/8" × 51/2" × 141/8"
Bottom	1/2" × 7" × 10"

HARDWARE AND SUPPLIES

1" brads (as needed)

2. Shape the back and sides. Make a grid of 1/2-inch squares and draw the *Side Pattern* on it. Transfer the pattern to the stock.

The sides are not identical. Orient the pattern to create a right- and left-hand side, positioning the miter as shown in the *Construction Overview.* Cut the curves in the back and sides with a band saw, scroll saw, or coping saw. Clean up the edges with a sanding drum or spokeshave.

SIDE PATTERN

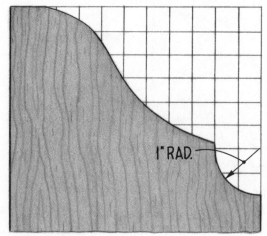

1" RAD.

ONE SQUARE = 1/2"

3. Make the bottom. Lay out the bottom so that the sides will cover the end grain, as shown in the *Construction Overview.* Lay out the straight edges so that they join at a 90 degree angle, as shown in the *Construction Overview.* You will trim this corner to fit later. Lay out the curve with a compass or a pair of dividers.

Set the table saw miter gauge to 45 degrees and cut the straight sides. Cut the round front edge with a band saw, jigsaw, or coping saw. Clean up the edge with a spokeshave or sanding disk.

ASSEMBLE THE PARTS.

1. Attach the sides. Drive four 1-inch brads through the back and into each side. Start the brads with the back flat on the bench and drive them at a 45 degree angle into the back edges of the sides. Secure the sides in a vise when driving the nails home (*Photo 1*).

Photo 1: Put a side in the vise and drive the brads through the back, parallel to the sides.

Photo 2: Position the side and back assembly on top of the bottom and draw a line on the bottom indicating the cut for the back.

2. Attach the bottom. Place the side and back assembly on the bottom (*Photo 2*). Trace along the inside of the back to lay out the final cut on the bottom.

Cut off the corner about ¼ inch outside this line. Test fit the bottom to the sides. Use a hand plane or a sanding disk to gradually trim the edge until the bottom fits tightly on all three sides. Drive two brads through each side and the back to attach the bottom.

3. Bevel the edges of the back. If you leave the edges of the back square, they will prevent the shelf from hugging the wall. Bevel the edges of the back with a block plane to match the angle of the sides.

PRIMITIVE COATRACK

This coatrack hung near the side door on my parents' farm in rural Massachusetts. As children, my eight siblings and I hung our coats here. It was seldom visible, for it only had four hooks, and each usually had up to three coats hanging from it.

The house was originally a small Cape Cod built in the late 1730s by a farmer named Nathan Stone. In the 1820s, Nathan's more prosperous grandson built a (then) modern two-story house, which used the Cape as a small wing, or ell. The grandson also updated the Cape's interior woodwork. Based on some educated guesswork, I'd say the grandson built this rack himself shortly after the renovations.

To begin with, the coatrack isn't nearly as refined as the Lord Coatrack (page 222). Its construction contrasts with the interiors of both the original Cape and the addition, both of which were built by a well-trained housewright. This makes me sure the farmer-grandson made it himself. This is not surprising; while much country woodwork was done by skilled craftsmen, much was done by untrained farmers.

Inventories left in the wills and other probate records of old-time farmers show that they usually owned some woodworking tools—usually a couple of bench planes, a few handsaws, and one or more molding planes. The

CONSTRUCTION OVERVIEW

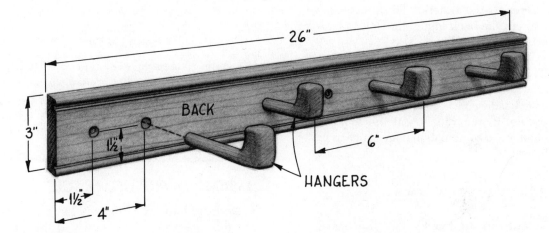

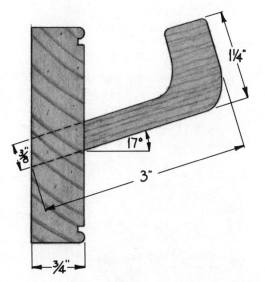

MATERIALS LIST

PART	DIMENSIONS
Back	$\frac{3}{4}'' \times 3'' \times 26''$
Hangers (4)	$\frac{7}{16}'' \times 1\frac{1}{4}'' \times 3\frac{1}{2}''$

HARDWARE AND SUPPLIES

#6 × 1½″ wood screws (as needed)

molding planes permitted this farmer to add a bit of decoration to his woodwork.

This rack was made with the kind of tools a farmer might have. The simplest of all was the pocket knife the builder used to whittle the hangers. But it's the molding, and the plane that made it, that helped me date the piece: The bead is offset by a flat-bottomed groove

called a quirk. This shape became popular about 1820, replacing the earlier version of the bead, which was offset by a beveled groove.

Furniture historians call work done by such farmers primitive, but it's not a negative term. Like this coatrack, much primitive woodwork has a very distinctive, naive charm.

The original pine rack has only four hooks and is 26 inches long. It fits on a short wall on one side of my parents' kitchen fireplace. You can make your rack to suit your purposes. Include as many hangers as you need and make the back as long as you like. I left my coatrack "in the white" (unfinished).

MAKE THE BACK.

1. Prepare the material. Thickness plane, rip, and cut the back to length. Hand plane it to remove any machine marks.

2. Mold the edges. Rout the top and bottom edges of the back with a ⅛-inch-diameter edge-beading bit. Feel free to substitute another profile. If you want to cut the moldings by hand, use a combination plane, such as a Stanley #45.

MAKE THE HANGERS.

1. Cut out the blanks. Cut the hangers to rough shape with a band saw, jigsaw, or coping saw.

2. Whittle the hangers. Whittle the hangers to shape with a jackknife or with a #3 sweep 35 mm carving gouge (*Photo 1*). Whittle the

Photo 1: Whittle the hangers with a simple pocketknife or a #3 sweep 35 mm gouge.

end of the hanger to form a ⅜-inch-diameter dowel. This dowel will fit into a hole in the back, as shown in the *Side View.*

TECHNIQUE TIP

Test the diameter of the hanger by fitting it in a ⅜-inch hole drilled in a scrap of softwood. Whittle the very end of the hanger to fit in the hole. Whittle your way up the hanger, testing the diameter in the hole as you go.

ASSEMBLE THE COATRACK.

1. Drill the holes. Lay out the hanger holes and the screw holes, as shown in the *Construction Overview.* Note that the screw holes are at a right angle to the surface, but the

---

TECHNIQUE TIP

If you do not have a drill press, you can drill angled holes with an electric hand drill. Set a sliding T-bevel to 17 degrees and hold it next to each hanger hole. Looking from the side, align the bit with the square.

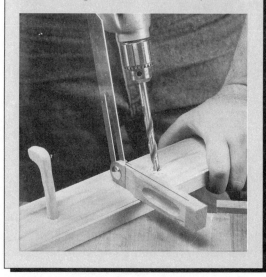

CONSTRUCTION TIP

To ensure the joint is tight, wedge the stems. Cut the slot for the wedge after you've glued and inserted the hanger stem. Cut the slot by driving a ⅜-inch chisel into the stem with a mallet. Make sure the slots are at a right angle to the back's grain. Smear a light layer of glue on a wedge and tap it into the split. Saw the wedge off flush and pare it smooth with a carving gouge.

hanger holes are at a 17 degree angle. Mark each type of hole with a different mark to avoid confusion. Drill all the holes and countersink the screw holes.

2. Attach the hangers. Swab the inside of each hole with yellow glue and insert the hanger stems. There should be about ½ inch of stem waste protruding from the rear of the back. Cut off this waste. Pare the stems flush with a #3 sweep 35 mm carving gouge.

LORD COATRACK

Today, as in the past, every country home needs a place to hang coats and jackets. The coatrack is a simple solution: a strip of individual hangers mounted on a wooden back. Most homes had at least a few coatracks, one in the rear entry as well as others in or near bedrooms.

Thus, coatracks were a universal piece of country woodworking. Most of today's woodworkers recognize the Shaker pegboard, but that is far from the only type that was made. In fact, coatracks were made in a such a wide variety of forms, they were bounded only by the imaginations of country woodworkers. Re-

flecting that diversity, this book contains two different coatracks. That way, I hope you will find one that suits your tastes, your tools, and your woodworking skills.

This coatrack requires neither a lathe nor drilled holes. It is a cabinetmaker's coatrack. I know that fact not just from looking at how it was constructed but from other evidence as well. While most country woodworking is anonymous, this piece is not. I know who made it, when it was made, and where it was used. In 1817, a young cabinetmaker named Ebenezer Lord moved into my house with his wife, Susan, who was pregnant with their

CONSTRUCTION OVERVIEW

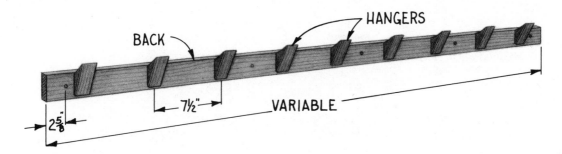

first child. The house had been built 16 years earlier by Susan's uncle, John Seaward, a ship's captain.

Through the 1820s, Ebenezer and Susan's family grew to include three daughters and a son. During the 1830s, there were 11 people in their household—themselves, their children, Lord's mother-in-law and her husband, two apprentices, and a maid. Lord was forced to add additional bedrooms. He built one in the attic for the apprentices. He made another for his daughters by dividing an upstairs sitting room with a partition wall of vertical feather-edge boards. I live in that house today, and as I write this chapter, I am sitting in that former bedroom only 2 feet from the wall's former location.

On the back side of the partition and adjacent to his bedroom door, Lord hung the coatrack from which this one is copied. This location was probably where he hung his work clothes. When restoring the house, I returned the sitting room to its original size so I could use it as an office. In the process I removed the wall and the coatrack and stored them in the attic.

The entire rack is made of eastern white pine, a wood that Lord had in abundance. That is what I selected to make my copy. The original rack had been painted several times,

MATERIALS LIST	
PART	**DIMENSIONS**
Back	$\frac{3}{4}'' \times 2\frac{1}{8}'' \times$ (variable)
Hanger stock	$\frac{3}{4}'' \times 10'' \times 6''$
HARDWARE AND SUPPLIES	
$1\frac{1}{4}''$ headless brads (as needed)	
#8 × 2'' drywall screws (as needed)	

probably by later occupants. A practical man like Lord would have left such a piece of purely utilitarian woodwork unfinished.

In Lord's shop, the coatrack was made with hand tools. He would have first beveled the back of the hangers with a hand plane, then he would have created the hangers' distinctive concave neck with a round-bottomed wooden plane called a hollow. Finally, he would have ripped the material into short, narrow strips to make the individual hangers.

In making your hangers, I suggest altering the process slightly to accommodate the tools you are likely to own. Rather than beveling my materials with a hand plane, I used a table saw. I then ripped the materials into strips and hollowed the individual hangers on the round end of a belt sander.

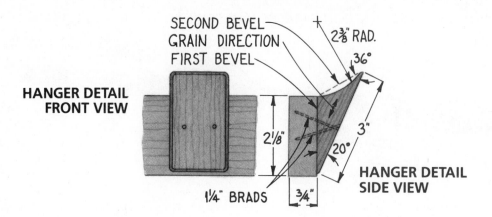

SECOND BEVEL
GRAIN DIRECTION
FIRST BEVEL

2⅜" RAD.

36°

**HANGER DETAIL
FRONT VIEW**

2⅛"

3"

20°

**HANGER DETAIL
SIDE VIEW**

¼" BRADS   ¾"

PREPARE THE MATERIALS.

1. Make the back. Joint, thickness plane, and rip the back to the dimensions given in the Materials List. The length is variable and you should fit it to your intended location. Hand plane all visible surfaces to remove machine marks.

2. Make the hanger material. Thickness plane the stock to ¾ inch and hand plane the visible surfaces. The grain in the hangers runs vertically. The most efficient way to make the hangers is to crosscut 3-inch-long strips of hanger material from a wide board, as specified in the Materials List. Go through the next few procedures before you cut the wide board into narrower hangers.

3. Bevel the hanger strips. Move your rip fence to the left side of the blade. Adjust the tilting arbor to 20 degrees and raise the blade enough to make the cut. Ripping a wide bevel in narrow stock can be dangerous because the stock tends to tip or get caught in the blade slot. To overcome the danger, clamp a guide block to the hanger stock (*Photo 1*). Make the guide block from a piece of scrap that is wider

than the fence is high. Clamping the guide block to the hanger stock will provide more stability and bearing surface during the cut. Make sure that the clamps clear the fence and the blade. Adjust the fence to the thickness of the guide plus ⅛ inch. Guide the stock with push sticks as you cut. After the first bevel has been cut, crosscut the hangers to length.

Photo 1: Clamp a guide block to the hanger stock to add stability while beveling.

4. Make the second bevel. It is easier to hollow the hangers if you have already removed most of the wood by cutting a second bevel, as shown by the dotted line in the *Hanger Detail Side View.* Once again, you can use the guide block to add stability to the stock when cutting. This time, however, tape the guide block to the stock with double-sided carpet tape (*Photo 2*). For this cut, set the saw's arbor to 36 degrees.

5. Rip the hangers. Set your miter gauge to 90 degrees and cut the wide hanger board into strips of hangers each 1⅝ inch wide.

TECHNIQUE TIP

Rather than measure each individual hanger, clamp a wide stop block to the saw table. Position the block 1⅝ inches to the side of the blade and 2 inches in front of it. After each cut, push the end of the material against the stop block before advancing the miter gauge. Each of the pieces will be exactly 1⅝ inches wide.

Photo 2: Tape the hanger stock to a guide block when cutting the second bevel.

Photo 3: Hollow out the top bevel on each hanger by holding it against the round end of a belt sander.

6. Hollow the hangers. Create the hollow in the hanger, as shown in the *Hanger Detail Side View*, with a drum sander or the round end of a belt sander (*Photo 3*).

7. Bevel the edges of the hanger. As shown in the *Hanger Detail Front View*, all the edges on the hanger's front surface are beveled. Cut the small bevels with a block plane to approximate those shown.

8. Round-over the upper end of the hangers. The sharp edge on the upper end of the hanger could damage clothing hung on it. To prevent this, round-over each upper edge with sandpaper.

ASSEMBLE THE RACK.

1. Attach the hangers to the back. With a square and a pencil, make light layout lines indicating the position of the hangers. Smear a light layer of glue on each hanger and clamp it in its location. With a try square, make sure the hanger is at a right angle to the back's edges.

When the glue is dry, secure each hanger with two 1¼-inch headless brads. Angle the brads, as shown in the *Hanger Detail Side View*.

TOOL TIP

Because of the hangers' sloping edges, conventional clamps will tend to slide off. Get a good grip on the hangers with some rubber-tipped spring clamps while gluing.

---

2. Drill the screw holes. Locate the screw holes, as shown in the *Construction Overview*, and drill them with a ¼-inch bit. Countersink each hole. Attach the coatrack to the wall with #8 × 2-inch drywall screws.

FIDDLE-BACK SCONCE

There was a time when houses were illuminated by the flame of either a lamp or a candle. Country homes were among the last to be electrified, and many country folk can still remember living, working, and playing by the light of a flame. Today, we still use candles, but mostly on special occasions, such as a romantic dinner for two.

When a candle is hung on the wall, it is held in a device called a sconce. In the days before electricity, sconces were usually made of tin because of its highly reflective quality. There were some exceptions, such as this sconce. I like this one because it is made of wood and I am a woodworker. The original was made by a Moravian craftsman working in the North Carolina settlement of Wachovia. It is a prime example of the country craftsman's use of geometric shapes—in this case, circles. They are cleverly assembled to create a very interesting and pleasing shape.

The candle has to be held in a socket. When the candle has burned to a nub, the flame may come in contact with the socket, so it shouldn't be made of wood. I made mine from a sheet of tin cut from leftover heating duct material. I simply soldered the seam.

Sconces are most commonly used in pairs. They are hung in a room in a manner that creates balance and symmetry—for example, on either side of a window or on opposite walls. Thus, you will probably want to make two sconces, so your planning should include sufficient materials for a pair—double the amounts listed in the Materials List.

You can make this sconce from just about any light-colored hardwood. The original was made of poplar. I used curly maple because

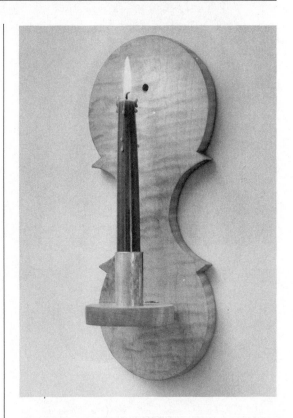

the flickering of a candle flame creates an interesting effect on this wood's strongly figured grain. I rubbed the sconce with wood finishing oil to bring out the depth of the grain.

MAKE THE PARTS.

1. Prepare the material. Thickness plane the wood to the dimensions given in the Materials List. Joint one edge of each piece, and square one end to the jointed edge. This squaring is important for laying out the arm mortise and tenon.

CONSTRUCTION OVERVIEW

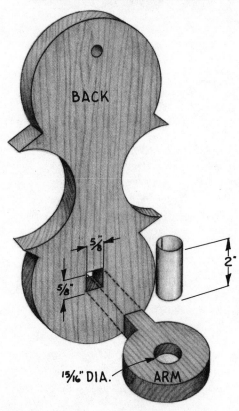

BACK

5⁄8"

5⁄8"

2"

1⁵⁄₁₆" DIA.   ARM

MATERIALS LIST

PART	DIMENSIONS
Back stock	5⁄8" × 5½" × 12½"
Arm stock	5⁄8" × 3¼" × 3¾"

HARDWARE AND SUPPLIES

2" × 2⅞" piece of sheet tin

2. Lay out the back. First, use the dimensions given in the *Back Layout* to lay out the back on a piece of posterboard. Next, draw a centerline on the back stock that is parallel to the jointed edge. Align the back pattern center-line with the centerline on the back stock and position the lower circle toward the squared end. Trace the pattern. To locate the arm mortise, make a mark by pushing an awl or a nail through the center point of the pattern's lower circle.

3. Lay out the arm mortise. Lay out the 5⁄8-inch square around the lower circle's center point, as shown in the *Back Layout*. Square the sides of the mortise with a try square set against the jointed side and squared end.

BACK LAYOUT

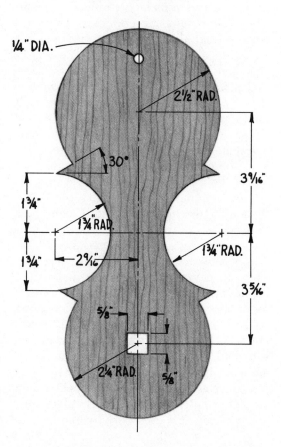

¼" DIA.

2½" RAD.

30°

3⁹⁄₁₆"

1¾"

1¾" RAD.

1¾" RAD.

1¾"

2⁹⁄₁₆"

3⁵⁄₁₆"

5⁄8"

2¼" RAD.   5⁄8"

ARM LAYOUT

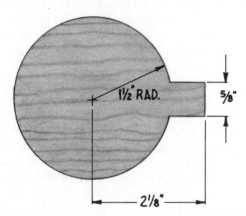

4. Lay out the arm. Draw a centerline on the arm stock. Measure ⁵⁄₁₆ inch to each side of the line and draw two more lines parallel to the first to form the tenon shown in the *Arm Layout*. Set a compass to 1½ inches. Set the compass point on the centerline, in 2⅛ inches from the squared end, and draw a circle around this point. The resulting layout includes a 3-inch-diameter circle with a tenon ⅝ inch long and ⅝ inch wide, as shown in the *Arm Layout*.

5. Shape the parts. Cut out the parts with a band saw or scroll saw, or by hand with a coping saw. Cut the arm tenon with a dovetail saw. Drill a ¼-inch-diameter hole in the center of the back's upper circle, as shown in the *Back Layout*.

Scrape and sand the two parts to remove the layout lines and saw marks.

JOIN THE PARTS.

1. Make the mortise. Drill a ⁹⁄₁₆-inch hole within the arm mortise layout. Square the edges of the through mortise with a sharp chisel.

TECHNIQUE TIP

When drilling and chiseling the mortise, back up the work with a piece of waste wood to prevent tear-out. The back of the sconce will seldom be seen, but the joint should look neat from that perspective as well.

2. Fit the tenon to the mortise. If necessary, pare the tenon with a sharp chisel to fit into the mortise.

MAKE THE CANDLE SOCKET.

1. Prepare the sheet tin. Use tin shears to cut a square of sheet tin to the dimensions given in the Materials List. In a pinch, even the smooth sides of a tin can will do. Clean the two long edges with either emery cloth or steel wool. Wrap the tin around a short length

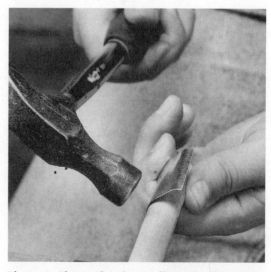

Photo 1: Shape the tin candle socket by wrapping the tin around a piece of ¾-inch-diameter dowel. Tap the tin into shape with a hammer.

Photo 2: Melt the flux with a solder iron and run a narrow bead of solder into the seam.

of ¾-inch-diameter hardwood dowel . Tap it lightly with a hammer to make it round (*Photo 1*).

2. Solder the socket. Remove the dowel and grip the tin in a vise so the two edges are squeezed together. Smear the seam with flux and heat it with a solder iron. When the flux melts, run a narrow bead of solder into the joint (*Photo 2*). Allow the tin to cool. The result is a socket with a $^{15}/_{16}$-inch outside diam-

eter and a $^7/_8$-inch inside diameter — just about the thickness of most commercial candles.

If you don't feel comfortable doing this metalwork, find a friend who does, or have the candle socket soldered at a local machine shop.

3. Drill the candle socket hole. Grip the arm in a vise. As shown in the *Construction Overview*, drill a $^{15}/_{16}$-inch-diameter hole centered on the arm. Drill the hole with a spade bit or Forstner bit, but don't allow the lead point to break through the bottom of the arm. The wax could run through the arm and onto the floor.

ASSEMBLE THE PARTS.

1. Fit the socket. Place the tin socket into the $^{15}/_{16}$-inch hole. Put the arm and socket assembly into a vise and squeeze the two together to make sure the socket is pressed as deeply into the hole as possible.

2. Attach the arm to the back. Spread glue into the arm mortise and fit the arm's tenon into it. Clamp the assembly and set it aside to dry.

When the glue is dry, clean away excess glue and finish sand the sconce.

CANTED DISPLAY SHELF

So many country shelves have survived that we can assume every home had several. Most shelves are made up of long horizontal boards, and the objects displayed on them are placed side by side. This shelf is very different in that it is tall and narrow. Because of its unique shape, each of its shelves results in a vertical cubbyhole large enough for only one object. The shelf must have been made specifically for displaying individual precious keepsakes that deserve their own space.

The back has a shape that is seen elsewhere in this book. A very similar outline, the fishtail, is used on the Pipe Box (page 159). If you look at the dimensions, you see that this shelf is considerably larger than the Pipe Box.

The original shelf is made of tulip and painted red. I made mine out of maple and finished it with Watco Danish Oil.

MAKE THE PARTS AND ASSEMBLE THE SHELF.

1. Prepare the stock. Joint, thickness plane, rip, and cut the back and side stock to the dimensions given in the Materials List. Joint and thickness plane the stock for the shelves. Hand plane the stock to remove machine marks.

2. Make the back. Lay out the back's canted sides, as shown in the *Construction Overview.* Cut along the layout lines with your band saw or jigsaw and smooth the cut with a hand plane. Lay out the fishtail shape with a compass and cut it out with a coping saw, band saw, or jigsaw. Clean up the edges with a spokeshave and sandpaper.

Drill a ¼-inch-diameter hole in the fishtail, as shown in the *Construction Overview*.

3. Cut the dadoes and rabbets. When making the dadoes, it is easier to have both edges of the sides straight. So, before you taper the sides, cut the dadoes on your table saw with a ⅜-inch-wide dado blade. Raise the blade to exactly ³⁄₁₆ inch and tilt your saw's arbor to 1½ degrees. Lay out the rabbets and dadoes on the sides and guide the stock with your miter gauge at 90 degrees as you make the cuts (*Photo 1*).

CONSTRUCTION OVERVIEW

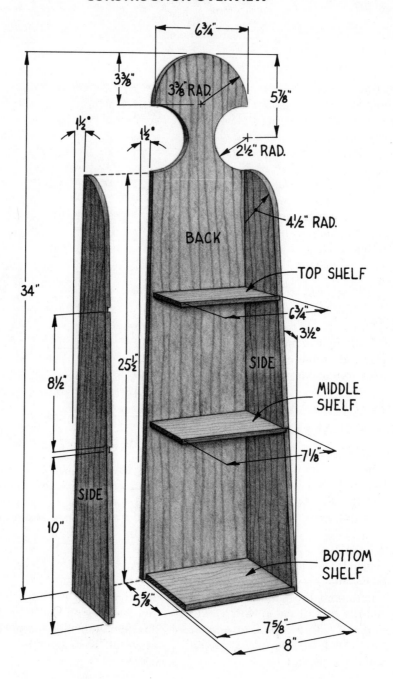

6¾"

3⅜"

3⅜" RAD.

5⅞"

2½" RAD.

1½°

1½°

4½" RAD.

BACK

TOP SHELF

6¾"

3½°

SIDE

34"

8½"

25½"

MIDDLE
SHELF

7⅛"

SIDE

10"

BOTTOM
SHELF

5⅝"

7⅝"

8"

MATERIALS LIST

PART	DIMENSIONS
Back	⅜" × 8" × 34"
Sides (2)	⅜" × 5⅝" × 25½"
Bottom shelf	⅜" × 5⅝" × 7⅝"
Middle shelf	⅜" × 5" × 7⅛"
Top shelf	⅜" × 4¼" × 6¾"

HARDWARE AND SUPPLIES

1" headless brads (as needed)

TECHNIQUE TIP

If you do not have a dado blade, make two cuts on each edge of each dado and rabbet with your regular blade. Pare the waste from the dadoes and rabbets with a very sharp ⅜-inch chisel.

Photo 1: Guide the side stock with a miter gauge as you cut the dadoes and rabbets. Align the layout line with the blade as you start the cut.

TOOL TIP

It is important to make the back's long edges taper at 1½ degrees, as shown in the *Construction Overview.* You have several options available when making this taper, including the band saw method described in step 2. The back can also be tapered on the table saw with a tapering jig as a guide. Tapering jigs are available from most catalog tool dealers, including Woodcraft, 210 Wood County Industrial Park, P.O. Box 1686, Parkersburg, WV 26102 (part #03R22).

Since the taper is very gradual, the work can also be done very easily with a jointer plane. Lay out the taper with a pencil and a straightedge. Grip the back in your bench's side vise and plane to the line.

These same techniques can also be used to taper the sides.

4. Taper the front edges of the sides. When the dadoes and rabbets have been cut, lay out the taper on the front edge of each side, as shown in the *Construction Overview.* Lay out the rounded top edge of each side with a compass and cut it to shape with a band saw, a jigsaw, or a coping saw. Smooth all the sawed edges with a block plane and sandpaper.

5. Attach the sides to the back. Clamp one side in a vise to hold it stable. Nail the back to the side with 1-inch headless brads. Repeat for the remaining side.

6. Make the shelves. Because the back and sides taper toward the top, the bottom shelf is both longer and wider than the top shelf, and the middle shelf falls somewhere in between. First, set your table saw's arbor to 1½ degrees and bevel one end of each shelf, then flip the shelves end for end and cut them to length. Compare the shelves with their dadoes or rabbets in the sides and gradually remove stock until they match perfectly.

Next, set your saw's arbor to 3½ degrees and bevel the front edge of each shelf. Reset the saw's arbor to 90 degrees. Measuring from the assembled sides and back, cut the shelves to slightly more than the measured width. To obtain a perfect fit, trim the rear edge with a block plane, testing the shelves in their dadoes to achieve a perfect fit.

CONSTRUCTION TIP

The fit of the shelves is very important. Before cutting them to the lengths given in the Materials List, measure the distance between the dadoes or rabbets in the back and side assembly, and use those measurements to fit the shelves.

7. Attach the shelves. One at a time, insert each shelf into its rabbet or dado and nail it in place with 1-inch brads.

CAPE COD CURTAIN HOLDER

Tab curtains were common in country homes. These curtains amount to little more than two strips of material, each slightly wider than half the window opening. A row of cloth loops, or tabs, is stitched across the top, and the curtains are hung by passing a rod (nothing more sophisticated than a ¾-inch dowel) through the tabs. The curtains hang loosely and are easily pushed aside to let in light and air.

The method for hanging these curtain rods evolved over time. At first, the rods were merely suspended on two nails, one driven into each upper corner of the window's trim. Later, some anonymous woodworker devised wooden brackets to hold the rod. Although very simple, these brackets have a much more finished appearance than the nails. These popular brackets somehow became associated with Cape Cod, the arm of land in Massachusetts that projects into the Atlantic Ocean, and they are now commonly called Cape Cod curtain holders.

Tab curtains are so simple they were usually hung in a house's informal rooms, but if you have a country parlor, you may want to

CONSTRUCTION OVERVIEW

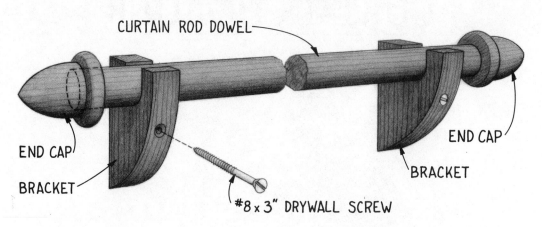

CURTAIN ROD DOWEL

END CAP

BRACKET

#8 x 3" DRYWALL SCREW

END CAP

BRACKET

use them there, too. I have included a common profile for turned end caps that add a bit of sophistication to a country curtain rod. The shape is inspired by the acorn—a popular symbol in early America. End caps were usually accented with a paint that contrasted with the trim, and sometimes they were gilded in a gold leaf. If you like the idea of gold leaf, you can use gold spray paint, available at most frame shops. The rod can be left unfinished.

The curtain rod bracket is probably the simplest project in this book, but it does present a different challenge. These brackets are seldom made as a single pair. Most rooms have more than one window, so you will likely need several pairs. These window brackets are an opportunity to practice making a wooden object in multiples.

Woodworkers who are in business often find it most efficient to make their products in production runs. This requires them to approach their woodworking differently than they would if they were making objects one at a time. They have to divide the project into the most efficient sequence of steps. The production woodworker sets up one step and performs

MATERIALS LIST	
PART	**DIMENSIONS**
Brackets (as needed)	¾″ × 2½″ × 3½″
End cap blanks (as needed)	2″ × 2″ × 2¾″
Curtain rod dowels (as needed)	¾″ dia. × (variable)
HARDWARE AND SUPPLIES	
#8 × 3″ drywall screws (as needed)	

that operation on all the parts. Then he sets up and completes the next step, then the next, and the next, until he has a pile of completed objects. I suggest making your curtain brackets in a production run, rather than one at a time.

MAKE THE BRACKETS.

1. Prepare the bracket stock. Calculate the amount of material required to make the number of brackets you need. If you buy rough-sawn lumber, joint and thickness plane the stock to the dimensions given in the Materials List. Rip the stock to 2½ inches wide, then hand plane it to remove the machine marks. Cut the stock into 3½-inch-long blanks.

TECHNIQUE TIP

Attach a stop block to your table saw's rip fence to regulate the length of the bracket blanks. Clamp a stop block to the rip fence just in front of the blade, adjusting the fence until the distance between the stop block and the blade is the same as the part's length (in this case 3½ inches). Before making each cut, press the end of the bracket stock against the stop block and use the miter gauge to push the material past the blade. This process is very fast and will render multiple parts of equal length.

2. Cut the brackets to shape. Draw a grid of ¼-inch squares on a piece of posterboard and plot the curve shown in the *Bracket Side Pattern.* Cut a template from the posterboard

BRACKET SIDE PATTERN

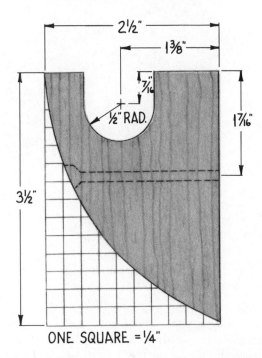

ONE SQUARE = ¼"

and trace the curve onto the bracket blanks. Cut the parts to shape with a band saw, scroll saw, or coping saw. Remove the saw marks from the curve with a spokeshave or belt sander or on a sanding disk.

3. Make the dowel notches. First, lay out the 1-inch-diameter dowel notch hole on one of the brackets, as shown in the *Bracket Side Pattern.* Put a 1-inch-diameter drill bit in the drill press. I drilled the hole with a Forstner bit, which cuts extremely accurate, smooth-sided holes. Clamp a fence to the drill press table and a stop block to the fence to position the bracket (*Photo 1*). Put a piece of scrap under the bracket to support the edge of the hole as the bit exits the stock. Once the fence and stop block are positioned correctly, drill the hole in each of the brackets.

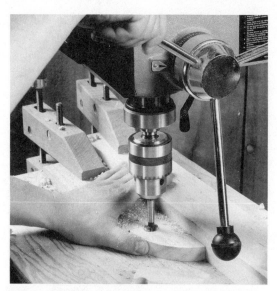

Photo 1: Clamp a fence and stop block to the drill press table to position the stock.

Once the holes have been drilled, finish off the top corners of each notch by cutting away the waste on the band saw, or grind away the corners and sand the notch at the same time with a ¾-inch-diameter drum sander. If you choose to use the drum sander, put it in the drill press and sand away the top corners of the notch to produce the profile shown in the *Bracket Side Pattern*.

4. Bore the screw holes. Each bracket is attached to the window trim with a 3-inch-long drywall screw, which passes through the bracket's width, as shown in the *Bracket Side Pattern*. First, bore the pilot hole for each screw with a ⅛-inch-diameter drill bit in a drill press. As when drilling the dowel notch, position the bracket with a fence and stop block clamped to the drill press table. Start boring each pilot hole slowly so that the bit has time to grab the stock. If you plunge too fast, the bit may try to follow the curve.

Next, replace the drill bit with a ¼-inch-diameter countersink bit, and countersink the pilot holes, as shown in the *Bracket Side Pattern*.

MAKE THE END CAPS.

1. Turn the acorn-shaped end caps. First, secure an end cap blank between centers on the lathe and turn the blank to a diameter of 1⅞ inches with a gouge. Define the ends of the end cap by making plunge cuts with the parting tool (*Photo 2*). Next, make a plunge cut with the parting tool to a diameter of 1⅜ inches just above the base of the end cap to define the top end of the acorn shape. When the ends and base have been defined, turn the end cap to the shape shown in the *End Cap Turning Layout* with a gouge (*Photo 3*), and sand the surface smooth. Remove the end cap from the lathe, cut off the waste, and turn the next end cap.

END CAP TURNING LAYOUT

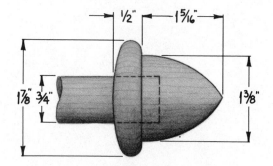

2. Drill the dowel holes. Drill a ¾-inch-diameter × ¾-inch-deep hole in the base of each end cap, as shown in the *End Cap Turning Layout*. To hold the end cap stable as you drill the hole, make a cap-holding jig from a 1½-inch-thick hardwood scrap. Drill a 1½-

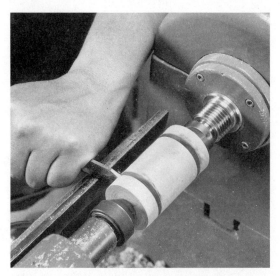

Photo 2: Define the ends of the end cap by making plunge cuts with the parting tool. Plunge down to a diameter of ½ to ⅜ inch.

Photo 4: Put the end cap in the cap-holding jig with the pointed end in the hole and the base resting firmly on top of the jig. Carefully support the stock with your fingers and drill the dowel hole.

Place the cap-holding jig and end cap on the drill press. Steady the base of the end cap in the jig with your fingers and drill the ¾-inch-diameter dowel hole (*Photo 4*). Drill a dowel hole in each end cap.

ASSEMBLE THE CURTAIN RODS AND HANG THE BRACKETS.

1. Attach the end caps. Paint or gild the end caps and arrange them in pairs. Glue one end

Photo 3: Carefully round and shape the end cap with a gouge. Use the parting tool cut as a reference as you turn the acorn shape.

inch-diameter hole through the scrap, and put the point of the end cap in the hole.

TOOL TIP

Drill the 1½-inch diameter hole in the cap-holding jig and the ¾-inch-diameter hole in each end cap with Forstner bits. Forstner bits drill smooth-sided, large diameter, flat-bottomed holes quickly and easily.

---

cap from each pair to the end of its curtain rod dowel. Push the remaining end cap from each pair on the other end of its curtain rod dowel, but don't glue the cap onto the dowel. (No glue is used so that the end cap can be removed when the curtains need to be taken down or hung up.)

2. Finish and hang the brackets. Paint or stain the brackets to match the window trim. When the finish is dry, lay out the position of the brackets on the window trim and drill pilot holes for the screws. Put a #8 × 3-inch drywall screw in the pilot hole, hold the brackets in place, and drive the screw.

HANGING QUILT RACK

In the past, rural households were usually much larger than they are today. A married couple would have numerous children of their own and might very well raise the children of a relative. Grandparents usually lived under the same roof with their children. Many households also employed hired help—unmarried men to work the farm and unmarried women to help in the kitchen. If the head of the family was a tradesman rather than a farmer, his household might include one or more apprentices. All these people created a small, self-contained community.

It was customary for many of the household's members—especially children or apprentices—to sleep together in the same bed. Doubling and tripling up, a large family would still own a half-dozen or more beds. All those beds required lots of bedclothes, including sheets, blankets, quilts, and coverlets.

All this bedding had to be stored, so rural families owned several blanket chests that were distributed throughout the house. Blanket chests take up a lot of floor space, and floor space was often at a premium in a crowded rural home. The genius of the quilt rack shown here is that it hangs on the wall. It stores a lot of bedclothes but takes up no floor space.

CONSTRUCTION OVERVIEW

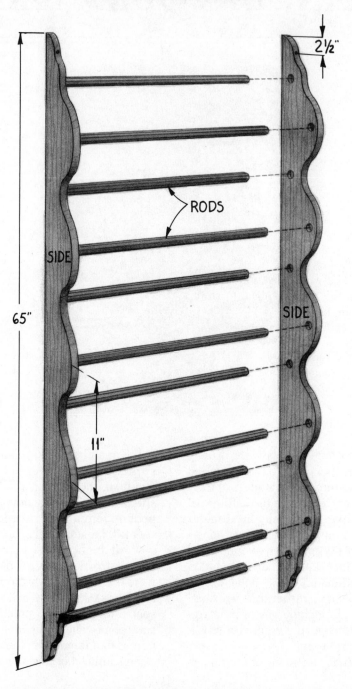

2½"

RODS

SIDE

SIDE

65"

11"

MATERIALS LIST

PART	DIMENSIONS
Sides (2)	$\frac{3}{4}'' \times 6'' \times$ (variable)
Rods (as needed)	$\frac{3}{4}'' \times \frac{3}{4}'' \times 23\frac{1}{2}''$

HARDWARE AND SUPPLIES

$1\frac{1}{4}''$ finishing nails (as needed)

CONSTRUCTION TIP

If you plan to customize the height of your quilt rack, calculate the new length of the sides and cut them to length. One repeating section of the side pattern equals 11 inches, so add or subtract 11 inches as necessary.

If you change the length of the sides, you will also need to add or subtract the number of rods to match.

These days, we are more likely to store linens and blankets in a closet. In my house, though, closet space is at a premium. So if you're like me, this quilt rack can be just as handy as it was to those early Americans. This quilt rack is able to hold a surprising number of sheets and blankets, and it can be hung in an out-of-the-way place. And, as its name implies, it's the perfect place to store beautiful handmade quilts.

The original quilt rack was handmade from pine. The rods were whittled, but you can use store-bought dowels. I whittled my rods to catch the country flavor of the original. The original quilt rack was 65 inches long, but you can make it longer or shorter to suit your needs. The undulating sides are composed of a repeating pattern, which can be added to or subtracted from to change the rack's length.

The original rack was painted gray. I left mine unpainted, or "in the white." I like the combination of unfinished wood and fabric.

MAKE THE PARTS.

1. Prepare the materials. Joint, thickness plane, rip, and cut the parts to the dimensions given in the Materials List. If you are using $\frac{3}{4}$-inch-diameter dowels for the rods, simply cut them to length. Hand plane the sides to remove machine marks.

2. Cut the sides to shape. Draw a grid of $\frac{1}{2}$-inch squares on a piece of posterboard and plot the shape of the side on it, as shown in the *Side Pattern*. Cut out the pattern and trace it onto the side stock. You will need to flip the pattern end for end several times to lay out the complete pattern on the sides—match your pattern carefully. Cut out the profile on a band saw. Clean up the sawed edges with a spokeshave and sandpaper.

TECHNIQUE TIP

In order to produce two matching sides, cut both at once. Clamp or tape the side stock together with the pattern layout visible, and cut the assembly to shape on the band saw.

---

3. Whittle the rods round. If you intend to whittle the rods from square stock, grip a piece of rod stock with one corner facing up between your bench's tail vise and a bench dog. Flatten the corner with a hand plane set to cut a moderately thick chip (*Photo 1*). I chose a #5 jack plane to flatten the corners. Do the same to the other three corners to produce an octagonal cross section. Soften the eight corners with a block plane set to take a light shaving. Repeat for the remaining rods.

SIDE PATTERN

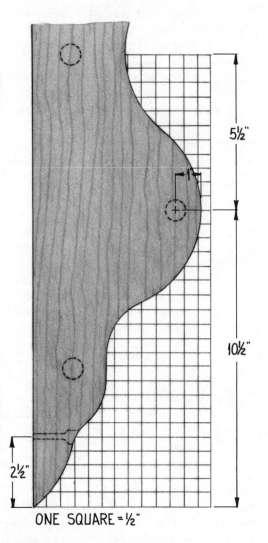

5½"

10½"

2½"

ONE SQUARE = ½"

Photo 1: Flatten the corners of the rod stock with a hand plane to turn the square stock into an octagon. Set your hand plane to take a moderately deep cut.

TOOL TIP

The rod holes are ½ inch deep, leaving only ¼ inch of material between the bottom of the hole and the outside surface of the sides. To avoid piercing the sides, use a bit with a short lead spur such as a Forstner bit or a brad-point bit.

ASSEMBLE THE PARTS.

1. Drill the rod holes. Locate and drill the ¾-inch-diameter rod holes on the inner surface of each side, as shown in the *Side Pattern*. Drill the holes with the depth gauge of your drill press set to ½ inch.

2. Drill the mounting screw holes. Drill the four ¼-inch-diameter mounting screw holes 2½ inches on center from the top and bottom of the sides, as shown in the *Construction Overview.* Countersink the holes.

3. Assemble the rack. Place all the rods in their holes in one side and tap them in place with a hammer. Put the second side in place and hold it lightly with a bar clamp. One at a time, align the rods with the holes in the second side. When all the rods are in place, lay the rack on one side and tap over each rod to ensure that they are seated in their second holes.

4. Nail the joints. Drive a 1¼-inch finishing nail through the edge of the sides and into each rod.

HANGING MAGAZINE RACK

In the past, a country house received far fewer magazines and newspapers than today's average home does. Without radio or television, these few periodicals were the source of most news and information. Therefore, country folk kept such valued reading materials around the house longer and read them more thoroughly than we do today. Storing periodicals neatly and in a handy place became important, and because we receive so many periodicals, it's still important to us today.

This hanging magazine and newspaper rack is one country woodworker's answer to storing periodical publications. It is a clever solution because, instead of standing on the floor where it would take up space, it is hung out of the way on the wall. It is also easier to use than a floor model. The magazine covers and newspaper headlines are all easily visible both above and between the evenly spaced front strips, eliminating the need to rummage around in the rack lifting out every magazine to find the one you want.

It is interesting to note that the size of most magazines and newspapers has not varied much over the many decades since the

CONSTRUCTION OVERVIEW

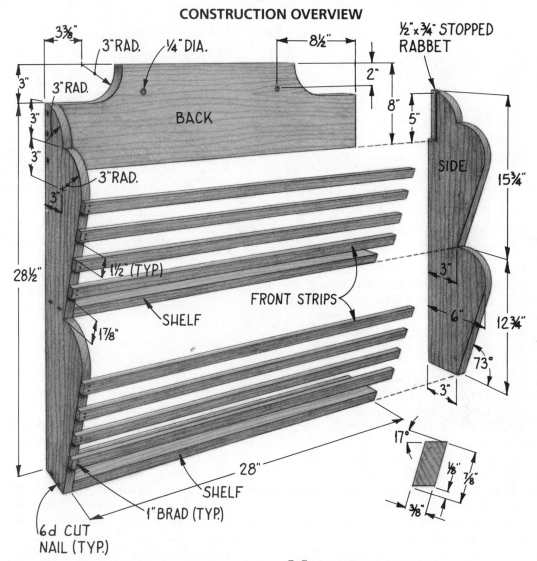

original rack was made. Two newspapers fit in it side by side with a slight overlap, and three magazines easily fit side by side.

The original rack was painted many times; it is not possible to determine the first color or wood species through all the layers. I made my magazine rack from pine. Paint or stain your magazine rack to match your decor.

MAKE THE PARTS.

1. Prepare the stock. Thickness plane the stock to ¾ inch, if necessary, and hand plane the surfaces and edges to remove any machine marks. Rip and cut the sides, back, and shelves to the dimensions given in the Materials List.

MATERIALS LIST

PART	DIMENSIONS
Sides (2)	¾″ × 6″ × 28½″
Back	¾″ × 29″ × 8″
Shelves (2)	¾″ × 28″ × 3¼″
Front strips (8)	⅜″ × ⅞″ × 29½″

HARDWARE AND SUPPLIES

6d cut nails (as needed). Available from
   Tremont Nail Company, 8 Elm Street, P.O.
   Box 111, Wareham, MA 02571.
   Part #N-21 Std.

1″ headless brads (as needed)

2. Cut the sides to shape. Lay out the curves and angles on the sides, as shown in the *Construction Overview,* with a compass and straightedge. Cut the sides to shape with a band saw or bow saw. Clean up the sawed edges with a spokeshave and sandpaper.

3. Cut the stopped rabbets in the sides. The back fits into ½ × ¾-inch stopped rabbets cut into the tops of the sides, as shown in the *Construction Overview.* Cut the rabbets with a ¾-inch-diameter straight bit in your router. Guide the cut with the router's fence attachment, and stop the cut 5 inches from the top of the side (*Photo 1*). For added security, clamp a stop block to the side to stop the router when it reaches the end of the cut. Square the rounded ends of the rabbet with a chisel.

4. Shape the back. Lay out the cutouts on the back, as shown in the *Construction Overview,* with a compass and straightedge. Cut the back to shape with a band saw or bow saw. Clean up the sawed edges with a drum sander or a spokeshave and sandpaper. Drill two ¼-inch-diameter holes, as shown in the *Construction Overview.*

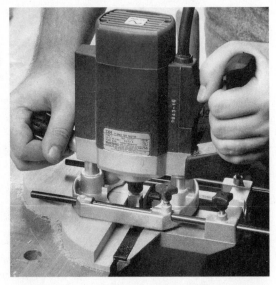

Photo 1: Guide the rabbeting cut with the fence attachment on your router. Clamp a stop block to the side to stop the cut at 5 inches.

5. Bevel the shelves. Set your table saw's arbor to 17 degrees and rip a bevel along the front edge of each shelf, as shown in the *Construction Overview.* Guide the stock against the table saw fence as you rip the bevel. Hand plane the beveled edge to remove any saw marks.

6. Make the front strips. With your table saw's arbor tilted at 17 degrees, bevel the front strips as you cut them to width. First, bevel one edge, then roll the strip 180 degrees and rip the second edge. The resulting profile should match that shown in the *Construction Overview* and *Strip End View.* Hand plane the sawed edges to remove any saw marks.

ASSEMBLE THE PARTS.

1. Nail the sides to the back and shelves. Nail through the sides and into the ends of the shelves with 6d cut nails. To control the path of the nails, drill a $\frac{3}{16}$-inch pilot hole for each nail. Square the shelves to the sides with a cabinet square. Nail the back into its rabbets with 6d cut nails.

CONSTRUCTION TIP

The back must support the weight of the magazine rack and its contents. For that reason the rabbet joints should be nailed in two directions—through the back *and* through the sides, as shown in the *Rabbet Joint Detail.*

2. Attach the front strips. Lay out and position the front strips, as shown in the *Construction Overview,* and attach the strips to the sides with two 1-inch headless brads at each end.

RABBET JOINT DETAIL

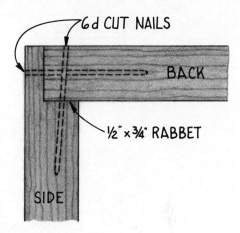

6d CUT NAILS

BACK

$\frac{1}{2}$" × $\frac{3}{4}$" RABBET

SIDE

PYRAMID SHELF

Like most country accessories, this set of shelves is very clever and very simple at the same time. It is little more than three boards held together by rawhide strips in the shape of a pyramid. Although this construction may sound crude or primitive, this shelf, when stretched taut on the wall, has the delicacy and grace of a spiderweb.

Further evidence contradicts any attempt to describe this shelf as primitive. It is too carefully planned. The maker used a 3:2 ratio between the neighboring shelves. The lower shelf is 9 × 18 inches, the middle shelf is 6 × 12 inches, and the upper shelf is 4 × 8 inches.

The same ratio is used in planning the distance between shelves. Obviously, the shelf was not thrown together by a farmer who needed shelf space in the barn.

The woodwork involved in making the shelf appears so basic as to present no challenge. True, making the shelves is very quick and simple. The effort is in drilling the holes. While the back string holes are drilled at simple angles from the shelf ends, the front holes are drilled at compound angles between the shelf ends and front edges. In making the shelf, it is important that the holes be angled correctly so the rawhide is stretched in straight lines.

CONSTRUCTION OVERVIEW

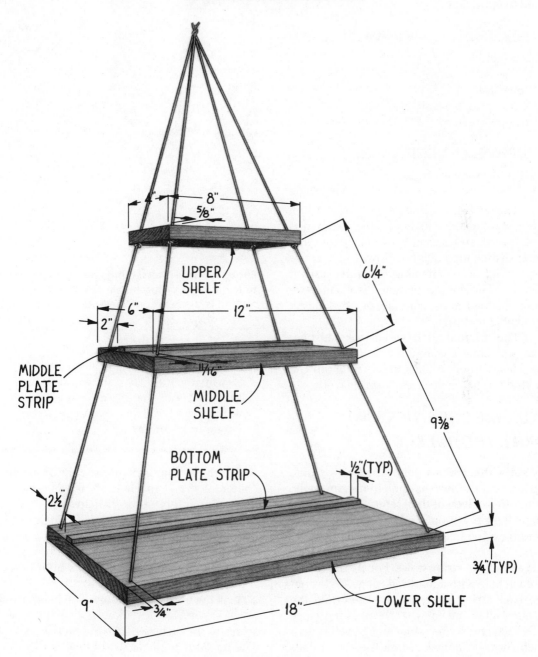

UPPER SHELF

8"

4"

5/8"

6¼"

MIDDLE PLATE STRIP

6"

2"

12"

MIDDLE SHELF

11/16"

9⅜"

BOTTOM PLATE STRIP

½"(TYP.)

2½"

¾"(TYP.)

9"

¾"

18"

LOWER SHELF

MATERIALS LIST

PART	DIMENSIONS
Lower shelf	¾″ × 9″ × 18″
Middle shelf	¾″ × 6″ × 12″
Upper shelf	¾″ × 4″ × 8″
Bottom plate strip	¼″ × ½″ × 18″
Middle plate strip	¼″ × ½″ × 12″

HARDWARE AND SUPPLIES

72″ rawhide shoelaces (2)

Photo 1: Scribe intersecting lines at each corner to lay out the string holes. The point of intersection is the center of the hole.

The bottom and middle shelves have thin strips of wood glued to them. This is known as a plate strip and is used to support plates and other disk-shaped objects. However, because the rawhide is very flexible and shifts easily if bumped, I do not recommend displaying anything made of glass, ceramic, or other easily breakable material.

The original shelf was never finished. The pine boards were left raw and, over the decades, turned a color very similar to the rawhide. I, too, left my copy unfinished.

PREPARE THE STOCK AND DRILL THE HOLES.

1. Make the shelves. Joint, thickness plane, rip, and cut the shelves and plate strips to the dimensions given in the Materials List. Hand plane the top, bottom, and edges of each piece to remove the machine marks.

2. Lay out the string holes. Locate the center of each hole with a marking gauge. To lay out the back string holes on each shelf and the upper shelf's front holes, set the marking gauge to ⅝ inch and scribe a line along each side of each corner (*Photo 1*). Mark the scribe lines on the top of the shelves only. The point at

---

TECHNIQUE TIP

To avoid confusion when drilling the holes, identify the front edge and top surface of each shelf with a pencil. I did this by lightly writing the letters F (front) and T (top) where appropriate.

---

which the scribe lines intersect indicates the center of the string hole. Make an impression at the intersection with an awl.

Repeat the process when laying out the other string holes, but reset the marking gauge to ¾ inch for the lower shelf's front holes and to ¹¹⁄₁₆ inch for the middle shelf's front holes.

3. Drill the back string holes. The back string holes are angled to follow the angle of the string, as shown in the *Construction Overview*. The angle of the holes can be approximated with a hand-held drill.

Photo 2: Match the angle on the drill bit with that of the sliding T-bevel's blade as you drill the back string holes.

Photo 3: Sight across the front and side of the sliding T-bevel to align the drill bit.

First, put a $\frac{3}{16}$-inch-diameter drill bit (preferably a brad-point bit) in your drill. Next, set a sliding T-bevel to 17 degrees and use it as a reference as you drill the angled holes (*Photo 2*). The handle of the sliding T-bevel should be parallel to the back edge of the shelves. Drill the angled back holes in the three shelves.

4. Drill the front string holes. The front string holes must be drilled at a compound angle to the sides and ends. First, set a sliding T-bevel to 20 degrees, then angle the base of the sliding T-bevel about 42 degrees from the front edge of the shelves. Align the bit with both the base and blade of the sliding T-bevel and drill the holes (*Photo 3*).

5. Attach the plate strips. Lay out the positions of the plate strips on the lower shelf and middle shelf, as shown in the *Construction Overview.* Spread a light layer of glue on the

bottom of the plate strips and clamp them to the shelves.

> **TOOL TIP**
>
> Spring clamps are the ideal tool for clamping delicate pieces like the plate strips. They can be operated with one hand while you hold the piece in place with the other.

ASSEMBLE THE SHELF.

1. Attach the lower shelf. Cut the rawhide shoelaces in half to produce four 36-inch-long lengths. Tie a half-knot, as shown in the *Half-Knot Diagram,* as close to one end of each piece as possible. Pass one length through each of the lower shelf's holes.

2. Attach the middle shelf. One at a time, draw the rawhide pieces taut. Be careful not to pull so tightly that they stretch. Make a

HALF-KNOT

SQUARE KNOT

mark with an ink pen on the rawhide laces 9⅜ inches above the lower shelf's front string holes and 9 inches above the lower shelf's back string holes. Tie a half-knot just above the ink mark on each lace.

Pass the four laces through the string holes in the middle shelf.

3. Attach the upper shelf. Repeat the knotting process described in step 2, but this time make marks on the laces 6¼ inches above the middle shelf's front string holes and 6 inches above the middle shelf's back string holes. Pass the laces through the upper shelf and tie a half-knot in each lace just above the mark, as shown in the *Half-Knot Diagram.*

4. Tie the lace ends. Tie the ends of the back laces in a square knot, as shown in the *Square Knot Diagram.* Hang the assembly against the wall on a nail. Raise the shelves' front edges by lifting the ends of the front laces. Rest a small level across the lower shelf's width and tie a square knot in the front laces at a point that allows the shelves to hang level. Loop the front laces over the nail.

SPOON RACK

Rural households stored their "everyday" knives and forks in a knife box like the one shown on page 181. The everyday spoons were stored in a vertical container called a spooner. Nearly every household also had a "best" set of spoons—these were used for tea or for dining. These spoons were often made of silver and were too nice to be stored where they could not be seen. For that reason many rural homes had a wall-hung spoon rack for displaying the family's silver spoons.

Most spoon racks are very much akin to more ordinary wall boxes. They have a back whose profile is the result of one or more geometric shapes. At the bottom they often have a storage box for holding the countless odds and ends that a household accumulates over time. Above the box are one or more horizontal racks with a number of evenly spaced spoon slots.

Silver spoons not only were functional, but also represented a store of wealth. In fact, the grade of metal used in most silver spoons was called coin silver because it was obtained by melting coins and had the same purity. These silver spoons were usually made and marked by a local silversmith and were personalized with the owner's monogram.

CONSTRUCTION OVERVIEW

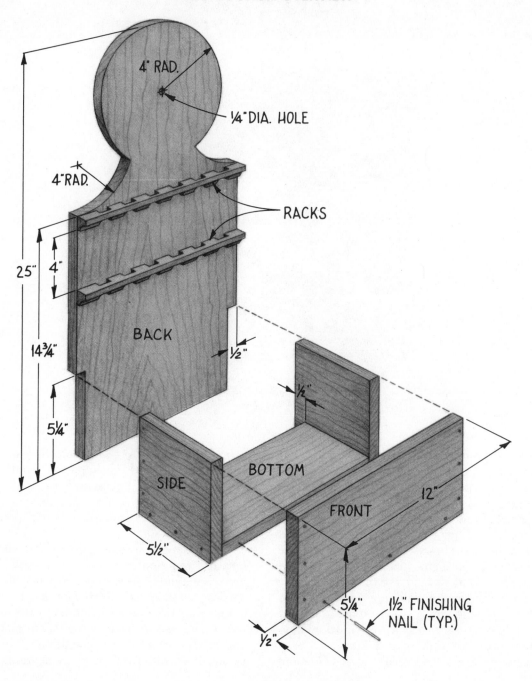

4" RAD.

¼" DIA. HOLE

4" RAD.

RACKS

25"

4"

14¾"

BACK

½"

½"

5¼"

SIDE

BOTTOM

FRONT

12"

5½"

5¼"

½"

1½" FINISHING
NAIL (TYP.)

MATERIALS LIST

PART	DIMENSIONS
Back	½″ × 12″ × 25″
Racks (2)	¾″ × ⅞″ × 12″
Sides (2)	½″ × 5¼″ × 5½″
Front	½″ × 5¼″ × 12″
Bottom	½″ × 5″ × 11″

HARDWARE AND SUPPLIES

1½″ finishing nails (as needed)

Coin silver spoons were made in such enormous quantities that they are a staple in every antique shop. I collect silver spoons made by silversmiths who worked in Portsmouth, New Hampshire — the city where I live.

My copy of this pine spoon rack, like the original, is painted blue. If you choose to paint your spoon rack, you might want to select a color that matches or complements the color of the room in which it will hang.

MAKE THE PARTS.

1. Prepare the materials. Joint, thickness plane, rip, and cut the stock to the dimensions given in the Materials List.

2. Shape the back. Lay out the back's 4-inch-radius curves with a compass, as shown in the *Construction Overview*. Cut the curves with a band saw or coping saw.

The back is cut out to accept the sides, as shown in the *Construction Overview*. Cut the joints with a band saw and, to keep the cuts straight, guide the back against a fence. Clean up the sawed edges with a spokeshave, chisel, and sandpaper.

3. Shape and notch the racks. First, rout a ½-inch-radius cove in the edge of each of the racks, as shown in the *Rack Detail*. Put the cove bit in a table-mounted router and guide the racks against a fence as you rout (*Photo 1*).

RACK DETAIL

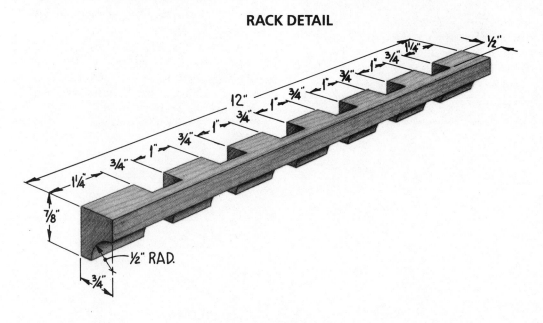

½″ RAD.

Photo 1: Rout the cove in the rack stock with a ½-inch-diameter cove bit in a table-mounted router. Bury the bit in the fence and guide the stock against the fence as you rout.

TOOL TIP

You can also cut the spoon notches on the table saw with a dado blade. Install a ¾-inch-wide dado blade in your table saw and raise it ½ inch above the surface of the table. Guide the stock with the miter gauge set at 90 degrees as you cut the notches.

Lay out the spoon notches in the racks, as shown in the *Rack Detail*. Continue the layout lines across the wide edges of the stock with a square and pencil. Cut along the layout lines with a fine dovetail saw and remove the waste with a sharp chisel.

ASSEMBLE THE PARTS.

1. Assemble the back, sides, front, and bottom. First, attach the sides to the back with 1½-inch finishing nails, as shown in the *Construction Overview*. Nail the front in place, then fit and nail the bottom to the box.

2. Attach the racks. Put a spot of glue on the end of each rack and one in the center. Attach the racks to the back with 1½-inch finishing nails, as shown in the *Construction Overview*.

TECHNIQUE TIP

It is generally considered poor construction to glue one piece of wood across the grain of another. Seasonal movement will either break the glue bond or split the wider piece of wood (in this case the back). However, the spoon notches make the racks flexible so that they will bend (imperceptibly) to adjust to the back board's seasonal expansion and contraction.

TOWEL ROLLER

Most of the projects in this book are copies of original pieces of country woodworking. This towel roller is an exception. Although it is inspired by an original, I have adapted it to serve a modern need.

The original towel roller held a continuous cloth towel. In the past, these were very common in rural households. Rollers for a continuous towel were found in nearly every kitchen and scullery.

Today, continuous towels are no longer the first choice, having gone out of favor when it was feared they were unsanitary. Still, many will remember them as a standard fixture in restaurant and gas station restrooms.

Today, few people would choose to have a continuous towel in a kitchen or bath. Instead, we are more inclined to use paper towels, which are used once and discarded, so I adapted this towel roller to hold a roll of paper towels.

A roll of paper towels is big and bulky in contrast to a continuous towel. For that reason, the original roller was much smaller than my adaptation. I really liked the original's side design, which was much more pleasing than

CONSTRUCTION OVERVIEW

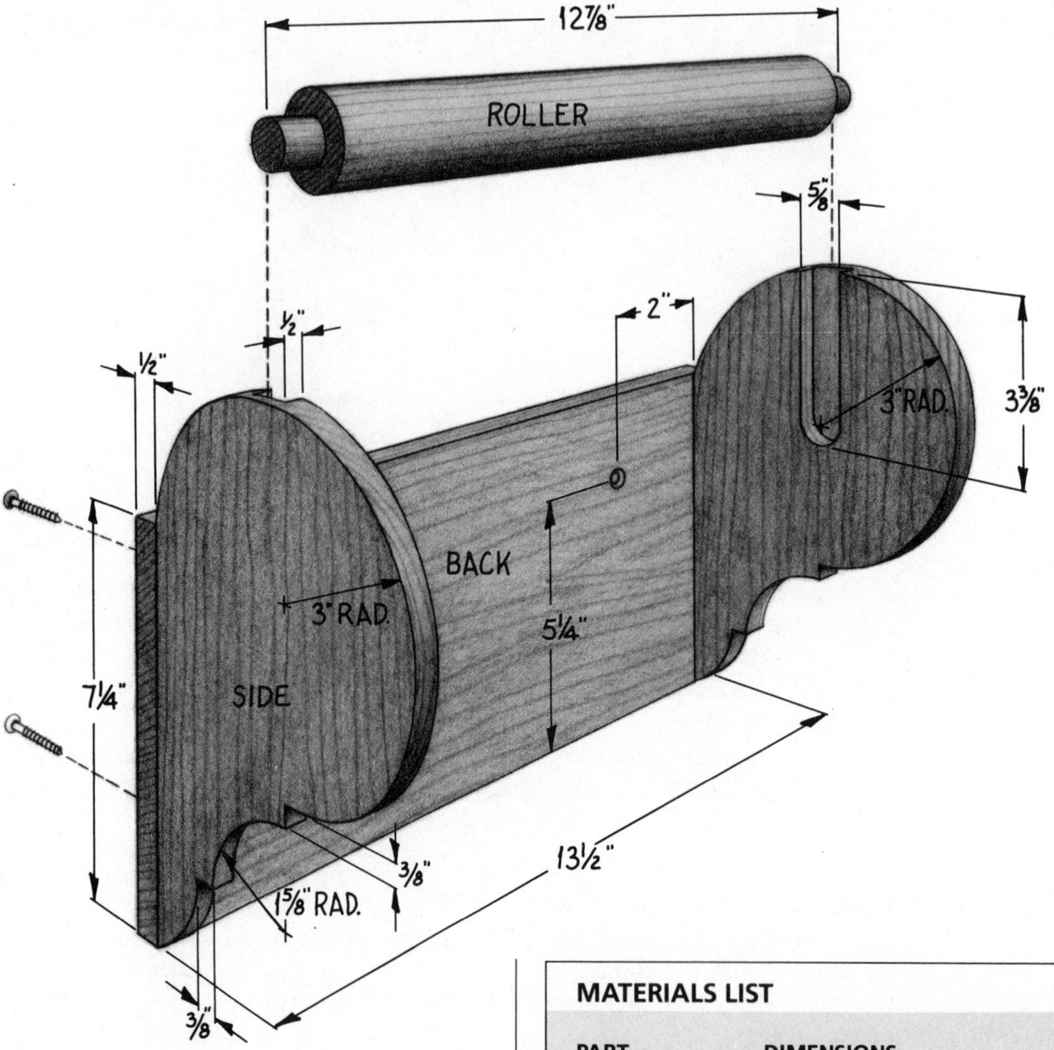
12⅞"
ROLLER
⅝"
2"
½"
½"
3" RAD.
3⅜"
BACK
3" RAD.
5¼"
7¼"
SIDE
13½"
⅜"
1⅝" RAD.
⅜"

most continuous towel holders. The maker chose to match the roller's side profile to a molding that was first developed by the classical Greeks and known as an astragal-and-cavetto. Later, the profile was used by the Romans. It was again discovered during the

MATERIALS LIST

PART	DIMENSIONS
Roller stock	1¼" × 1¼" × 13⅞"
Sides (2)	¾" × 6" × 10"
Back	½" × 7¼" × 13½"

HARDWARE AND SUPPLIES

#8 × 1¼" drywall screws (6)

Renaissance and has continued in use through all succeeding architectural styles.

To make the original into a paper towel roller, I merely doubled the size of the sides and cut the roller's diameter in half. Except for the size changes, the roller is a faithful copy, including the slots that allow the roller to be lifted out of the ends.

The original towel roller was made of maple and painted white. Because my adaptation has larger sides that are more visible, I made my roller of cherry, which I finished with linseed oil.

MAKE AND ASSEMBLE THE PARTS.

1. Prepare the materials. Joint, thickness plane, rip, and cut the side and back stock to the dimensions given in the Materials List. Hand plane the sides and back to remove the machine marks.

2. Make the sides. Lay out the side shape on the side stock with a ruler and compass, using the dimensions shown in the *Construction Overview.* Lay out the bottom curve so it pleases your eye.

While the stock is still a rectangle, lay out and rout the roller grooves. Put a ⅝-inch-diameter straight bit in a table-mounted router and raise the bit to ½ inch. Guide the end stock against a fence as you rout each groove.

When the grooves have been routed, cut the ends to shape with a band saw or coping saw. Clean up the sawed edges with a spokeshave, file, or sandpaper.

3. Drill the mounting holes in the back. Drill and countersink two ⅛-inch mounting holes for #8 drywall screws, as shown in the *Construction Overview.*

4. Make the roller. You have the choice of buying a birch dowel for your roller (available from The Woodworkers' Store, 21801 Industrial Boulevard, Rogers, MN 55374; part #20800) or turning your roller on the lathe.

If you decide to purchase a 1¼-inch-diameter dowel, you will still need to tenon the ends. First, put a ¾-inch-wide dado blade in your table saw and raise it ⅜ inch above the saw table. When the dado blade has been set up, clamp a stop block on the rip fence to gauge the tenon length. The stop block should be positioned ¾ inch from the far side of the dado blade. Next, hold the dowel firmly against a miter gauge set at 90 degrees and butt the

ROLLER TENON DETAIL

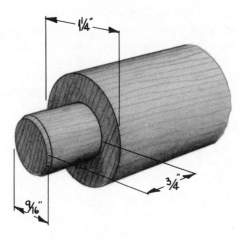

Photo 1: To cut tenons in the dowel stock, hold the dowel firmly against the miter gauge and pass it over the blade. Make several more passes over the blade, each time rotating the dowel slightly.

dowel's end against the stop block. To cut the tenon, slowly push the dowel into the blade with the miter gauge. When the first cut has been made, rotate the dowel slightly and make a second pass (*Photo 1*). Continue rotating the dowel with each pass until a cylindrical tenon has been formed. Cut the second tenon in the same way.

If you decide to turn the roller, secure the roller stock between centers on the lathe and turn it round to a 1⅜-inch diameter with a gouge. Next, smooth the stock while you reduce the diameter to 1¼ inches with a skew (*Photo 2*). Lay out the position of the tenons on the ends of the stock, as shown in the *Roller Tenon Detail*, by holding a pencil against the spinning stock. Define the steps between the roller body and tenons by pushing a parting tool into the stock just to the outside of the tenon layout lines (*Photo 3*). The diameter of the tenon should be ⁹⁄₁₆ inch, as shown in the *Roller Tenon Detail*. Finish shaping the tenon with a small spindle gouge.

Photo 2: Smooth the roller by planing the spinning stock with a skew. Hold the skew against the stock, as shown, and slowly raise the handle until a thin shaving begins to spin off the stock.

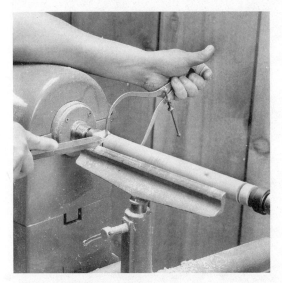

Photo 3: Push the parting tool into the stock just to the outside of the tenon layout lines. Continually check the diameter at the base of the tenon and stop cutting when a $\frac{9}{16}$-inch diameter has been achieved.

5. Assemble the towel roller. Attach the back to the sides with #8 × 1¼-inch drywall screws. Drill and countersink holes for the screws approximately where shown in the *Construction Overview.* Screw the back to the sides and finish sand the towel roller.

After the finish has been applied, mount the towel roller on the wall by driving screws through the mounting holes, then slip the roller in place.

CORNER SHELF

This corner shelf is a quintessential country accent. Much of the charm of country woodwork resulted from naive attempts to imitate the work done in cities, but sometimes the country design is total whimsy. That is the case here. This shelf's outline relates to no other shape with which I am familiar. It was certainly created out of its maker's mind. In fact, I suspect the woodworker drew the pattern freehand, adapting the curves and shapes to accommodate the shelf's placement.

It is interesting that the design — as flamboyant and incoherent as it is — works visually. It is thoroughly charming.

The shelf is also useful. Like other shelves in this book, its purpose was to display a few small objects that were precious to its owner, and it makes use of the wasted space created by the intersection of two walls.

I made my copy of pine and painted it with pumpkin-colored milk paint.

MAKE THE PARTS.

1. Prepare the materials. Buy ½-inch-thick surfaced pine at the local lumberyard, or joint and thickness plane rough-sawn stock. Rip and cut the parts to the sizes given in the Materials List and hand plane the parts to remove any machine marks.

CONSTRUCTION OVERVIEW

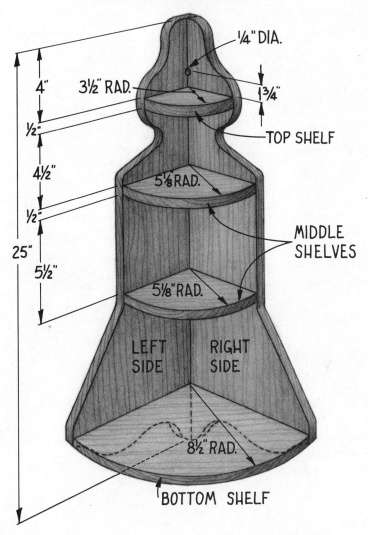

2. Cut the sides to shape. Make a grid of 1-inch squares on a large piece of posterboard and draw the side shape on it, as shown in the *Side Pattern*. Cut the pattern from the posterboard and transfer it onto the stock. When you are transferring the pattern to the stock, remember that the left side is ½ inch wider than the right side and position the pattern accordingly.

Cut the sides to shape with a band saw or bow saw and clean up the sawed edges with a spokeshave, file, and sandpaper.

MATERIALS LIST

PART	DIMENSIONS
Right side	½″ × 8½″ × 25″
Left side	½″ × 9″ × 25″
Bottom shelf	½″ × 8½″ × 8½″
Middle shelves (2)	½″ × 5⅛″ × 5⅛″
Top shelf	½″ × 3½″ × 3½″

HARDWARE AND SUPPLIES

1″ brads (as needed)

SIDE PATTERN

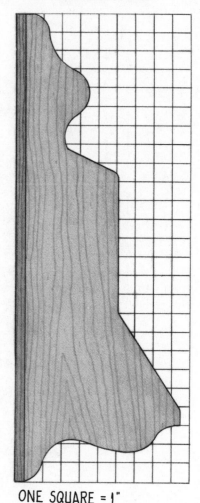

ONE SQUARE = 1″

3. Cut the radii in the shelves. Lay out the radius of each shelf, as shown in the *Construction Overview,* with a compass or a pair of dividers. Cut the shelves to shape with a band saw or bow saw and clean up the sawed edges with a spokeshave and sandpaper.

ASSEMBLE THE SHELF.

1. Join the sides. Grip the narrow right side board in a vise and lay the wider side on it so it overlaps the right side's back edge and forms a right angle, as shown in the *Construction Overview.* Drive 1-inch brads through the wider left side and into the right side to join the parts.

TECHNIQUE TIP

Joint the back edge of the narrow right side before you nail the parts together. The jointed edge should keep the shelf square. Even if the sides are slightly out of square, they will be brought into place when the shelves are added.

2. Attach the shelves. Lay out the position of each shelf, as shown in the *Construction Overview.* Put the bottom shelf in place and secure it with one 1-inch brad. Square the shelf's surface to the side with a try square, then add several more brads to secure it in place.

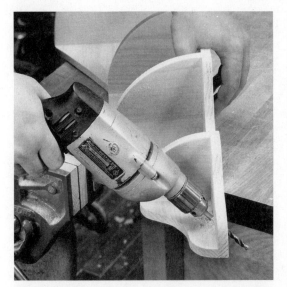

Photo 1: Drill a ¼-inch-diameter mounting hole through the corner of the shelf. Position the hole 1¾ inches above the top shelf.

When the first shelf is in place, position the remaining shelves and secure them in place with brads.

3. Drill the mounting hole. Lay the shelf on the corner formed by its two sides and drill a ¼-inch-diameter mounting hole through the corner 1¾ inches above the top shelf (*Photo 1*).

KIDS'
STUFF

SPINNING TOP

Tops are among the most ancient toys known, and they continue to amuse children today. The original of the top shown here was made long ago for a child by some unknown country woodworker. All I can say about that woodworker is that he had a lathe and he loved that child.

This top is more sophisticated than many. Most tops are set spinning by wrapping a plain string directly around the body; in this case, the string is wrapped around a long stem that fits into a special holder. The string also has a turned handle that provides a better grip.

To use the top, you wind the string around the stem where it is exposed within the open holder. Then you hold the top an inch or so above the floor and give the string a determined pull. When the string has been pulled free, the top falls out of the handle and starts twirling.

The top stands on its point as it spins and creates considerable friction, so it has to be made of a dense hardwood that will hold up over the years. The original is maple, but any hardwood—native or exotic—of equal hardness will do. The other parts are also made of maple, but you could use contrasting woods if you prefer.

STRING HANDLE TURNING LAYOUT

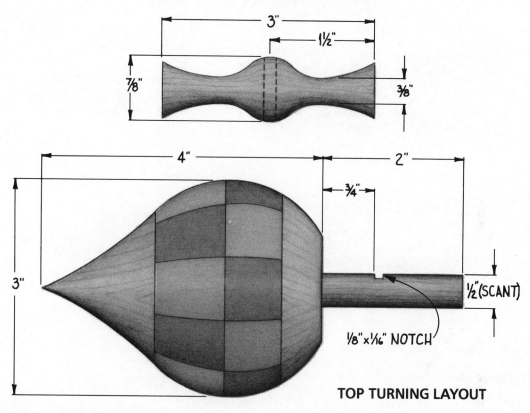

TOP TURNING LAYOUT

MATERIALS LIST

PART	DIMENSIONS
Top stock	3¼″ × 3¼″ × 6½″
String handle stock	1″ × 1″ × 3½″
Holder stock	1½″ × 1½″ × 9½″

HARDWARE AND SUPPLIES

36″ length cotton twine

The top is decorated with a band of red and green painted squares laid out in a grid two rows deep. As the top spins, these squares flash by, creating an effect that the eyes find dazzling. The country woodworker who made the top had a steadier hand when turning than when painting. His squares do not all have straight edges. In fact, some look more like spots than squares, giving the top a charming, primitive appearance. I am sure the child who owned the top never noticed.

You can use colors other than red and green, but they should be bright colors and have an equally strong contrast so they flash as the top spins. Use child-safe enamel, and apply it with a fine artist's paintbrush. If you doubt the steadiness of your hand, the top can be decorated with simple horizontal bands rather than squares.

HOLDER TURNING LAYOUT

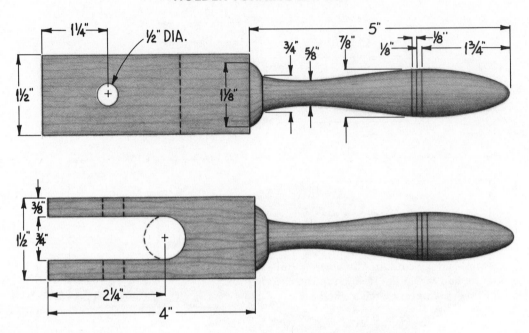

MAKE THE PARTS.

1. Prepare the materials. Rip and cut the turning blanks for the top, holder, and string handle to the dimensions given in the Materials List. Each piece has an extra ½ inch added to the length for waste. If necessary, glue up stock for the body turning blank. Locate the center on each end of the turning blanks by drawing an X diagonally across the corners.

2. Turn the top. First, turn the blank round to the largest diameter of the top with a gouge (*Photo 1*).

SAFETY TIP

Always make sure that the blank will miss the tool rest by turning it one revolution by hand before you turn on the lathe.

Photo 1: Turn the top blank round with a gouge.

Photo 2: Make a deep cut with the parting tool to divide the body from the stem. Stop the cut when the stem diameter equals ½ inch.

Next, lay out and divide the stem of the top from the body with a parting tool. Push the parting tool into the wood until it reaches the ½-inch diameter of the stem (*Photo 2*).

Photo 3: Plane the body smooth with the skew.

When the division has been made, begin shaping the body of the top with a ½-inch gouge. When the shape of the body is approaching that shown in the *Top Turning Layout*, switch to the skew and carefully plane the body smooth (*Photo 3*).

When the body has taken shape, turn the stem down to a scant ½-inch diameter. The stem must pass easily through the ½-inch-diameter hole in the holder.

Sand the stem smooth. File a string notch in the handle where indicated in the *Top Turning Layout*.

SAFETY TIP

Always wear safety glasses when you are using the lathe. The high-velocity chips produced in turning are not very friendly to unprotected eyes.

---

3. Lay out the painting grid. The grid for the painted squares can be laid out with a center locator while the top is still on the lathe. A center locator is an easy-to-make jig that works in conjunction with your lathe's index head. It has two parts—a flat base that slides on the lathe's bed and an adjustable upright that holds a pencil. For center locator building directions, see "Lathe Center Scribe" on page 27.

Set the base of the center locator on the lathe bed and adjust the pencil height so it is even with the lathe centers. Lock your lathe's index head in place and run the pencil along the top's body. The pencil will draw a center-line along the surface. Move the index head in even increments and draw coinciding pencil lines that divide the turning into even horizontal segments (*Photo 4*). The original top had eight roughly equal segments.

To divide the turning vertically, as shown in the *Top Turning Layout*, walk off even increments (1¾ to 2 inches) along one of the horizontal lines with a compass. Hold the pencil point against the top at one of the marks and rotate it by hand to produce the vertical lines. The original top's grid was divided into two horizontal bands, as shown in the *Top Turning Layout*.

Remove the top from the lathe and remove any waste.

4. Make the string handle. Put the string handle blank on the lathe and turn it round with a gouge. Turn the string handle to the profile shown in the *String Handle Turning Layout* with a ½-inch gouge and sand it smooth. Make a light vertical layout line centered on the handle's length with a skew.

Remove the string handle from the lathe, cut off the waste, and drill a ³⁄₁₆-inch string hole through the string handle on the vertical layout line.

Pass the cotton twine through the string hole and knot both ends.

Photo 5: Make two side-by-side parting cuts on the handle side of the scribe line. Stop the cut when the diameter equals 1⅛ inches.

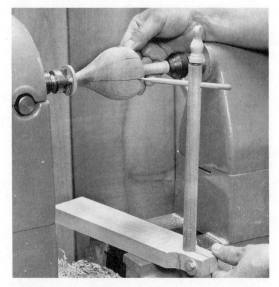

Photo 4: Guide the center locator along the lathe bed to lay out the horizontal segments.

5. Turn the holder. The holder is divided into two sections—the head and the handle. Only the handle is turned. Scribe a deep line around the holder blank that indicates where the handle begins. Guide a utility knife against a square to scribe the line.

Put the holder blank between centers on the lathe and turn on the lathe. Divide the handle from the head with two side-by-side parting tool cuts (*Photo 5*). Push the parting tool into the wood until the outside diameter of the handle's base has been reached. Check the diameter with calipers.

When the parting tool cuts have been made, turn the handle round with a gouge, then turn it to the shape shown in the *Holder Turning Layout* with a ½-inch gouge and a skew. Make the decorative rings on the handle with the edge of the skew (*Photo 6*).

Sand the handle smooth.

Press firmly on the utility knife so that the surface fibers are severed as you scribe the line that separates the head from the handle. If the fibers are not severed, the wood grain may tear as you make the cuts with the parting tool.

6. Drill the stem hole and cut the holder slot. Drill a ½-inch hole for the top's stem, as shown in the *Holder Turning Layout.*

Create the slot in the holder by first drilling a ¾-inch hole, as shown in the *Holder Slot Detail.* Then, set a marking gauge to ⅜ inch and scribe layout lines on the holder that meet the edges of the hole. Cut along the scribe lines with a band saw or a fine-tooth backsaw and remove the waste. File away any saw marks from the slot.

Photo 6: Lightly press the heel of the skew straight against the holder handle to make the decorative rings.

NOISEMAKER

This device has no name of which I am aware. Since its sole purpose is to make noise, I have dubbed it a noisemaker. I am sure that long ago it gave vent to some youngster's need to make noise. The original was crudely painted in red, white, and blue—most likely for use on the Fourth of July.

The noisemaker is a simple, two-sided box that holds a hardwood tongue. The box's end is weighted to add some momentum as you swing it 'round and 'round on the handle. As the box swings, the tongue strikes against the teeth of a wooden gear. This results in a loud cracking sound as each tooth on the gear bends and releases the tongue in rapid succession.

The original noisemaker was very primitive, and its handle was whittled rather than turned. Since I enjoy wood turning, I could not resist the urge to improve my copy by turning the handle. I patterned the handle on the holder for the Spinning Top on page 270. If you do not have a lathe, or if you choose to more closely emulate the original, you can whittle the handle.

The gear teeth on the original noisemaker were cut freehand using a dovetail saw. No effort was made to lay them out evenly or to make them uniform. I very much like the spontaneity of the original gear, so I duplicated this feeling in mine.

CONSTRUCTION OVERVIEW

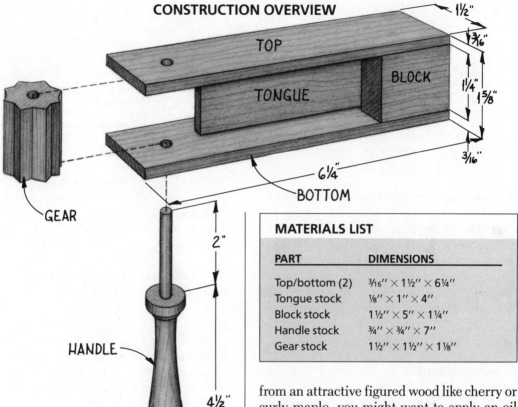

MATERIALS LIST

PART	DIMENSIONS
Top/bottom (2)	³⁄₁₆″ × 1½″ × 6¼″
Tongue stock	⅛″ × 1″ × 4″
Block stock	1½″ × 5″ × 1¼″
Handle stock	¾″ × ¾″ × 7″
Gear stock	1½″ × 1½″ × 1⅛″

from an attractive figured wood like cherry or curly maple, you might want to apply an oil finish, too, but your noisemaker, like the original, could also be decorated with the colors of the flag.

MAKE THE PARTS.

1. Make the top, bottom, and tongue. Rip the top, bottom, and tongue stock to the widths and thicknesses given in the Materials List. Cut the top and bottom to length. Hand plane or sand the stock to remove the saw marks.

2. Drill the stem holes. Clamp the top and bottom together and lay out the ⁵⁄₁₆-inch-diameter stem hole where indicated in the *Top View.* Drill the hole through the top and bottom at the same time on the drill press.

The original noisemaker was made entirely of maple. I made mine with a maple handle, but I made the rest out of cherry. You should use some similar even-grained hardwoods. Like some other small projects in this book, this one is a good chance to use up some scrap. I finished my noisemaker with oil to show off the nicely grained cherry. If you make yours

TOP VIEW
(TOP REMOVED)

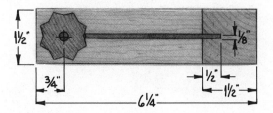

3. Make the tongue slot and cut the block to size. Because it would be unsafe to cut the tongue slot in the small block on the table saw, cut the block to its final size after the slot has been cut. Cut the slot in the block stock with a standard ⅛-inch-wide table saw blade. Guide the stock against the rip fence as you cut the ½-inch-deep slot, as shown in the *Top View*.

When the tongue slot has been cut, cut the block to its final width of 1¼ inches.

4. Make the handle. You can either whittle or lathe turn the handle. If you choose to whittle the handle, simply cut and file it to approximate the shape shown in the *Handle Profile*. Pay special attention while filing the stem at the top of the handle to a ⁵⁄₁₆-inch diameter.

If you choose to turn the handle, rip and cut the turning blank for the handle to the

dimensions given in the Materials List. Put the handle blank in the lathe and turn it to a ¾-inch diameter with a gouge. Turn the handle to the profile shown in the *Handle Profile* with a spindle gouge and skew. Be especially careful when turning the fragile ⁵⁄₁₆-inch-diameter stem.

5. Cut the gear teeth. First, cut the gear stock to the dimensions given in the Materials List, then find the center on the top of the gear stock by drawing an X diagonally across the corners. Drill a ⁵⁄₁₆-inch hole through the center of the gear stock on the drill press.

Next, cut off the corners of the gear stock with a dovetail saw or backsaw to produce a rough octagon (*Photo 1*).

When the octagon has been cut, lay out the teeth on the top of the gear stock with a pencil. The exact angle of the teeth is not crucial. Simply try to approximate the gear shape shown in the *Top View*.

HANDLE PROFILE

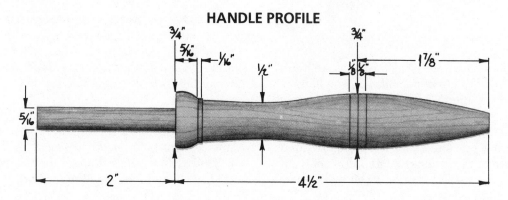

When the teeth have been laid out, clamp the gear stock in a vise and cut the waste from between the teeth with a dovetail saw (*Photo 2*). Sand the gear.

ASSEMBLE THE PARTS.

1. Attach the tongue to the block. Glue the tongue into the tongue slot in the block. If necessary, reduce the tongue's thickness with a block plane until it fits in the slot. Center the tongue in the slot between the edges of the block.

2. Attach the gear to the handle. First, pass the handle stem through the hole in the noisemaker's bottom. Next, spread glue in the gear

Photo 1: Cut away the corners of the gear stock with a dovetail saw to produce an octagon.

Photo 2: Clamp the gear stock in a vise and cut the teeth to shape.

hole and slide the gear over the handle stem, as shown in the *Construction Overview*. Wipe off any excess glue with a damp cloth.

3. Attach the top and bottom to the block. Pass the handle stem through the hole in the noisemaker's top. The handle stem will protrude slightly above the top. Glue and clamp the block between the top and bottom, as shown in the *Construction Overview*, and allow the glue to dry.

When the glue is dry, apply the finish and go make some noise.

TOY HORSE

I found a toy horse like the one shown here in an antique shop. Judging from wear, it had experienced the play of many children—perhaps several generations worth. Perhaps this horse would be suitable for a child in your life, or for use in a doll collection.

I was attracted to this horse because of the clever solution its maker devised for joining the head and front legs so they could pivot as a unit. He used a double-threaded pipe nipple, available at any plumbing supply store and most hardware stores. Such a simple, innovative solution is typical of country work.

The horse's body can be made from a softwood like pine, but the wheels should be made of hardwood that will resist wear. The horse can be given a natural finish, but I think it's most appropriate to paint it to resemble a real horse. Do not be daunted by this task. The little people who use the horse will not demand perfection. In fact, an amateur paint job will enhance the toy's primitive look.

Paint the horse a base color and, to imitate a breed or particular type of horse, paint a colored pattern over the base color. For example, random spots will imitate a dappled horse, while large solid spots will make it look more like a pinto. Also paint in such details as the eyes, mouth, bridle, reins, and so on.

Remove the wheels for finishing. The wheels will receive a lot of wear, so oil (like Watco Danish Oil), which can occasionally be

CONSTRUCTION OVERVIEW

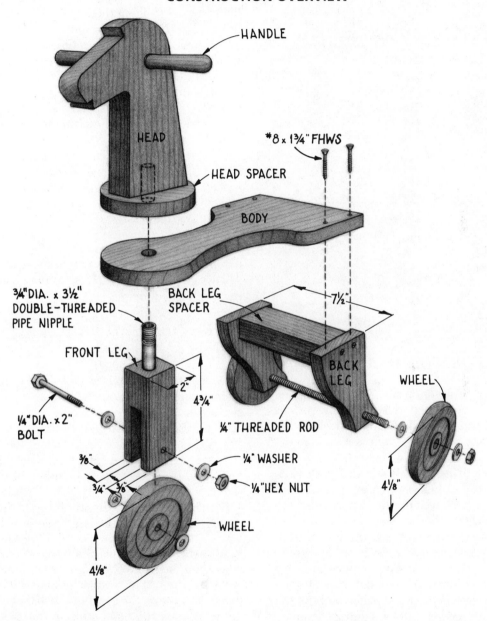

HANDLE

HEAD

HEAD SPACER

#8 x 1¾" FHWS

BODY

¾"DIA. x 3½"
DOUBLE-THREADED
PIPE NIPPLE

BACK LEG
SPACER

7½"

FRONT LEG

2"

4¾"

¼"DIA. x 2"
BOLT

BACK
LEG

WHEEL

¼" THREADED ROD

⅜"

¾"   ⅜"

¼" WASHER

¼"HEX NUT

4⅛"

WHEEL

4⅛"

renewed, is the best finish for them. When the finish is dry, mount the wheels for the final time. Flatten and spread the ends of the threaded rod and bolt with a ball-peen hammer so that there are no sharp edges to scratch tiny legs and so the nuts cannot come loose.

MATERIALS LIST

PART	DIMENSIONS
Head	1½″ × 6½″ × 10″
Body	¾″ × 7½″ × 16″
Back legs (2)	¾″ × 5¼″ × 4¾″
Front leg	1½″ × 2″ × 4¾″
Head spacer	¾″ × 5⅜″ × 5⅜″
Wheels (3)	½″ × 4⅛″ × 4⅛″
Handle	¾″ dia. × 7½″
Back leg spacer	1½″ × 2¼″ × 6″

HARDWARE AND SUPPLIES

#8 × 1¾″ flathead wood screws (12)

½″ I.D. double-threaded pipe nipple

¼″ dia. × 2″ bolt (1)

¼″ hex nuts (3)

¼″ washers (6)

¼″ dia. × 9⅜″ threaded rod (1)

4d finishing nail (1)

MAKE THE BODY PARTS.

1. Prepare the materials. Thickness plane, joint, and cut the materials to the dimensions given in the Materials List. Hand plane the parts to remove any machine marks.

2. Cut out the head, body, and back legs. Make a grid of ½-inch squares on a piece of posterboard. Lay out the patterns for the head, body, and back legs on the grid, as shown in the *Patterns.* Cut the patterns from the posterboard, then trace the shapes onto their respective stock. Cut the parts to shape with a band saw or bow saw. Smooth the straight edges with a hand plane, and smooth the curved edges with a sanding drum, a spokeshave, or a rasp and sandpaper. Drill the holes where indicated in the head, body, and back legs.

3. Shape the front leg. First, drill a ¼-inch-diameter axle hole in the front leg, as shown in the *Construction Overview.*

When the axle hole has been drilled, cut ⅛-inch chamfers in the edges of the stock, as shown in the *Construction Overview.* Use a chamfer bit in a table-mounted router. While you have this setup available, also chamfer the back leg spacer, as shown in the *Construction Overview.*

Next, cut the wheel notch in the front leg with a band saw, as shown in the *Construction Overview.* Clamp a fence to the band saw table to ensure straight cuts. Remove the fence and cut out the waste.

4. Shape the head. Make the head more life-like by relieving its edges with a spokeshave. Always cut with the grain. Sand the head to remove any tool marks.

MAKE THE HEAD SPACER, WHEELS, AND HANDLE.

1. Make the head spacer. Cut the 5⅜-inch-diameter head spacer on the drill press with a circle cutter (available from The Woodworkers' Store, 21801 Industrial Boulevard, Rogers, MN 55374; part #42887), or lay out the circle with a compass and cut it out on the band saw. Sand the edge smooth on a belt or disk sander.

Drill a $^{13}/_{16}$-inch-diameter pivot hole through the center of the head spacer.

2. Make the wheels. Cut the 4⅛-inch-diameter wheels on the drill press with a circle cutter, or lay out the wheels with a compass and cut them carefully on the band saw. If you cut out the wheels on the band saw, drill a ¼-inch-diameter axle hole on the mark left by the point of the compass. A circle cutter automatically drills an axle hole.

PATTERNS

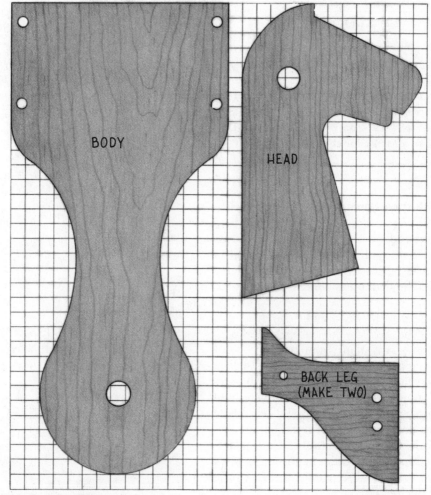

BODY

HEAD

BACK LEG
(MAKE TWO)

ONE SQUARE = ½"

Round-over the edges of the wheels, as shown in the *Construction Overview,* with either a sanding disk in a table saw or a stationary belt sander.

3. Shape the handle. If you prefer, you can leave the handle dowel plain, but I think shaping the dowel gives the horse a more finished appearance. Clamp the handle dowel in a vise, and file and sand contours in the handle that roughly match those shown in the *Con-*

struction Overview. You could also turn the handle to shape on a lathe.

ASSEMBLE THE HORSE.

1. Assemble the head and head spacer. Put the head upside down in a vise, and center the head spacer on it. Screw the head spacer to the head with two #8 × 1¾-inch flathead wood screws.

CONSTRUCTION TIP

If you plan to give your horse a clear oil finish, consider accenting the handle by making it from a walnut or cherry ¾-inch-diameter dowel (available from The Woodworkers' Store, 21801 Industrial Boulevard, Rogers, MN 55374; part #21030 for walnut, and part #21097 for cherry).

Photo 1: Assemble the support stand as shown above, and place the head and head spacer assembly upside down in it.

2. Drill the pivot holes in the head and front leg. Drill a ¾-inch-diameter × 1⅛-inch-deep hole centered on the top of the front leg. Drill the hole with a ¾-inch-diameter bit in a drill press. Rest the base of the front leg firmly on the drill press table as you drill the hole.

To steady the head and head spacer as you drill the hole in the base of the head, make a support stand from two ¾ × 5 × 10-inch uprights and a ¾ × 1½ × 5-inch spacer. Nail the spacer between the uprights to create the support stand, and put the head and head spacer assembly upside down in it (*Photo 1*). Place the support stand and head assembly on the drill press table. Center the ¾-inch-diameter bit in the head spacer pivot hole and drill the 1⅛-inch-deep hole in the base of the head.

3. Assemble the head and front leg. The head is attached to the front leg with a double-threaded ½-inch I.D. pipe nipple.

First, put the head upside down in a vise and screw the pipe nipple into the hole in the base of the head with a pair of vise grips. As the pipe nipple's threads bite into the soft wood of the head, try to keep the pipe nipple as straight as possible.

Next, put the body's pivot hole over the pipe nipple, and carefully turn the front leg

onto the pipe nipple (*Photo 2*). Once again, make sure the nipple enters the hole as straight as possible. Align the front leg with the head,

Photo 2: Pass the pipe nipple through the head spacer and screw it into the head, then put the body in place. Finally, screw the front leg in place to complete the assembly.

and leave enough play so that the head and front leg can turn easily.

CONSTRUCTION TIP

To ensure that the pipe nipple holds firmly in the head and front leg, pour some epoxy into the pipe nipple before you screw the front leg in place. Once the front leg is screwed on, turn the horse over a few times to spread the epoxy evenly in the hole.

4. Attach the back legs and spacer. Screw the back legs and back leg spacer to the underside of the body with #8 × 1¾-inch flathead wood screws, as shown in the *Construction Overview*.

5. Mount the wheels. Bolt the front wheel into the front leg. Place a washer on each side of the wheel, one under the nut, and one under the head of the bolt.

Cut the threaded rod to length and insert it through the holes in the back legs. Place a washer on each side of each wheel and turn the nuts onto the threaded rod.

Flatten and spread the ends of the threaded rod with a ball-peen hammer.

6. Mount the handle. Insert the handle into the hole in the head. Secure it in place by driving a 4d finishing nail through the back of the head. Countersink the nail.

Fill the nail hole with wood filler. Allow the filler to dry and sand it smooth. Sand the entire horse.

DOLL CRADLE

Little children have been playing with dolls since time immemorial, and for just as long, parents and grandparents have been making doll clothes and doll furniture. Some time during the mid-1800s, a country woodworker designed and built this little cradle for his child or grandchild. Surely your child would be delighted, as I'm sure that country woodworker's child was, to receive a copy of it.

There were lots of doll cradles made in rural America, and many of them have survived. This one is a very typical example: It has a simple shape, it is made of pine, and it is decorated with paint. It is atypical in that it is larger than most I've found. Old-fashioned dolls tended to be much smaller than most today, and the cradles were made to match. This cradle, however, makes a great resting place for large dolls and for stuffed animals.

As with other projects in this book that were originally intended for children, the cradle can be made for someone who just wants to create a "lived-in" country decor. It also can be made for someone who collects dolls.

This pine cradle is sponge painted. First, a base color of light blue was laid down with a brush. Then, after the base coat was dry, a darker blue was dappled on with a sponge. When the second color was dry, white paint was dappled on.

CONSTRUCTION OVERVIEW

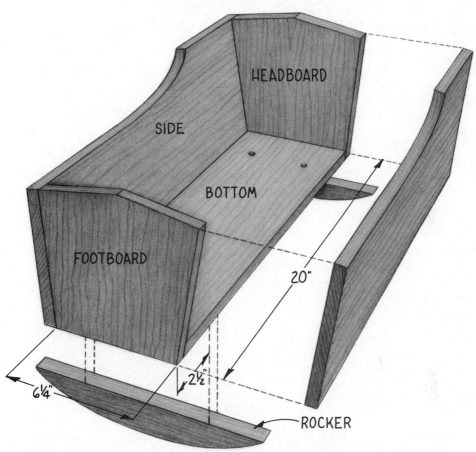

HEADBOARD

SIDE

BOTTOM

FOOTBOARD

20"

2½"

6¼"

ROCKER

MAKE THE PARTS.

1. Prepare the stock. Joint and thickness plane the stock to ¾ inch. Hand plane the surfaces to remove any machine marks.

2. Make the bottom. First, cut the stock to the length given in the Materials List.

Next, bevel the edges of the bottom as you rip it to width. Tilt your table saw's arbor to 10 degrees and rip one edge. Guide the stock against the fence as you make the cut. When the first edge has been beveled, bevel

the second edge as you rip the bottom to a width of 6½ inches. Orient the bevels as shown in the *End View.*

When the edges have been beveled, pre-drill and countersink pilot holes for the screws that attach the bottom to the rockers. Position the holes where shown in the *End View* and the *Construction Overview,* and size each hole to accommodate a #6 × 1½″ flathead wood screw.

3. Make the sides. Cut the stock to the length given in the Materials List. Tilt your table saw blade to 10 degrees and bevel the bottom

MATERIALS LIST

PART	DIMENSIONS
Bottom stock	¾" × 7" × 18½"
Sides (2)	¾" × 8¹⁄₁₆" × 20"
Headboard stock	¾" × 10" × 8¾"
Footboard stock	¾" × 9" × 6⅞"
Rocker stock (2)	¾" × 1¾" × 12½"

HARDWARE AND SUPPLIES

1½" finishing nails (as needed)
#6 × 1½" flathead wood screws (4)

edge of each side. Make a grid of ½-inch squares on a piece of posterboard and draw the side shape on it, as shown in the *Side Pattern*. Cut the shape out and trace it onto the sides. Shape the sides on the band saw and smooth the sawed edges with a spokeshave and sandpaper.

4. **Make the headboard and footboard.** Cut the stock to the dimensions given in the Materials List and lay out the angles on the stock, as shown in the *End View*.

First, set your table saw's miter gauge at 80 degrees and cut the angled ends. Next, cut the peaked side. Set the miter gauge at 90 degrees and place the angled ends against it as you cut along the layout lines.

CONSTRUCTION TIP

If either the headboard or footboard does not fit perfectly, trim it on a disk sander or with a block plane on a shooting board.

---

5. **Make the rockers.** Lay out the 13½-inch-radius curved edges with a pair of dividers (*Photo 1*). Cut the rockers to shape on the band saw and clean up the sawed surfaces with a spokeshave and sandpaper. Round the ends with a belt sander or spokeshave.

END VIEW

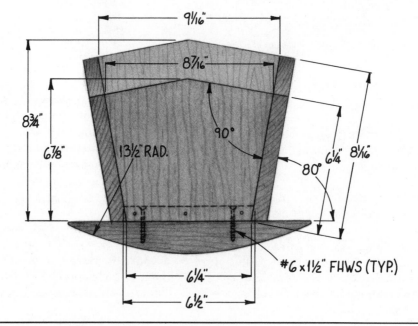

SIDE PATTERN

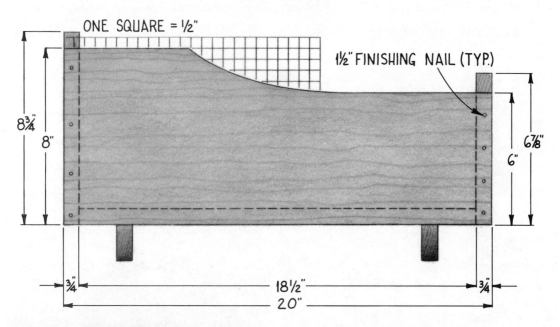

ONE SQUARE = 1/2"

1/2" FINISHING NAIL (TYP.)

8 3/4"

8"

6 7/8"

6"

3/4"

18 1/2"

20"

3/4"

Photo 1: Clamp the rocker stock to your bench and, with the help of a square, measure back 13½ inches from the front center of the stock. From that point, swing a pair of dividers to lay out the 13½-inch-radius rocker curve.

ASSEMBLE THE CRADLE.

1. Nail together the sides and ends. Secure the sides to the bottom with 1½-inch finishing nails. One at a time, fit the headboard and footboard between the sides and nail them to the sides and bottom.

2. Attach the rockers. Position the rockers under the bottom, as shown in the *End View* and the *Construction Overview.* Pass #6 × 1½-inch screws through the holes in the bottom and drive them into the rockers.

SAFETY TIP
To make the doll cradle more child-safe, lightly round all the square edges and corners with sandpaper. A child could easily be scratched by sharp corners.

CHILD'S HUTCH TABLE

Country woodworkers often made toys for their children, and, like those we buy or make for our children today, early toys were often miniature copies of objects used by adults. This child's hutch table (also called a chair table) is a good example.

Rural households were large and crowded. To make the best use of limited space, much early rural furniture could be collapsed to take up less space, or it could be altered to serve more than one purpose. Most of the time, an adult-size hutch table was placed against a wall with its top up. In this position it served as a chair. When a flat surface was needed for eating, working, or writing, the

top was pushed down into a horizontal position. The child's hutch table will do exactly the same for a little person. When a child needs a surface for coloring or eating milk and cookies, the top is easily lowered. When the top is raised, the hutch table can be placed against a wall to provide miniature seating. The hutch table, when used as a chair, is also a good place to display special dolls or stuffed animals.

The original piece was made completely of pine, with the exception of the maple hinge pins. The hinge pins can be turned or whittled. The original hutch table was painted red. When making my copy, I used the same wood and finished it the same way. Note that the

CONSTRUCTION OVERVIEW

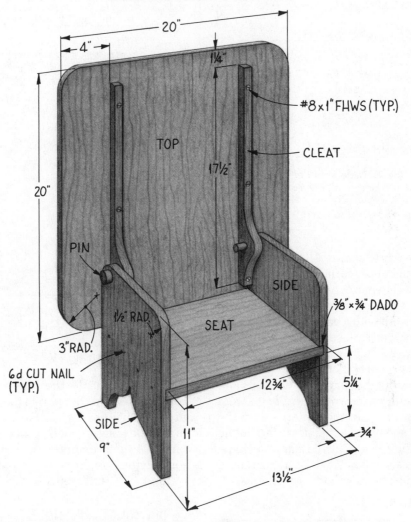

20"

4"

1¼"

#8×1"FHWS (TYP.)

TOP

CLEAT

17½"

20"

PIN

SIDE

⅜"×¾" DADO

1½" RAD.

SEAT

3" RAD.

6d CUT NAIL
(TYP.)

12¾"

5¼"

SIDE

11"

¾"

9"

13½"

---

edges and the top's corners are all rounded to help avoid injury.

Notice that the top is not centered on the base, but is offset in the direction opposite the pins. When the child uses the table, make sure he or she sits on the extended side. Not only will the extended side provide more leg room, but the top will not lift when this side is leaned on.

MAKE THE PARTS.

1. Prepare the stock. If necessary, joint and thickness plane all the stock (except the pin stock) to ¾ inch. Glue up enough stock to make a 20-inch square top. Cut and rip the stock to the dimensions given in the Materials List. Hand plane all surfaces to remove machine marks and glue spills.

MATERIALS LIST

PART	DIMENSIONS
Top	¾″ × 20″ × 20″
Cleats (2)	¾″ × 1¾″ × 17½″
Sides (2)	¾″ × 9″ × 11″
Pin stock (2)	1″ × 1″ × 3½″
Seat	¾″ × 9″ × 12¾″

HARDWARE AND SUPPLIES

6d cut nails (8). Available from Tremont Nail Company, 8 Elm Street, P.O. Box 111, Wareham, MA 02571. Part # N-21 Std.
#8 × 1″ flathead wood screws (6)

2. Cut the parts to shape. All four corners of the top and the upper corners on each side are rounded, as shown in the *Construction Overview.* Lay out the corner radii with a compass and cut them out with a band saw or bow saw. Smooth the sawed surfaces with a spokeshave and sandpaper.

Make a grid of ½-inch squares on posterboard and lay out the shapes of the cleats and the side cutout, as shown in the *Cleat Detail* and *Side Pattern.* Cut the patterns from the posterboard and use as templates to lay out the shapes on the stock. Cut the parts to shape with a band saw or bow saw. Use a spokeshave and sandpaper to smooth the sawed edges.

SIDE PATTERN

½″ DIA. HINGE PIN HOLE

1″

1½″ RAD.

1″

ONE SQUARE = ½″

3. Turn or whittle the hinge pins. If you have a lathe, turn the pins to the shape shown in the *Hinge Pin Detail.* First, put the hinge pin stock (long enough to make both hinge pins) between centers on the lathe and turn it round with a gouge. Next, lay out the position of the heads and stems by holding a pencil

CLEAT DETAIL

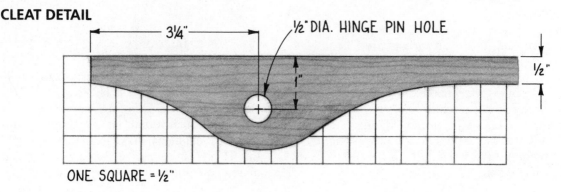

3¼″

½″ DIA. HINGE PIN HOLE

½″

1″

ONE SQUARE = ½″

against the spinning stock.

When the layout lines have been drawn, divide the heads from the stems with a parting tool (*Photo 1*). Be careful not to cut beyond the stems' ½-inch diameter with the parting tool. When the parting tool cuts have been made, shape the stems and heads with a gouge (*Photo 2*).

Finally, sand the hinge pins smooth and remove them from the lathe. Cut off the waste with a dovetail saw.

If you would prefer to whittle the hinge pins, cut the hinge pin stock into two 3½-inch lengths. First, clamp each pin in a vise and round the hinge pins with a spokeshave and file. Next, define the base of the head of each pin by making cuts with a backsaw (*Photo 3*). When the head has been defined, clamp each hinge pin's head in a vise and carefully shave its stem to a ½-inch diameter with a chisel and file (*Photo 4*).

FIT AND ASSEMBLE THE PARTS.

1. Cut the dadoes in the sides. Rout the seat dadoes in the sides with a ¾-inch-diameter

HINGE PIN DETAIL

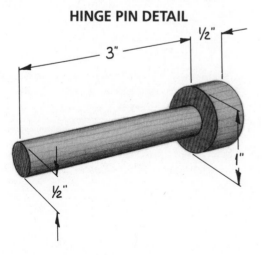

Photo 1: Divide the hinge pin head from the hinge pin stem with a parting tool. Check the stem's diameter with a pair of calipers or a depth gauge on your parting tool. Stop cutting when the stem is ½ inch in diameter.

Photo 2: Gradually shape the head and stem with a spindle gouge. Be careful not to let the gouge catch on the head as you shape the stem.

Photo 3: When whittling hinge pins, lay out and define the base of the head with several shallow backsaw cuts.

Photo 4: With the pin clamped upside down in a vise, carefully pare the stem down to its ½-inch diameter with a sharp chisel.

straight bit, as shown in the *Construction Overview.* Clamp a straightedge to the sides to guide the router as you rout the dadoes.

2. Drill the hinge pin holes and cleat screw holes. Drill ½-inch-diameter holes for the hinge pins in the sides and the cleats, as shown in the *Side Pattern* and *Cleat Detail.*

Drill and countersink each cleat for three #8 × 1-inch flathead wood screws, as shown in the *Construction Overview.*

TECHNIQUE TIP

To save time and ensure accuracy, drill the hinge pin holes in the sides in one operation. Before drilling, clamp the sides together with the dadoes facing in, then drill the hinge pin holes through the clamped sides on the drill press.

The holes in the cleats can be drilled in the same way.

---

3. Nail the sides to the seat. Place the seat ends in their dadoes and nail the joints with 6d cut nails, as shown in the *Construction Overview.* While nailing, square the sides to the seat with a try square.

4. Attach the cleats. Screw the cleats to the top's underside surface, as shown in the *Construction Overview.*

TECHNIQUE TIP

To ensure the cleats are square and parallel, lay out a pair of guide lines with a framing square or a draftsman's T-square.

---

5. Attach the top. Align the cleats' hinge pin holes with those in the sides and insert the pins.

CHILD'S WING CHAIR

Early American homes were drafty because they were heated with stoves and fireplaces, which draw cold air through cracks around doors and windows. In the city, wealthy urban dwellers sat in very expensive upholstered wing chairs that protected them from cold drafts on three sides, while the open front was turned toward the fire. Less affluent rural residents found other ways to protect themselves from the cold. Any chair could be made more comfortable by draping a shawl over its back, but a wooden wing chair with a shawl was almost as good as its more expensive city cousin.

Of course, little ones, too, had to be protected from the cold. A growing family had several times more children than adults, which probably explains why child-size wooden wing chairs like the one shown here are far more common than the adult-size version. Besides being common, most of these child's wing chairs are very boxy and use very basic construction. I chose this one because it is much more imaginative than most I've seen and its construction is more challenging. It has details that I, as a woodworker, appreciate.

The chair's shape is derived from an upholstered wing chair, which its maker had proba-

CONSTRUCTION OVERVIEW

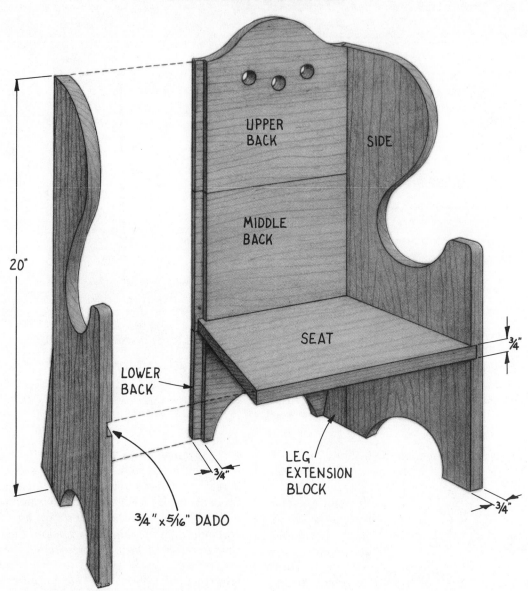

UPPER
BACK

SIDE

MIDDLE
BACK

20"

SEAT

3/4"

LOWER
BACK

LEG
EXTENSION
BLOCK

3/4"

3/4"

3/4" x 5/16" DADO

bly seen on a trip to the city. That influence is apparent in the shape of the serpentine back and the side wings. While many of these child's wing chairs are square, this one has canted sides and canted back legs. These features make the chair more interesting visually and, at the same time, make the chair more stable. However, the same features that make the

MATERIALS LIST

PART	DIMENSIONS
Side stock (2)	¾″ × 9″ × 20″
Leg extension blocks (2)	¾″ × 1½″ × 6¼″
Seat stock	¾″ × 7⅝″ × 12″
Upper back	¾″ × 8″ × 9¹¹⁄₁₆″
Middle back	¾″ × 7¼″ × 9¹¹⁄₁₆″
Lower back	¾″ × 6⁹⁄₁₆″ × 9¹¹⁄₁₆″

HARDWARE AND SUPPLIES

1½″ finishing nails (as needed)

chair more stable also complicate its joinery. The back's rabbets are angled, and the lower back is trapezoidal rather than rectangular.

Many of these chairs have a hole cut out of the seat so the chair can be used as a potty chair. Although the original did not have that feature, you can easily add it. The three finger holes in the upper back make grabbing and moving the chair easy.

I made my chair of white pine, like the original. The original had been stripped and I do not know how it was finished. I decorated my wing chair in false grain with a very bold Chinese red base and a flat black, glazed wood figure. One of the nice things about false graining is you can ignore the wood's real grain direction. I ran my painted grain across the grain on the seat and back. For instructions on applying a false grain finish, see "False Graining" on page 8.

CUT AND SHAPE THE SIDES AND SEAT.

1. Prepare the materials. All of the stock is ¾-inch-thick pine, which you can buy presurfaced from any lumber supply company. If you choose to use rough-sawn lumber, joint and thickness plane the stock to ¾ inch.

Rip and cut the parts to the dimensions given in the Materials List. Hand plane the stock to remove any machine marks.

2. Cut the dadoes in the side stock. Mark the position of the front edge, top edge, and inside face on each piece of side stock. While both edges are straight and square, cut dadoes

SIDE PATTERN

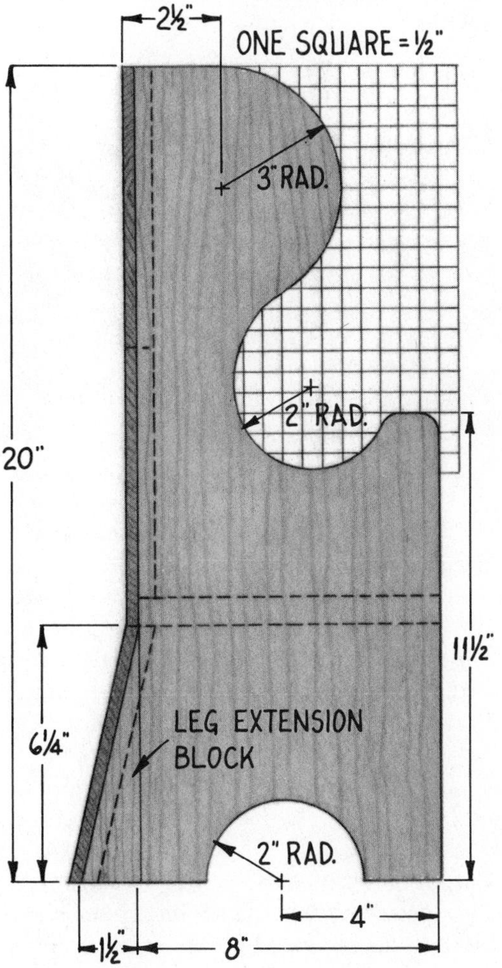
2½"
ONE SQUARE = ½"
3" RAD.
2" RAD.
20"
11½"
6¼"
LEG EXTENSION BLOCK
2" RAD.
4"
1½"
8"

on the inside face of the side stock to hold the seat, as shown in the *Construction Overview* and the *Side Pattern.* Cut the ¾-inch-wide dadoes with a dado blade in your table saw. Adjust the dado head carefully to create tight, friction-fit dadoes, and raise the blade ⁵⁄₁₆ inch above the saw table. Guide the stock against the rip fence as you cut the dadoes.

3. Bevel the front edges of the sides. Put the regular saw blade back into the table saw and set the table saw's arbor to 12 degrees. Bevel the front edges of the sides as you rip them to width.

TECHNIQUE TIP

When you rip the front edges of the sides, you make them into a right and left side. On a standard table saw with the fence to the right of the blade, bevel both sides with the dado facing up. Guide the right side into the saw blade with the top end leading, and guide the left side into the saw with the bottom end leading. To avoid confusion, use a pencil to mark the sides Right and Left.

---

4. Attach the leg extension blocks and cut the sides to shape. First, glue and clamp the leg extension blocks to each side, as shown in the *Construction Overview* and the *Side Pattern.* When the glue is dry, hand plane the extensions to remove any excess glue and to even the extension and side surfaces.

While the leg extension blocks are still square, make a grid of ½-inch squares on a piece of posterboard and draw the side shape on it, as shown in the *Side Pattern.* Cut the shape from the posterboard and transfer it to the stock. When the curves have been laid out on the stock, draw a line across the corners of

the leg extensions to produce the wedge shape shown in the *Side Pattern.*

Shape the sides and leg extensions with a band saw or bow saw and clean up the sawed edges with a spokeshave and sandpaper.

5. Make the seat. The seat's ends are angled in toward the back of the chair, as shown in the *Top View.* Lay out the angles on the stock with a sliding T-bevel. Guide the seat stock with your table saw's miter gauge set at 78 degrees and cut along the layout lines.

CUT AND SHAPE THE BACK BOARDS.

1. Bevel and shape the upper back and middle back. Bevel the ends of the upper back and middle back, as shown in the *Top View* and *Upper Back: Back View.* Set the table saw blade to 12 degrees and carefully bevel the ends. Guide the stock against the fence as you make the cuts.

When the ends have been beveled, make a grid of ½-inch squares on a piece of posterboard and draw the upper back's shape

TOP VIEW

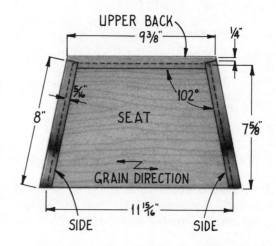

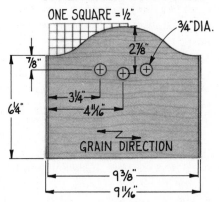

UPPER BACK: BACK VIEW

ONE SQUARE = ½"

¾" DIA.

⅞"

2⅞"

3¼"

4¹¹⁄₁₆"

6¼"

GRAIN DIRECTION

9⅜"

9¹¹⁄₁₆"

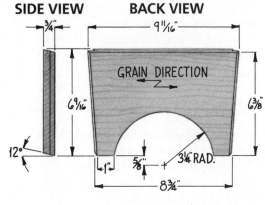

LOWER BACK: SIDE VIEW

LOWER BACK: BACK VIEW

¾"

9¹¹⁄₁₆"

GRAIN DIRECTION

6⁹⁄₁₆"

6⅜"

12°

1"

⅝"

3¼" RAD.

8¾"

on it, as shown in the *Upper Back: Back View*. Cut the shape from the posterboard and transfer the pattern onto the stock. Cut the upper back to shape with a band saw or bow saw. Smooth the sawed edges with a spokeshave and sandpaper.

Lay out and drill the ¾-inch-diameter finger holes in the upper back, as shown in the *Upper Back: Back View*.

TECHNIQUE TIP

Make an extra middle back as a test piece for adjusting the dado blade when you are getting set up to cut the angled rabbets for the sides.

---

2. Bevel, angle, and shape the lower back. Since the lower back slants outward at the bottom of the chair, the edges are beveled to match the slant, as shown in the *Lower Back: Side View*. Set your saw's arbor to 12 degrees and carefully rip the bevels in both edges. Guide the stock against the fence as you rip the bevels.

When the edges have been beveled, bevel and angle the ends, as shown in the *Lower Back: Back View*. Lay out the angles on the

stock with a sliding T-bevel set to 12 degrees off square (78 degrees), and make sure that the resulting length dimensions are consistent with those shown in the *Lower Back: Back*

Photo 1: To cut the first combination angle and bevel on the left end of the lower back, tilt the saw blade to 12 degrees and the miter gauge clockwise to 78 degrees. Put the bottom edge of the stock against the miter gauge with the outside surface facing up, and align the layout line with the blade.

View. Next, tilt the table saw blade to 12 degrees and set the miter gauge clockwise to 78 degrees. Insert the miter gauge in the slot to the right of the saw blade. Put the lower back on the saw table with its outside surface facing up, and rest its bottom edge against the miter gauge. Align the saw blade with your layout line as you cut the first combination angle and bevel (*Photo 1*).

When the first end has been angled and beveled, reset your miter gauge counterclockwise to 78 degrees. Rotate the lower back 180 degrees with the outside surface still facing up, and rest the top edge against the miter gauge. Align the second layout line with the blade and cut the combination angle and bevel (*Photo 2*).

When the ends have been beveled and angled, lay out the semicircular "bootjack"

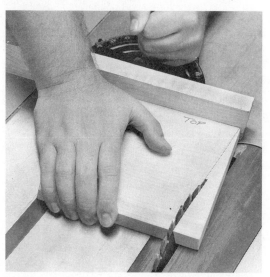

Photo 2: To cut the second combination angle and bevel on the right end of the lower back, reset the miter gauge counterclockwise to 78 degrees. Put the top edge of the stock against the miter gauge with the outside surface still facing up, and align the layout line with the blade.

opening in the lower back, as shown in the *Lower Back: Back View.* Cut out the semicircle with a band saw or bow saw and clean up the sawed edges with a spokeshave and sandpaper.

3. Rabbet the back boards to accept the seat and sides. First, cut a ¾ × ⁵⁄₁₆-inch rabbet in the bottom edge of the middle back to accept the seat. Mount a ¾-inch-wide dado blade in your table saw and clamp a 1-inch-thick wooden auxiliary fence to the left side of the rip fence. Crank the dado blade below the surface of the table, move the wooden fence into a position that slightly covers the blade, and slowly raise the spinning blade so that it cuts about ⅜ inch into the wooden fence. Reposition the fence so that the full ¾-inch width of the blade is exposed and raise the blade to ⁵⁄₁₆ inch. Guide the bottom edge of the middle back against the auxiliary fence to cut the rabbet (*Photo 3*).

Next, cut the angled rabbets on the edges of the back boards. Tilt the dado blade to 12 degrees and crank it down below the surface of the table. Clamp the auxiliary fence to the right side of the rip fence and again raise the dado blade into it. Adjust the blade height and fence position to produce the rabbets shown in the *Top View.* Test the setup by cutting the rabbets in pieces of scrap, then make any necessary adjustments. Cut the rabbets by guiding the ends of the back boards against the fence (*Photo 4*).

ASSEMBLE THE CHAIR.

1. Test fit the parts. Assemble the chair without glue to make sure that all of the angles, bevels, rabbets, and dadoes have been cut correctly. Make any necessary adjustments.

Photo 3: Guide the bottom edge of the middle back against an auxiliary fence clamped to the left side of the rip fence to cut the rabbet for the seat.

Photo 4: Guide the ends of the back boards against an auxiliary fence clamped to the right side of the rip fence to cut the rabbets for the sides. The dado blade is tilted at 12 degrees to produce a beveled rabbet.

TOOL TIP

You may find that the dado blade table insert for your table saw is not designed to accommodate a tilted dado blade. If that's the case, you will have to make one.

Start by thickness planing a piece of hardwood to the thickness of your regular table insert. Then, trace the shape of your regular table insert onto the hardwood table insert stock and cut it to shape on the band saw. Next, lower the tilted dado blade below the surface of the table and slip your new hardwood table insert into place above it. When the hardwood table insert is in place, reposition the rip fence so that the wooden auxiliary fence is above the insert but just to the side of the dado blade. Make sure that the metal fence is positioned clear of the blade, then lock the fence in place.

With everything in position, turn on the saw and *slowly* raise the blade. When the blade begins to bite into the hardwood table insert, back the blade off a bit, then slowly raise it into the hardwood table insert again. Repeat the process until the blade is through the hardwood table insert and about ½ inch above the surface of the table.

2. Assemble the chair. Put a bead of glue into one of the side dadoes and press the seat into it. Spread some glue into the lower back's rabbets and hold it in place as you join the other side to the seat. Gently tap the sides with a mallet until the seat is set into the bottom of the dadoes. Spread some glue into the upper back and lower back rabbets and lower them into place.

TOOL TIP

If any of the back boards don't fit properly, make the necessary adjustments with a shoulder rabbet plane. Rest the side of the plane on the rabbet's wide edge. The wide edge holds the plane at the proper angle to shave the shoulder. You can also use the plane to trim the wide edge by guiding it against the shoulder.

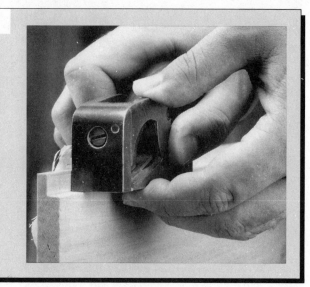

When the parts have been fit together, secure each joint with a few 1½-inch finishing nails. After the glue is dry, remove any excess glue and even up the joints with a block plane.

ROCKING CAT

Rocking animals were popular with country woodworkers and the children in their lives. The rocking toys were usually cut in the shape of a horse, swan, or some other animal on which a child could imagine riding or even flying. A cat, however, is an unusual choice for a rocking toy.

I was quite amused with the original rocking cat because the maker broke with the norm in another way that I find very clever. Usually the animal's head is in profile and the same face is painted on both sides, but in this case, the head is turned to the side. Instead of painting a face on both sides, the maker painted the full face on the right side and the back of the cat's head on the left side.

Because the piece gave me so much enjoyment, I made a copy of the original for my nephew, Thomas Earl Wallace, when he was a toddler. It was an appropriate gift, for at the time, his family's pet also happened to be a fat tiger cat.

In Thomas's imagination the rocking cat was his "Space Cat." He would sit in it dressed in his Superman costume and pretend that his cat could transport him anywhere in the universe. In later years Garfield became Thomas's favorite cartoon character, and I always won-

CONSTRUCTION OVERVIEW

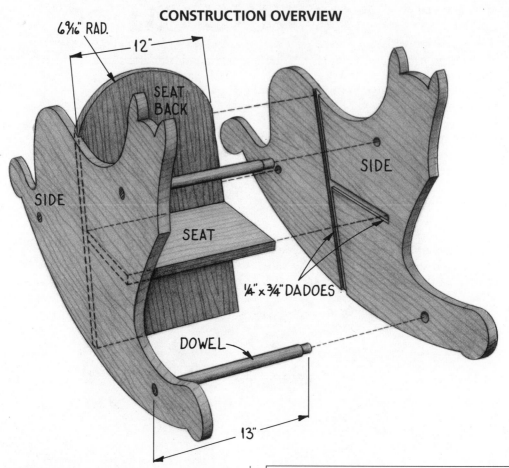

6⁹⁄₁₆" RAD.

12"

SEAT BACK

SIDE

SIDE

SEAT

¼" × ¾" DADOES

DOWEL

13"

dered if his rocking tiger cat was responsible.

As I write this chapter and think about making and painting this project, I find myself smiling in amusement as I did when I first saw the original, but my pleasure is bittersweet. About a month before I wrote this chapter, Thomas, age 13, died of leukemia. His family and I miss him.

I painted my pine cat and the dowels with two coats of mustard milk paint. The markings (tiger stripes) are done in black milk paint. The nose, ears, seat, and back are barn red milk paint. The whites of the eyes and pupils are done with oil paint.

MATERIALS LIST

PART	DIMENSIONS
Side stock (2)	¾" × 26" × 39½"
Seat	¾" × 8¼" × 12"
Seat back	¾" × 12" × 20½"
Dowels (3)	⅞" dia. × 13"

HARDWARE AND SUPPLIES

6d finish cut nails (as needed). Available from Tremont Nail Company, 8 Elm Street, P.O. Box 111, Wareham, MA 02571. Part #N-19 Std.

MAKE THE PARTS.

1. Prepare the stock. Buy ¾-inch-thick surfaced pine from a local lumberyard, or joint and thickness plane rough stock to ¾ inch. Glue up stock for the sides, seat back, and seat, and rip and cut it to the dimensions given in the Materials List. As you rip the seat to width, bevel the end that will meet the seat back at 8 degrees on the table saw. Hand plane the stock to remove excess glue and machine marks.

Cut the ⅞-inch-diameter dowels to the length given in the Materials List.

2. Cut the sides and seat back to shape. Make a grid of 1-inch squares directly on the side stock and draw the cat pattern on it, as shown

in the *Side Pattern*. Be sure to include the layout lines for the dadoes and dowel holes on the grid. Cut the sides to shape on the band saw and smooth the sawed edges with a spokeshave, file, and sandpaper.

Lay out the curve of the seat back, as shown in the *Construction Overview*. Cut the curve on the band saw and smooth the edges with a spokeshave and sandpaper.

TECHNIQUE TIP

Before laying out the dadoes, clearly mark the inside surface of each side with an X, then lay out the dadoes on the marked surfaces. If you take this extra precaution, you will end up with a left side and a right side.

SIDE PATTERN

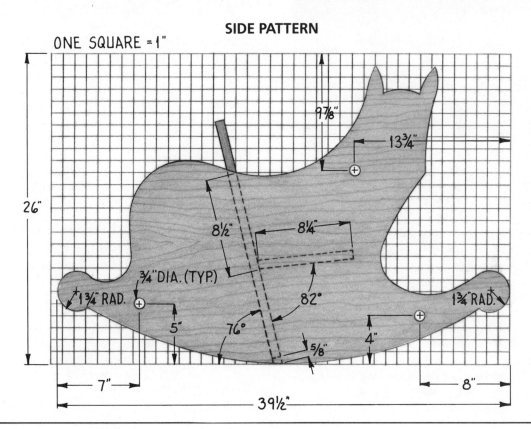

ONE SQUARE = 1"

26"

9⅞"

13¾"

8½"

8¼"

¾"DIA. (TYP.)

1¾" RAD.

1¾"RAD.

5"

82°

76°

4"

⅝"

7"

8"

39½"

CONSTRUCTION TIP

In order for the cat to rock evenly, it is important that the curves of the rockers be identical. To even up the rockers, clamp the sides together and use a hand plane to smooth the curves.

CUT THE JOINTS.

1. Tenon the dowels. The dowels have ¾-inch-diameter × ¾-inch-long tenons on each end to fit into the sides. First, put a ¾-inch-wide dado blade in your table saw and raise it ¹⁄₁₆ inch above the saw table. When the dado blade has been set up, clamp a wooden auxiliary fence to the rip fence and align it with the edge of the dado blade. Next, hold the dowel firmly against a miter gauge set at 90 degrees

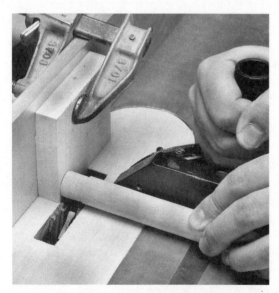

Photo 1: Guide the dowel with the miter gauge as you make the cuts. Rotate the dowel with each pass until the tenon is round.

and butt the dowel's end against the auxiliary fence. Begin cutting the tenon by slowly pushing the dowel into the blade with the miter gauge. When the first cut has been made, rotate the dowel slightly and make a second pass (*Photo 1*). Continue rotating the dowel with each pass until a cylindrical tenon has been formed. Cut the remaining tenons in the same way.

2. Cut the dadoes. As shown in the *Construction Overview,* the seat and seat back fit into ¾-inch-wide × ¼-inch-deep dadoes that are cut into the sides. The dadoes were laid out before you cut the sides to shape. Cut the dadoes with a router and a ¾-inch-diameter straight bit. Clamp a straightedge parallel to the layout lines to guide the router as you cut the dadoes. To position the straightedge correctly, divide your router's base diameter by 2 and subtract ⅜ inch (one-half the bit's diameter) from that figure: *(base/2) − ⅜ = distance from layout lines.*

First, rout a dado for the seat back in each side (*Photo 2*). When the seat back dadoes have been cut, reposition and clamp the straightedge for the seat dado. Start cutting the seat dado by dropping the spinning bit into the seat back dado, then push the router forward along the straightedge until the bit reaches the end of the layout lines (*Photo 3*). Square the ends of the seat dadoes with a chisel.

3. Drill the dowel holes. Drill ¾-inch-diameter dowel holes in the sides, as shown in the *Side Pattern.* To be sure the holes are aligned and the rockers are even on both sides, clamp the two sides together with the rockers' bottom edges aligned. Drill each pair of holes at the same time on the drill press. To avoid tear-out, back up the stock with a piece of scrap wood as you drill the holes.

Photo 2: Clamp a straightedge to the side to guide the router as you cut the seat back dado.

ASSEMBLE THE CAT.

1. Glue the joints. First, lay one of the sides face down on the workbench and swab glue in the dowel holes. Next, insert the dowels in their holes and put the seat and seat back in their dadoes.

When the parts have been inserted in the first side, swab glue into the dowel holes in the second side and put it in place.

Set the cat upright and hold it together with bar clamps.

Photo 3: Drop the bit into the seat back dado as you begin to cut the seat dado. Guide the router along the straightedge until the bit reaches the end of the layout lines.

2. Secure the joints. First, drive 6d cut nails through the sides and into the seat and seat back. When the seat and seat back are secure, drive 6d cut nails through the seat back and into the seat.

When all of the nails have been driven, remove the clamps and plane the ends of the dowels flush with the sides. Sand the entire cat rocker and apply the finish.